经典汉语教材系列（影印版）

汉语教科书（上）

MODERN CHINESE READER（I）

北京大学外国留学生中国语文专修班 编

北京语言大学出版社
BEIJING LANGUAGE AND CULTURE UNIVERSITY PRESS

图书在版编目（CIP）数据

汉语教科书．上 / 北京大学外国留学生中国语文专修班编．-- 北京：北京语言大学出版社，2020.11

ISBN 978-7-5619-5760-8

Ⅰ．①汉… Ⅱ．①北… Ⅲ．①汉字－对外汉语教学－教材 Ⅳ．① H195.4

中国版本图书馆 CIP 数据核字（2020）第 188831 号

汉语教科书（上）

HANYU JIAOKESHU（SHANG）

排版制作：北京创艺涵文化发展有限公司
责任印制：周 燚

出版发行：北京语言大学出版社
社　　址：北京市海淀区学院路 15 号，100083
网　　址：www.blcup.com
电子信箱：service@blcup.com
电　　话：编 辑 部　8610-8230 3647/3592/3724
　　　　　国内发行　8610-8230 3650/3591/3648
　　　　　海外发行　8610-8230 3365/3080/3668
　　　　　北语书店　8610-8230 3653
　　　　　网购咨询　8610-8230 3908
印　　刷：北京中科印刷有限公司

版　　次：2020 年 11 月第 1 版　　印　　次：2020 年 11 月第 1 次印刷
开　　本：787 毫米 × 1092 毫米　1/16　　印　　张：25.5　插页：1
字　　数：320 千字
定　　价：88.00 元

PRINTED IN CHINA

出版说明

新中国的国际中文教育（时称“对外汉语教学”）事业肇始于1950年清华大学东欧交换生中国语文专修班，至今已有七十年历史。七十年于人而言，已是古稀；于学科而言，仍为少年。作为一个年轻的学科，国际中文教育正处于旺盛的成长期。目前，全世界有3万多所中小学开设了中文课程，4000多所大学设立了中文院系或开设了中文相关课程，还有4.5万所华文学校和培训机构开展中文教育，全球学习中文的人数超过2500万人。[1]国际中文教育的开展在促进中外人文交流、加深中国与其他各国彼此间了解与互信等方面发挥了极为关键的作用。

展望未来，我们充满信心；回首往昔，我们坚定不移。据史料记载，最早的汉语作为第二语言教学可上溯至汉代，两千年来汉语教学绵延不绝，直至今日。古时从事汉语教学的师者及其所使用的教材由于时间久远，存世稀少，我们难以考证；但是近代以来，在汉语教学过程中所使用的教材有幸保留下来，并得以传承，其中既包括外国传教士在中国境内教汉语所使用的教材，也包括华人在海外教汉语所编写的教材。

这些珍贵的史料，不仅反映了当时汉语教学的方法和思路，也从侧面记录了彼时社会的语言面貌和人文风貌。我们广泛收集有关史料，认真遴选其中极具学术价值和史料价值的代表书目，通过高清扫描、图片修复等技术，最大限度还原原书的本来面貌，汇编结集成这套“经典汉语教材系列（影印版）”。为进一步彰显该丛书的历史意义和学术价值，我们还精选了学界前贤关于各册经典教材的评论文章，以期帮助读者进一步加深对教材编写背景和历史价值的了解。

北京语言大学出版社

2020年11月

1　该数据信息来自“孔子学院总部/国家汉办”新闻中心关于“2019国际中文大会”相关报道，参看http://www.hanban.org/article/2019-12/11/content_795884.htm。

前　言

《汉语教科书》是中华人民共和国成立以来正式出版的第一部供外国人学习汉语使用的教材，也是第一部极具对外汉语教学特点的教材，开创了中国对外汉语教材编写事业的先河，在对外汉语教学史上具有不可替代的作用。

本书是北京大学外国留学生中国语文专修班使用的基础汉语教材，分上、下两册，上册42课，下册30课，适用于汉语零起点水平的外国留学生。本书的编写以语法为纲，编写者根据汉语语法特色和汉语教学特点，有针对性地对汉语教学语法进行了甄选和编排，并在此基础上兼顾词汇、课文以及汉字的选择与编排。本书所创立的语法体系奠定了对外汉语教学语法体系的基础，对此后对外汉语教材的编写影响深远。

本次影印出版，我们特别挑选了原书1958年第1版第1次的版本，采用高清扫描、图片修复等技术，最大限度还原了原书的本来面貌。由于受年代和当时印刷技术的局限，原书部分语句具有鲜明的时代性，局部存在印刷和排版错误。本着尊重历史的原则，我们完整地保留了教材的原貌，希望为汉语教材的研究、编写和出版提供参考和借鉴。

为使读者进一步了解教材的历史意义和学术价值，我们特将钟梫先生对参与《汉语教科书》编写和出版的相关回忆进行整理，置于上册文前，帮助读者进一步了解原书出版的时代背景和曲折经历。另外，我们还特地选择了吕文华先生评述《汉语教学书》语法体系的文章，置于下册文前，帮助读者进一步加深对《汉语教科书》语法体系的认识和了解。

北京语言大学出版社

2020年11月

《汉语教科书》的编写*
（代序）

1. 出版过程

在五十年代我们觉得教材是最重要的，所以就集中力量编教材，就是《汉语教科书》。中国语文专修班刚开始上课时用的是油印的教材，邓懿一写出来，我们就连夜刻蜡板，油印，第二天早上学生拿到的经常是油墨未干的。那时候我们痛感油印的教材给学生带来了很多麻烦，所以当时我们下决心铅印。后来这本教材交五十年代出版社[1]出版，而且有多种语言版本，除了英文版，还有俄文版和德文版。邓懿也看出来了，太玩儿命了。五十年代出版社的总部就在和平门那儿，我们就在下头印刷厂盯着。我、马欣华、许德楠，就我们三个人盯着，一直盯到这本书出来，就是英文版的《汉语教科书》，1958 年出版的。

因为邓懿得在学校里头主持教学，不能让她总跑和平门。有问题就问她，那得多少问题啊！油印的稿子，再改到那上头，排版，英文部分、中文部分，出现的问题太多了，所以后来邓懿就让我在那儿全权负责。

我们没白天没黑夜地干，晚上要从和平门回来都是 10 点以后了，在外头随便吃一点儿。那时搞教材开夜车，一直搞到早上 5 点，回来睡一会儿，8 点钟又上班，你算算一天就睡两个小时吧。搞教材到最关键的时候就我、许德楠、马欣华，所以我说他们两个的功劳很大，中文部分全部由他们两个校对。

记得当时出版社有什么问题，就在那儿当场解决，我们仨都在那儿，工人就在旁边干，1958 年不是大跃进么，工人也是加班。这儿排版，那儿改版，有什么问题，随提随改，“老钟，这个字是用这个还是用那个？”就到这个程度，这样才把《汉语教科书》突击出来。突击出来以后，质量还不错。

---

* 本文选自崔希亮主编《北京语言大学对外汉语教学名师访谈录 · 钟梫卷》“四、教材编写与词典编纂”中钟梫先生关于《汉语教科书》编写的相关回忆内容。

1 钟先生回忆说是“五十年代出版社”，施光亨在《新中国对外汉语教学40年大事记》（《世界汉语教学》1990年第2期）中说是“时代出版社”，文中保留钟先生原话。两位先生回忆的名称不同，但所指相同，即商务印书馆。

2. 语法体系的形成

我常常说新中国对外汉语的源头应该是赵元任，从赵元任到邓懿，邓懿从五十年代初开始编《汉语教科书》，这条路是这么下来的。

邓懿非常忠实于赵元任的教材，她是赵元任的助教，从他那儿她学了不少语音、语法的知识，我们最开始用的教材就是邓懿翻译赵元任的。但是我们也得从实际出发，赵元任在美国用的教材不完全适用于我们，所以，词汇上的改动大一些。句型，也就是 sentence patterns 用的是赵元任的，例句根据实际情况做了一些改变。语法上我们参考了很多，比如胡裕树的、张志公的，有冲突的我们还是用邓懿（赵元任）的。这个语法体系我们既没有用张志公的系统，也没有用王力的系统，更没有用北师大的系统，黎锦熙的更没法用，最接近的还是张志公的。

总结一下的话，就是刚开创的时候，各种各样的说法比较多。邓懿开始的时候就是搬来赵元任的，后来我们在使用中发现不合适的再一点一点改进。就这么一个过程，一个正常的过程。

所以，这套教材首先归功于赵元任，然后是他的接班人邓懿，我只是一个参加者。

后来在出版的时候，附上了汉语语法复习提纲，这个是跟我有关系的。

3. 汉语基本语法复习提纲

我一个学期要教好几个班，有一个班说考试要复习，最好有个复习的提纲给他们，所以我就搞了个汉语语法复习提纲，叫基本语法复习提纲。当时邓懿编的最后没有一个提纲性的东西。国际上有一些，但那些东西对我们不合适。后来学生就要求说能不能帮他们编一个基本语法复习提纲。也没有人要求我这么做，我只是觉得学生应该有一个这样的提纲，总复习就得有一个纲吧。于是我就从邓懿编的那些课文中抽取语法点，先是我手写的，后来给邓懿看，邓懿说不错，就油印了。我没有走一个大家去讨论什么的路子，就在自己班用。

后来这些油印教材商务印书馆要去出版了，要印成那个《汉语教科书》。邓懿说汉语语法复习提纲正好附在里头，归总了。前头的那些，不管是先讲体词谓语句，还是先讲形容词谓语句，最后复习提纲都按一定顺序把它排出来了。比如补语，整本书讲了多少个补语，我们都把它列出来。就这样子，把它放在整本书的后头，作为整本书的一个语法体系。原来没有往这个上头想。

我是觉得这个语法复习大纲是在实践当中形成的，学生需要。我辅导学生的时候，学生说：老师，我们要考试了，能不能稍微归纳归纳？特别是那个年纪大的，说人家不是分词类、语法、句法嘛，能不能按词法句法给我们分一下？哎，我说对呀。我是搞英文、搞俄文过来的，所以我马上就接受了。所以，我的那个复习提纲就分成词法、句法，句法用 syntax，词法是 morphology，把这两个先分开。词法里头分词类、词尾什么的，句法分句子分类、句子成分什么的。就这么样地搞。

所以我觉得我们这个就是水到渠成，没有刻意去追求个什么，完全是出于实践，出于学生需要。

节选自《北京语言大学对外汉语教学名师访谈录·钟梫卷》

崔希亮主编，北京语言大学出版社，2010 年

MODERN CHINESE READER

Part 1

COMPILED BY THE CHINESE LANGUAGE SPECIAL
CLASS FOR FOREIGN STUDENTS IN
PEKING UNIVERSITY

"Epoch" Publishing House
Peking, 1958

汉語教科書

（上　册）

北京大学外国留学生中国語文專修班編

时代出版社
1958年·北京

內容提要

本書是北京大學外国留学生中国語文專修班一年級第一学期前十几个星期的教科書，分上下两册，上册 42 課，下册 30 課，并附有小詞典．內容包括語音和語法，講解深入淺出．学完本書不但可以应付日常生活，而且可以閱讀簡易的文章，为进一步学習專业打好汉語基础．本書不仅可作外国留学生的教科書，而且也可以供一般外国人学習汉語之用．

This book is used as text-book by the Chinese Language Special Course for Foreign Students in Peking University, covering the first three months of the first term. It consists of two parts. In part I there are forty two lessons, and in part II there are thirty lessons and an appendix of vocabulary at the end. The contents of this book are Chinese phonetics and grammar which are explained in simple words. After studying this book, one can not only speak and write simple Chinese in daily life, but also can read simple articles, and thus is qualified for further study in any specialized field. Besides its use as a text-book for foreign students, it can also help any foreigner study the Chinese language.

时 代 出 版 社 出 版

北京市書刊出版业營业許可証出字第45号

（北京东总布胡同10号）

新 华 書 店 發 行

北京五十年代印刷厂印刷　　北京京華印書局裝訂

1958年10月北京初版　　1958年10月第1次印刷

開本：850×1168 1/32　印张：12 6/16　字数：336千字　插頁：5

印数：1—1,800 册　　定价（10）2.50 元

上 册 目 錄

Part I

Contents

* 原书页码有误，为方便读者查阅，本版增加页码勘误表，特此说明。

		勘误

說　明

1. 本書是北京大学外国留学生中国語文專修班第一学期所用的語音和語法的教材．几年来到我国来学習的留学生逐年增加，他們都要首先学好汉語才能学習專业，迫切地需要汉語教科書．另一方面，自从中华人民共和国成立以来，很多外国朋友对汉語發生了兴趣；但因缺乏适当的課本，学習很感困难．为了适应这个情况，我們决定把这本教科書付印，以滿足我班学生和别的国际朋友們的需要．

2. 本書以初学汉語的外国学生为对象，并以实用为目的．編排次序和重点的分配，都以切合具体对象的需要为原則．过細过深的理論，不易为初学者所接受的，都不收在本書里面．

3. 本書包括緒論、語音、語法三部分．緒論給我們所要学習的現代汉語作了一个輪廓的介紹，可以使学生在学習之前对汉語特点有所了解．前十二課是語音，其中理論八課、口語練習四課，共用教学时間二週．后六十課是語法，每六課构成一个單元，其中前五課是新課，后一課是复習；教学时間一共十週．本書学完以后，学生除了語音和基本語法之外，还学習詞彙 864 个(包括汉字 746 个)．这时候，他們不但应該能以簡單口語应付日常生活，而且可以閱讀淺易的文章，具备了进一步学習短文的条件．如果一位外国朋友不能拿出全部时間学習汉語，每天一課的分量当然显得太重，也可以适当地延長学習的时間．假如用作选修課程的教材，每週上課二三次，改为全年的教材也是可以的．

4. 关于語法部分，需要特別提出来下列各点：

(1) 为了重点突出、眉目清楚，在書中把基本語法抽繹为若干点，以便学生預習和复習．但在課堂教学时，教师应該先給例句、后給理論，尽量貫徹"从感性到理性"的原則．例句里尽量不用当課的生詞，以免分散学生对語法的注意力．

(2) 除了每个單元的复習課以外，每課的第一項都是"生詞"．实際上，这一項下也包含着大于詞的語和小于詞的詞素；"生詞"只是个極籠統的說法．生詞排列的次序是根据它們在語法項下的例句和課文中出現的先后而定的．詞的音、义之外，还注了詞类（所用簡号在第十三課前有說明）．第十四課介紹名量詞，从那課起，名詞之后兼注常用的特定量詞（如果特定量詞是一个生字，兼注讀音）；用量詞"个"的，省去不注．

(3) 为了外国学生的方便，語法的例句和課文採用了詞兒連写的办法．但因沒有大家公認的連写規則，我們試拟了一个規則（見附錄四）．連写的目的在于帮助学生朗讀，連写在一起的并不限於严格意义的"詞"，而是还有大于詞或小于詞的單位．这时候，除了考虑什么是詞以外，也考慮如何帮助学生讀得連貫、自然．

(4) 每課之后附有課外練習，这些練習都是为了檢驗学生是否掌握当課的語法重点而設的．同时，也适当地照顧到詞彙的复習．当然，不能指望作了这些練習就能达到熟練的目的．本書只是講授課用的教材，練習課和复習課材料并不包括在內．

(5) 为了減少学習汉字的困难，我們除了在語音阶段加入字素帮助学生分析汉字的組成部分以外，在語法阶段中，新課后面都附有汉字表．每課生詞中出現的新汉字都在汉字表中加以分析，分析出来的部分如果不是学生学过的，还把笔顺标出，以便学生能正确地書写．遇見曾經作为汉字組成部分出現过的字素或汉字，便不再給笔順或分析．書后附有汉字組合一覽（見附錄二），把学过的生詞排列在組成生詞的汉字下面，也是为了帮助学生学習生詞和記忆汉字而設的．

5. 本書注音根据 1958 年 2 月 11 日第一屆全国人民代表大会第五次会議批准的汉語拼音方案．

6. 国务院在 1956 年 1 月 28 日決議公布了"汉字簡化方案"，到目前为止，已先后在全国各报刊圖書上正式推行了三批簡化汉字，共計 425 个字．本書所用簡字就是这些正式推行的簡化汉字（見附录三：繁簡字对照表）．

7. 本書由北京大学外国留学生中国語文專修班汉語教研室集体編写．我們懇切地希望各地讀者不吝指正．

1958 年 8 月

EXPLANATIONS

1. This book contains the phonetic and grammar materials used for the first term by the Chinese Language Special Course for Foreign Students in Peking University. In recent years, more and more foreign students have come to China to study. They have to learn Chinese first before pursuing other professional studies, and so are in urgent need of a Chinese text-book. Besides, since the founding of the People's Republic of China, many foreign friends have become interested in Chinese. Without the help of a handy text-book, they are at a loss how to learn. To meet the demand of both the foreign students of our Course and international friends, we decided to put this text-book into print with an English translation.

2. This book is compiled for the use of foreign students. The lessons and the points in each lesson are arranged in accordance with the practical needs of foreign students in the process of learning. Learned theories or detailed explanations unacceptable to beginners, are not included in this book.

3. This book consists of three parts: introduction, phonetics and grammar. The introduction will give the students a general idea about the characteristics of modern Chinese. The first twelve lessons deal with phonetics, eight lessons on theory, and four lessons for oral practice, all of them to be given in two weeks. These are followed by sixty grammar lessons, every six lessons forming a unit, five of which are new lessons and the last one is a general review; all the grammar lessons will take ten weeks. Students, after finishing this book, will have learned 864 words (including 746 characters), aside from the phonetics and grammar. By this time, the students will not only have been able to speak simple Chinese of daily life, but also able to read simple writing; they will have been qualified for the further study of short essays and stories. If a foreign friend is not in a position to learn Chinese all the time, of

course one lesson per day is probably too much. In that case, he may take as much time as he thinks necessary. If this book is adopted in school using it for two or three hours a week, it will take a whole year to complete the course.

4. In the following are five points to be noticed concerning the grammar:

(1) For the sake of conspicuousness and orderly arrangement, the basic grammar in this book is given in the form of points, so that the students may easily prepare and review the lessons. But in class, the teacher must explain the grammar rules as illustrated by previously given example sentences in strict accordance with the principle, "from the sensational to the rational". The new words of each lesson are not used in the examples given in that lesson, in order that the students may concentrate their whole attention upon the new grammar rules.

(2) The first part of each lesson, with the exception of the general review at the end of each unit, gives the vocabulary or "new words". In fact, this part sometimes contains phrases which are larger units than words, and word elements which are smaller units than words; the term "new words" is used not in the strict sense. The new words are arranged according to their order of appearance in the example sentences under grammar rules and in the texts. We not only give the pronunciation and meanings of the words, but also indicate to what parts of speech they belong (the list of initial characters used for representing the parts of speech is given before the thirteenth lesson). The nominal measure words are dealt with in the fourteenth lesson, and from that lesson on, the specific nominal measure words are given in the new words column (if any of the specific measure words is a new character, its pronunciation is also given); the measure word 个, which is used for almost all nouns, is always omitted.

(3) The example sentences under grammar rules and the texts are written with the words separate from each other,

so that the foreign students may read them easily. But there are, as yet, no universally recognized rules of the separate writing of words; we are obliged to make some rules by ourselves (See Appendix 4). Since the separate writing of words is only to facilitate reading, they are separated not in strict accordance with the meaning of words, for some of them may be larger or smaller than the unit of a word. In separating words, our consideration is not limited to the word unit, but also how best to enable the students to read the texts with fluency and naturalness.

(4) At the end of each lesson, there is home work, this is to test whether the students have mastered the important points of grammar in that lesson or not. There is also a review of the vocabulary. Of course, it cannot be expected that all this home work will enable a student to master all the vocabulary and grammar. This book contains only mateiials for explanations, exercises and review materials are not included.

(5) In order to lessen the difficulty of the students in learning Chinese characters, a number of the components of Chinese characters are inserted in the phonetic part, with a view to helping the students in analyzing characters; in the grammar part, each lesson has also a table of Chinese characters. All the characters appearing in the new words of each lesson are analysed in the table, and if there is any component of a character that is new to the students, the order of strokes is also given, so that the students may write the character correctly. But all the components and characters which have already been given as the components of other characters are not analysed a second time, nor is the order of strokes indicated. At the end of this book, there is a table of the combination of Chinese characters (See Appendix 2), in which each of the words learned by the students is put under the character that is used to form the word, so that the students may learn and memorize the words and characters easily.

5. The phonetic annotations in this book follow the Phonetic Scheme approved by the 5th session of the 1st National People's Congress on the 11th of February, 1958.

6. Since the decision made by the State Council on the simplification of Chinese characters on January 28, 1956, 425 simplified characters appearing respectively in three different lists have been formally adopted by the newspapers, magazines and books throughout the country. All these publicly accepted simplified characters are used in this book (See Appendix 3, Table of Simplified Characters Placed against Their Original Complicated Forms).

7. This book was complied by the whole faculty of the Chinese Language Special Course for Foreign Students in Peking University. For the further improvement of this book, we sincerely hope that our readers will give us their criticisms and instructions.

August, 1958

緒　論

汉語是中国主要的語言，也是世界上使用人数最多的語言，并且是世界上最發达的語言之一.

中国是一个統一的多民族的国家. 全国人口有六亿多，90% 以上是汉民族. 各兄弟民族都各有自己的語言；汉語是汉民族的語言，又是民族間交际的共同語言.

汉語方言，就現在知道的情况，可以分成八个大方言：北方話，江浙話，湖南話，江西話，客家話，閩北話，閩南話，广东話. 說北方話的人数最多，約佔使用汉語的人口 70% 以上. 北方話的区域实际上包括長江以北地区，長江以南鎮江以上九江以下沿江地带，湖北（东南角除外），四川，云南，貴州四省以及湖南的西北角. 这么多的人口，这么大的地区，語言如此一致，在世界上是絕无仅有的. 各方言的語法基本上是一致的，詞彙絕大多数是相同的；語音的差别比較大，可是相互之間的对应关系还是很清楚的. 汉語的口語，目前的情况是：一方面固然还有方言的存在，另一方面中国正在推广以北京音为标准音的普通話，以逐漸統一汉民族的共同語言.

中国長时期使用的統一的汉語書面語"文言"，最初必然是在口語的基础上产生的，但是后来跟口語有了越来越远的距离. 因此另外出現了一种新的書面語言，更直接地紀录了活的口語，与口語一直保持着最密切的联系. 这就是現在通常所說的"白話"，也就是我們現在的汉民族共同語書面形式的主要来源. 各种用"白話"写的作品的方言基础，总的說来都是北方話. 同时以北京話为代表的北方話也逐漸成为方言区之間的交际工具，而被称为"官話". 1919年"五四"运动反对文言文，提倡白話文，动摇了文言的統治地位，汉民族共同語的書面和口头的統一形式逐漸形成，"普通話"这个名称也就代替了"官話". 1949 年中华人民共和国成立以来，書面語已基本上統一於"白話"，达到了原則上的"言文一致"，同时口語也得到了进一步的發展.

由於历史的原因，汉語發展到現在还沒有完全达到統一的地步，但是汉語統一的基础已經存在了，这就是以北京語音为标准音，以北方話为基础方言，以典范的現代白話文著作为語法規范的普通話．我們講授的現代汉語就是这样的标准語．

現在簡略地談談現代汉語在語音、語法、詞彙和文字等几方面的主要特点．

語音 (1) 元音(母音)佔优势　紀录汉語的每一个字是一个音节．这个音节是由單独的元音、复合元音或带輔音（子音）的元音构成的，而單独的輔音既不能构成音节，也就不能代表汉語里的一个字．例如：

[hàn (1) yǔ (2) kě (3) ài (4)]（汉語可爱．）

这四个音节（四个字）就是分别由單独的元音 (2)、复合元音 (4)、元音前带輔音 (3) 和元音前后带輔音 (1) 构成的．

(2) 声調　代表每一个字的每一个音节都有自己的固有声調．例如，mǎi（买）是降升調，mài（卖）是全降調．二者音素和結构虽然完全相同，只是因为声調的不同，意义也就两样了．

(3) 送气和不送气　一个音节开头的輔音送气和不送气的对立也是区别意义的重要因素．例如 bǎo（飽）和 pǎo（跑）的不同，完全在於音节开头輔音的送气不送气．

語法和詞彙 (1) 詞序固定　汉語里的詞序是一种很重要的表意方法．例如，"我帮助你"和"你帮助我"的意思恰好相反．"他念書"不能說成"書念他"．"(一朵) 香花兒"是詞組，而"(这朵) 花兒很香"就是句子了．修飾語一般在被修飾語之前．例如，"白馬"("白"，定語；"馬"，中心語) 和"慢慢兒地走"("慢慢兒地"，状語；"走"，中心語)．

(2) 助詞　助詞是汉語虛詞里的一种．它不表示实在的意义，不能作句子成分，更不能單独成句；主要的功用就是表示語法关系；可以附着於詞、詞組或句子，帮助詞語的結构（如結构助詞）或傳达句子的語气（如語气助詞）．

(3) 字和詞　汉語里的一个音节用文字紀录下来就是一个汉字．汉語里有單音节詞和多音节詞．單音节詞用一个汉字表示．例如：

人 rén　　来 lái　　好 hǎo

但是有例外，例如"花兒"两个汉字是一个音节 huār．多音节詞里最多的是双音节詞，用两个汉字表示．例如：

人民 rénmín　　幸福 xìngfú　　我們 wǒmen

此外还有三音节詞和四音节詞.

(4) 單純詞与复合詞　从上面的叙述可以知道,一个詞可以用一个字表示，也可以用两个或两个以上的字表示；但是并不是每个字都能成为一个詞. 1，有的字能够單独成为一个詞，例如“人”. 2，有的字也能表示一点意义，这样的字不能單独成为一个詞，只能成为詞里的一个成分，如“語”和“言”；可是它們結合起来能够构成一个具有明确意义的詞“語言”. 3，能够成詞的一个字也可以跟另一个字結合起来构成另一个詞，这另一个字可以是能够單独成詞的，也可以是不能單独成詞的，前者如“鉄路”，后者如“人民”. 4，有的字只出現在一个詞里，如“葡萄”，“葡”和“萄”單独都不能表示什么意义，也不能單独再跟任何别的字組成另一个詞. 1 和 4 所説的是單純詞，2 和 3 所説的是复合詞，复合詞的构成方式，多种多样，这里所談的只是举例的性質. 为了清楚起見，現在把以上説到的几点列表如下:

	單純詞							
字	葡	萄	鉄	路	人	民	語	言
			复合詞					

汉字　汉語的書写符号汉字，根据地下發掘的材料，也已經有三千年以上的历史了. 汉字虽然来源於一种象形文字，但早就越过了象形文字的阶段. 例如古文字里的“”(側面的“人”形)和“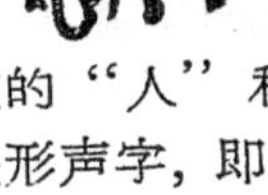”(側面的“象”形)，还可以看出来所象的形状，現在的“人”和“象”字就看不出那样的形状来了. 汉字絕大多数是形声字，即一部分表意，一部分表声的字. 例如:

油　yóu　　氵(即水，表意)
　　　　　　由 (yóu，表声)
桐　tóng　　木 (表意)
　　　　　　同 (tóng 表声)

但是由於汉字字形和汉語語音的变化，很多字的表声部分已經很难

辨認或者失去标音(調)作用了. 例如:

1. 江 jiāng: 工 gōng
2. 鴿 gē: 合 hé
3. 筒 tǒng: 同 tóng
4. 念 niàn: 今 jīn
5. 圈 quān: 卷 juàn
6. 問 wèn: 門 mén

为了辨認和書写的方便, 按照汉字的形体結构, 可以分为两类: 第一类是独体字, 本身是一个整体, 不能再加分析, 例如 "人" 和 "水". 第二类是合体字, 由两个或两个以上的独体字合成, 形声字都属於这一类. 合体字虽然比較复杂, 但是只要認識清楚了它的每一个組成部分, 也就沒有多大困难了.

汉字的字数虽然很多 (康熙字典收有 47,021 字, 不計或体), 然而实际上通用的大致不出五六千字; 据統計, 如果学会 1,556 字, 讀一般書籍的时候, 95 %的字都可以認識.

汉字在中国人民的悠久的文化历史上有过偉大的功績. 几千年来, 中国古代丰富的文献典籍依靠汉字保存下来. 在中国的社会主义建設时期, 汉字正在被广大人民群众更广泛地使用. 在長远的将来, 汉字也将繼續存在, 并且一定有許多人研究. 但是为了更好地普及文化敎育, 中国正在进行文字改革. 1956 年 1 月中华人民共和国国务院公布了汉字簡化方案, 簡化汉字就是把笔画繁复的字簡化, 并且在重复的字里选用一个, 廢用異体. 1958 年 2 月 11 日第一屆全国人民代表大会第五次会議又批准了汉語拼音方案. 这个方案的主要用途是給汉字注音, 帮助敎学汉字, 統一讀音和推广普通話. 外国人通过拼音字母学習汉語汉字, 也有極大的便利. 此外, 語文工作者也可以用这套拼音字母研究和实驗中国文字的进一步改革.

INTRODUCTION

The Chinese language (or the Han language) is the chief language of China, and also one of the most popular and developed languages in the world.

China is a country of many nationalities, and has a population of six hundred million, over 90% of which are of the Han nationality. Each of the national minorities has its own language. The Chinese language is the language of the Han nationality, and also the common social language used among all the nationalities.

The Chinese language, according to present data, consists of eight principal dialects: the Northern dialect, the Kiangsu-Chekiang dialect, the Hunan dialect, the Kiangsi dialect, the Hakka dialect, the northern Fukien dialect, the southern Fukien dialect and the Kwangtung dialect. Above 70% of the population who use the Chinese language speak the Northern dialect. The Northern dialect district includes, in fact, the wide area north of the Yangtze River, the tract of land to the south of the Yangtze River, the west of Chenkiang and the east of Kiukiang, the four provinces of Hupeh (excepting the south-east corner), Szechwan, Yunnan and Kweichow, and last of all, the north-western part of the Hunan province. It is seldom found in the world that so many people of so wide a region speak one and the same dialect. The grammar of all the dialects is fundamentally the same, the majority of words are the same, and only the pronunciation is rather different, but in spite of that, there exist among the various dialects some corresponding phonetic relations. The present condition of the spoken Han language may be described as follows: though the various dialects are still in use, the Chinese people are taking measures to spread the popular language with the Peking speech sounds as the standard so as to unify gradually the various dialects and form a common national language.

The "ancient literary language" (文言) of the Han nationality, which was once universally used in China for so long a period, must have become established on the basis of the spoken language, but it gradually deviated more and more from the spoken language. Hence, there appeared later a new type of written language, which directly recorded living speech, and kept close to the spoken language all the time. This is what we now call the "colloquial language" (白話), which is the source of our present national language in writing. All the works written in the "colloquial language" are, generally speaking, based upon the Northern dialect. At the same time, a branch of the Northern dialect, which represented the local speech of Peking, gradually become the means of social intercourse in the various dialect districts, and was called the "Mandarin language" (官話). The May 4th movement in 1919 stood for writing in the colloquial language and against writing in the ancient literary language, and destroyed the authoritative position of the ancient literary language. As a result, the common language of the Han nationality became gradually unified in its written and spoken forms. The term "popular language" (普通話) was adopted instead of the "Mandarin language". Since the founding of the People's Republic of China in 1949, the written language has become closer to the "colloquial language", and a fundamental union of the written and spoken languages is thus brought about; while the spoken language is further developed.

Because of various historical reasons, the Chinese language did not reach a total unification till now. But a basis has been established for the unification of the Chinese language, that is, the formation of a popular language, based upon the Peking speech sounds as the standard sounds, the Northern dialect as the basic dialect and modern classic works written in the colloquial language as grammatical models. The modern Chinese, which we purpose to teach, is just such a standard language.

Here are some of the chief characteristics of modern Chinese with respect to speech sounds, grammar, words and characters:

Speech sounds (1) The predomination of vowels. Every character, used in the Chinese language, is a syllable by itself. The syllable may consist of a single vowel, a compound vowel or a vowel preceded or followed by a consonant; but a single consonant can never form a syllable by itself, and so it cannot represent any Chinese character. e. g.

hàn (I) yǔ (2) kě (3) aì (4)

(The Chinese language is very charming.)

These four syllables (four characters) are formed respectively by a single vowel (2), a compound vowel (4), a vowel preceded by a consonant (3) and a vowel between two consonants (1).

(2) Tones. Every syllable representing a character, has its definite tone, e. g. "mǎi" (to buy) is pronounced in a falling and rising tone, and "mài" (to sell) in a completely falling tone. The difference in tone makes for the difference in meaning, though both have the same sound elements.

(3) Aspiration and non-aspiration. Whether the beginning consonant of a syllable is aspirated or unaspirated is quite essential for ascertaining the meaning represented by the syllable, e. g. the different meanings of "bǎo" (to have eaten enough) and "pǎo" (to run) are determined by the aspiration and non-aspiration of the beginning consonant of each syllable.

Grammar and words (1) Uniformity of syntax. The word order in Chinese is very important. For example, 我帮助你 (I help you) and 你帮助我 (you help me) are opposite in meaning. 他念書 (he reads a book) cannot be changed into 書念他. 一朵香花兒 (one fragrant flower) is a word group, while 这朵花兒很香 (this flower is very fragrant) is a sentence. A modifier is usually put before that which is modified, e. g. 白馬 (a white horse), in which 白 is an adjective modifier and 馬 the central word or the word modified, and 慢慢兒地走 (walk slowly), in which 慢慢兒地 is an adverbial modifier and 走 the central word.

(2) Particles. Particles are considered a kind of weak or form word in the Chinese language. No particle possesses any concrete meaning. It cannot be used as any sentence element, and therefore cannot form any sentence by itself. Particles are used chiefly for expressing grammatical relations: they may help words in forming grammatical constructions (such as structural particles) and may express sentence moods (such as modal particles) when they are used after words and sentences.

(3) Characters and words. In Chinese, a syllable is a character in writing. There are monosyllabic words and polysyllabic words in Chinese. A monosyllabic word is represented by a character, e. g.

人 rén (man),

来 lái (to come),
好 hǎo (good).

But there are exceptions, e. g. 花兒 (flower) consisting of two characters are pronounced as one syllable (huār). Most of the polysyllabic words are dissyllabic ones, each of which is represented by two characters, e. g.

人民 rénmín (people)
幸福 xìngfú (happiness)
我們 wǒmén (we, us)

Besides, there are also words of three syllables and four syllables.

(4) Simple and compound words. From what has been said above, it is clear that a word may be represented by one character, two characters or more than two; but not every character can form a word. 1. There are characters which can each form a word, e. g. 人 (man). 2. There are characters which may each express a bit of meaning, but cannot stand alone as a word, and can only be a part of a word, e. g. 語 and 言; but these two characters can be combined into a word with a definite meaning: 語言 (language). 3. One character, which can be a word by itself, may, in combination with another character, form another word, and the second character sometimes may form a word by itself, such as 鉄路 (railway), or it may not, such as 人民 (people). 4. There are some characters which only appear in one word, such as 葡萄 (grapes), for neither 葡 nor 萄 can express any meaning by itself, and therefore cannot form another word with any other character. The words given under 1 and 4 are simple words, and those under 2 and 3 are compound words. There are various formations of compound words, and the few instances given here are used only as illustrations. For the sake of clearness, the contents of the above four points may be summed up in the following table:

	Simple words							
Characters	葡	萄	鉄	路	人	民	語	言
			Compound words					

Chinese characters: The writing symbols of the Chinese language, the characters, have a history of more than three thousand years, according to excavated evidence. Notwithstanding the fact that the Chinese characters originated from a kind of hieroglyphs, they have already advanced far ahead of the stage of hieroglyphs, e. g. from these two ancient characters  (the side view of a man) and  (the side view of an elephant), we can see what they symbolize, but this pictorial form is lost in the same two characters in modern writing, 人 and 象. Most of the Chinese characters indicate shape and sound, that is, one part of each character represents the sense and the other part the sound, e. g.

油 yóu (oil) 氵 (meaning water, representing the sense)
由 ("yóu" representing the sound)

桐 tóng (tree of tung oil)
木 (meaning wood, representing the sense)
同 ("tóng" representing the sound)

But owing to the change of character writing and speech sounds, the sound part of a great number of characters has almost lost its function and no longer represents the sound and tone of the character, e. g.

1.	江	jiāng	(river):	工	gōng
2.	鴿	gē	(dove):	合	hé
3.	筒	tǒng	(tube):	同	tóng
4.	念	niàn	(to read):	今	jīn
5.	圈	quān	(circle):	卷	juàn
6.	問	wèn	(to ask):	門	mén

For the convenience of discriminating and writing characters, they may be divided into two kinds according to their structure. Characters of the first kind are basic characters, each of which consists of a simple unit, that cannot be analyzed, e. g. 人 (man) and 水 (water). Those of the second kind are mixed characters, each of which is composed of two or more than two simple units. The characters of shape and sound belong to this kind. Comparatively speaking, a mixed character seems somewhat complicated, but it is not really difficult as soon as one makes out each component part of the character.

The number of characters is very great (the Kan-hsi Dictionary records 47,021 characters, not counting the alternative forms), but actually those in common use are only about five or six thousand. According to recent statistics, any one who knows 1,556 characters, is actually in command of 95% of the characters in general use.

The Chinese characters have played brilliant and important role in the long history of Chinese culture. All the splendid ancient classical literature of China is preserved in these characters. In the period of the Chinese socialist construction, the Chinese characters are now used by the masses throughout the country. In the far future, they will continue to exist, and will be studied by many people. But in order to facilitate the popularization of culture and education, the characters are undergoing a reform. In January, 1956, the State Council of the People's Republic of China promulgated the Plan of the Simplification of Characters. It aims at simplifying the characters composed of too many strokes, and at selecting one form of a character when there are two or more than two forms.

On the 11th of February, 1958, the 5th session of the 1st National People's Congress approved the Phonetic Scheme for Annotating Chinese Characters. This scheme chiefly serves to annotate the pronunciation of Chinese characters alphabetically, to facilitate the teaching of them, to unify the speech sounds and to popularize the common language. Foreigners will find it very convenient to learn the Chinese language and characters with the help of the phonetic alphabet. Teachers and research students of the Chinese language may also consider further possible reforms of the Chinese characters on the basis of the phonetic alphabet.

語音　Phonetics

第一課　Lesson 1

1.1　母音　a, o, e, i, u, ü
Vowels: "a" "o" "e" "i" "u" "ü",

1.2　子音　b, d, g
Consonants: "b", "d", "g"

1.3　拼音
Spelling

1.4　声調 (一)
Tones (1)

1.1　母音　a, o, e, i, u, ü

現代汉語語音以北京語音为标准音，北京語音有六个基本母音: a, o, e, i, u, ü. 現在講这些母音的發音:

1.1 Vowels: - "a", "o", "e", "i", "u" "ü".

The standard speech sounds of modern Chinese are based upon the speech sounds of Peking dialect. There are six basic vowels in Peking dialect: "a", "o", "e", "i", "u", "ü". Here is the pronunciation of these six vowels:

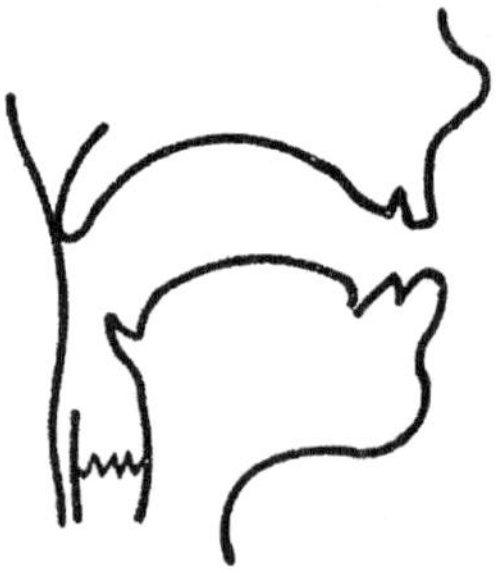

a: 舌下降至最低，口大張，唇不圓，气流通暢流出.

"a": It is produced by lowering the tongue, with the mouth and lips wide-open. The breath comes out freely.

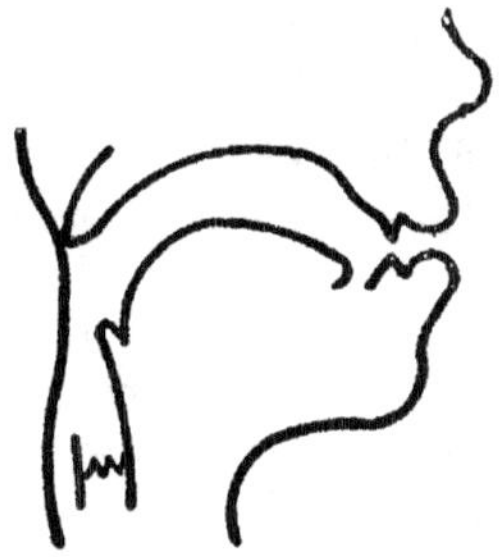

o: 舌根向軟顎上升，舌位半高，口稍微張开，唇略圓.

"o": It is produced by keeping the tongue in a half raised position with the back of the tongue towards the soft palate, the mouth a little open and the lips slightly rounded.

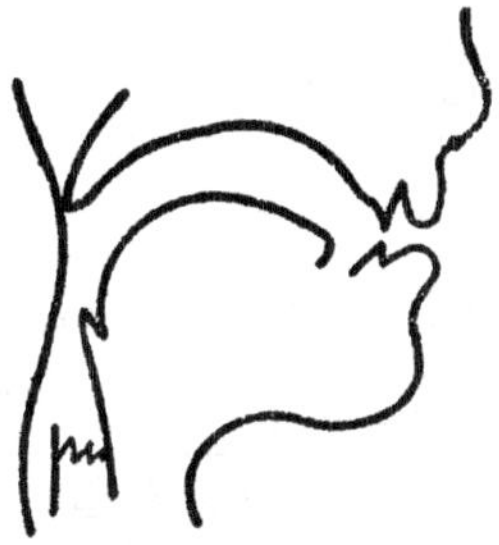

e: 舌根向軟顎上升，舌位比 o 略低，口半开，唇不圓，是与 o 相配的不圓唇母音.

"e": It is produced by raising the back of the tongue towards the soft palate, with the mouth half open and the tongue a little lower than in the case of "o". "e" is the unrounded vowel corresponding to the rounded vowel "o".

i: 舌面前部上升和硬顎相近，开口度很小，唇扁平，使气流由硬顎和舌面間向外送.

"i": It is produced by raising the front blade of the tongue towards the hard palate, with the mouth a little open and the lips flat, and then letting the breath come out between the hard palate and the blade of the tongue.

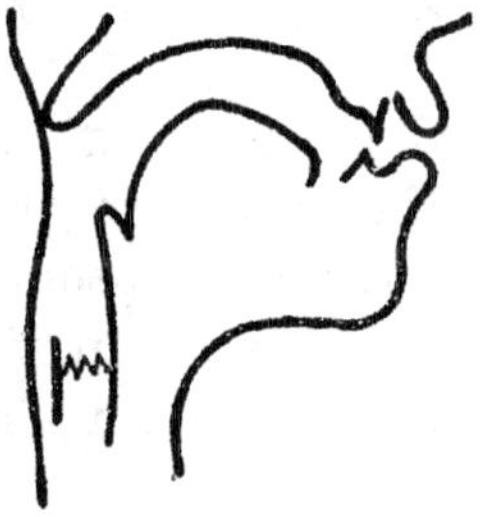

u: 舌根上升和軟顎相近，开口度和 i 相同，唇最圓，使气流由軟顎和舌根間向外送.

"u": It is produced by raising the back of the tongue towards the soft palate, and rounding the lips, with the mouth open as little as in pronouncing "i", and then letting the breath come out between the soft palate and the back of the tongue.

ü: 舌位和 i 相同，但唇形不同；唇形和 u 相同，但舌位不同；而开口度和 i，u 都相同．ü 是和 i 相对的圓唇母音，因此只要保持 i 的舌位，把嘴唇变成 u 的最圓形，就得到 ü 音．

"ü": The position of the tongue is like that of "i", but the shape of the lips is different; the shape of the lips is like that of "u", but the position of the tongue is different; the mouth is kept open as little as in pronouncing "i" and "u". "ü" is the rounded vowel corresponding to the unrounded vowel "i", and hence "ü" is produced only by keeping the tongue in the same position as in pronouncing "i" and the lips as rounded as in pronouncing "u".

1.2 子音 b, d, g

北京語音共有二十四个子音(包括 y, w)，按照發音方法和發音部位的不同，可以把这些音素分成若干組，現在講 b, d, g 的發音．这三个子音是不送气的清塞音，發音时开始气流通路完全阻塞，然后讓气流突然爆發出來．b 是双唇音，d 是舌尖音，g 是舌根音．

1.2 Consonants:- "b", "d", "g"

There are 24 consonants (including two semi-vowels "y" and "w") in Peking dialect. So far as their different positions and manners of pronunciation are concerned, they can be classified into several groups. In this lesson, only "b", "d" and "g" are introduced. These three consonants are unaspirated, voiceless, plosive sounds, because in pronouncing these consonants the passage of the breath is obstructed, and the pent-up air comes out with a pop. According to their positions of pronounciation, "b" is a labial plosive, "d" an alveolar plosive and "g" a velar plosive.

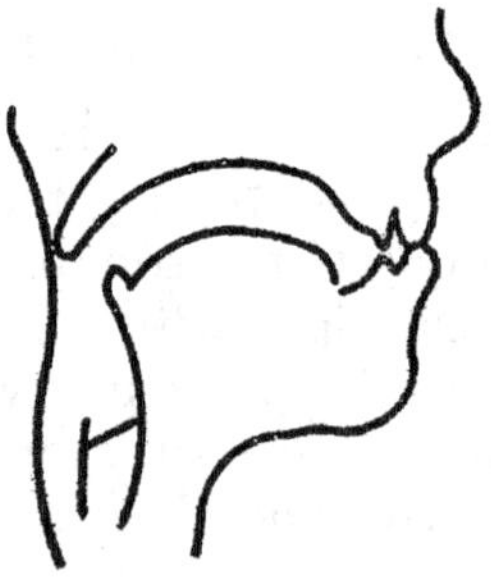

b: 双唇紧閉，口腔充滿气息，猛开双唇，使气流破唇而出，但不要尽量送气．声带不振动．

"b": It is produced by pressing the lips together, keeping the breath in the mouth for a moment, and then, opening the mouth and letting the pent-up air come out. Don't send forth too much air. The vocal cords do not vibrate.

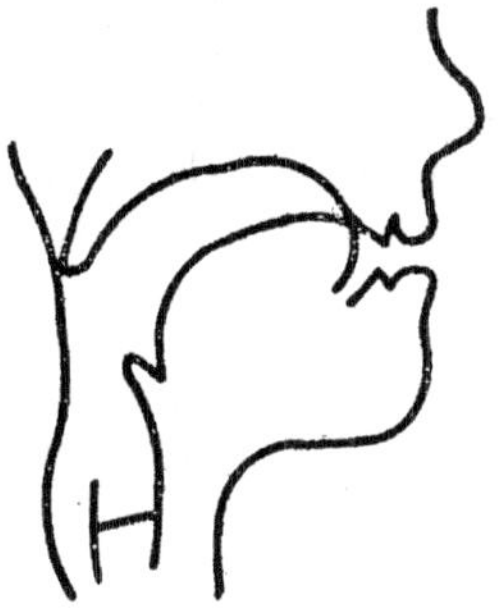

d: 舌尖頂上齿齦，口腔充滿气息，猛把舌尖移下，使气流爆發而出，但不要尽量送气．声带不振动．

"d": It is produced by raising the tip of the tongue against the gum of the upper teeth and then drawing it away to release the pent up air with a pop. Don't send forth too much air. The vocal cords do not vibrate.

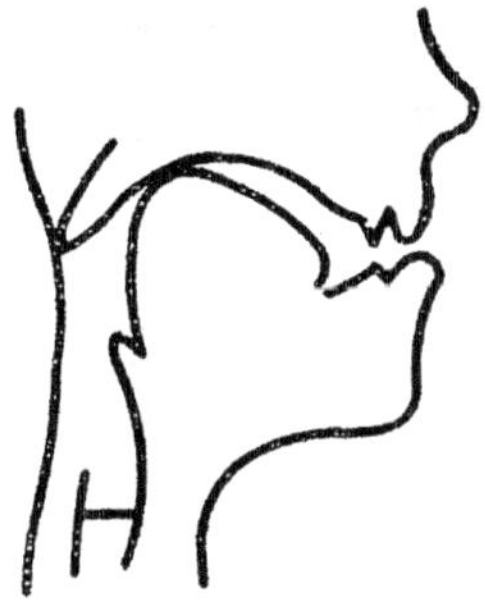

g: 舌根頂住軟顎，猛使舌根离开軟顎，使气流爆發而出，但不要尽量送气．声带不振动．

"g": It is produced by raising the back of the tongue against the soft palate, and then drawing it away to release the pent-up air with a pop. Don't send forth too much air. The vocal cords do not vibrate.

1.3 拼音

拼音就是两个或两个以上的音素連在一起，拼成一个音．如：

1.3 Spelling: —

Spelling is the joining of two or more sounds into one syllable. e. g.

b+a ⟶ ba
g+u ⟶ gu
d+i ⟶ di

1.4 声調（一）

声調是音高的变化状态（上升、下降或持續）．声調的升降是滑行的，不是跳跃的．在汉語里，每一个音节都有一定的声調，所以声調跟組成音节的母音、子音同样重要．有同样音素的詞，常因声調不同，就会表示出不同的意义．

1.4 Tones (1): —

The tone is the variation of pitch (rising, falling or continuing). The tone rises and falls by gliding and not by bounding. Every syllable in Chinese has its definite tone, and, therefore, tones are as important as vowels and consonants in forming syllables. It is only because of the difference of tones, that the meanings of words are different, although the spelling is the same.

北京語音的基本声調共有四个. 如果我們用一条直綫代表一个人說話的音高变动范圍，把这条直綫分为四等分，从下向上数，綫上有五个点，就可以分别代表五个音高:

There are four tones in Peking dialect. Let us draw a short vertical line to represent the range of the variation of pitch and divide it into four equal intervals with five points. These five points, counted from the bottom to the top, represent the five degrees:

5	高 调	the high-pitch
4	半高调	the mid-high pitch
3	中 调	the middle-pitch
2	半低调	the mid-low-pitch
1	低 调	the low-pitch

北京語音的四个基本声調，可以用下圖的 (1)、(2)、(3)、(4) 表示出来.

The four tones in Peking dialect are represented by (1), (2), (3) and (4) in the following fig. :

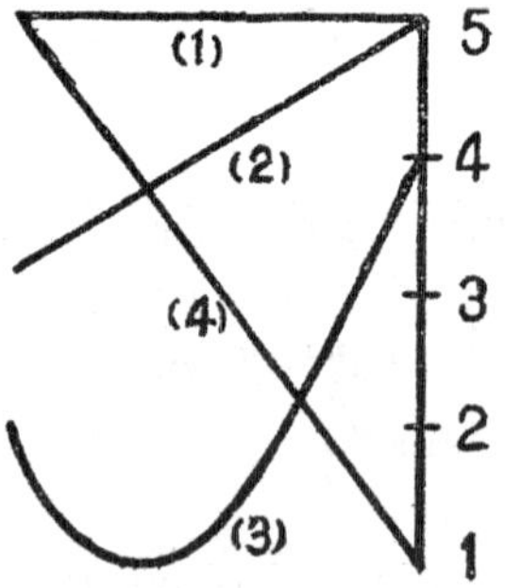

我們可以用声調符号 ˥，˧˥，˨˩˦，˥˩ 来描写这四个声调；为了簡便起見，平常簡写作 一，ˊ，ˇ，ˋ. 声調符号标在一个音节的母音（如果只有一个母音）或主要母音上.

We use the pitch-graphs "˥，˧˥，˨˩˦，˥˩ "to represent the four tones. But they can be simplified as follows: —，ˊ，ˇ，ˋ. They must be placed on the vowel (if there is only one vowel) or on the main vowel of a syllable.

本課先講第一声和第二声.

In this lesson we only deal with the 1st and 2nd tones.

第一声 (55) 是高平調. 我們用符号 "—" 表示. 如: gū, bā.

The 1st tone (55)、is a "high-level" tone. In writing it is represented by the pitch-graph "—". e. g. "gū", "bā".

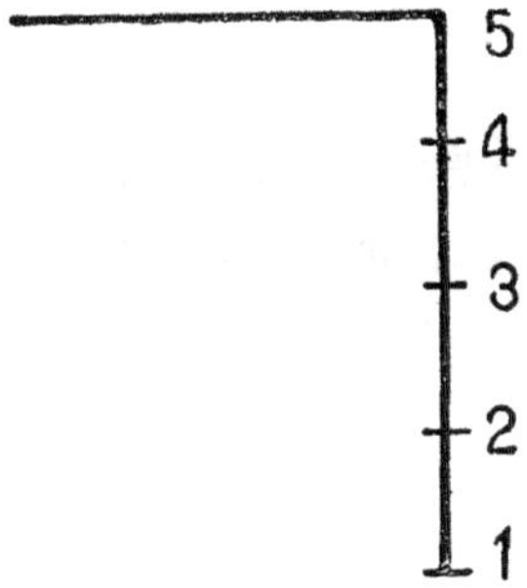

第二声 (35) 是高升調. 我們用符号 "ˊ" 表示. 如: dá, gé.

The 2nd tone (35) is a "high-rising" tone. It is represented by the pitch-graph "ˊ". e· g. "dá", "gé".

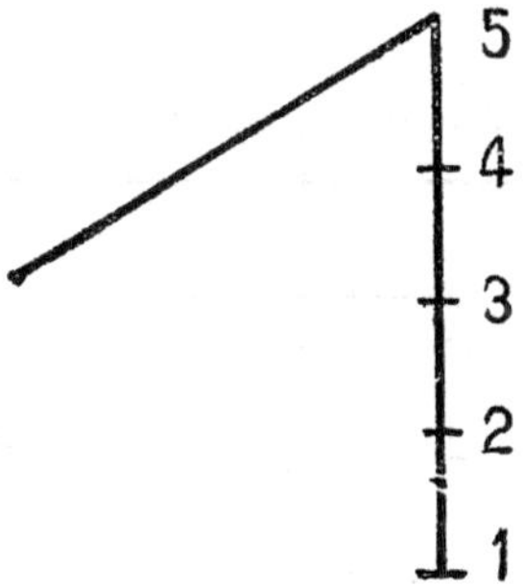

練習 Exercises

一、讀下列母音字母:

1) Read the following vowels:

a o e   a o e

a a   o o   e e

a o   a o   a o   a o

o e   o e   o e   o e

a e   a e   a e   a e

i u ü   i u ü

i i   u u   ü ü

i ü   i ü   i ü

u ü   u ü   u ü

a o e   i u ü

二、讀下列音节，注意音节中子音的發音:

2) Read the following syllables, paying attention to the pronunciation of the consonants:

bo de   bo de

ge bo   ge bo

de ge   de ge

bo de ge   bo de ge

bo de ge   bo de ge

bo bo   de de   ge ge

三、練習拼音:

3) Practise the following spellings:

	a	o	e	i	u	ü
b	ba	bo	—	bi	bu	—
d	da	—	de	di	du	—
g	ga	—	ge	—	gu	—

四、練習拼音及声調:

4) Practise the following spellings and tones:

ā	ā	á	á	
ǖ	ǖ	ǘ	ǘ	
bā	bā	bá	bá	
	bā	bá	bā	bá
dā	dā	dá	dá	
	dā	dá	dā	dá
bō	bō	bó	bó	
	bō	bó	bō	bó
gē	gē	gé	gé	
	gē	gé	gē	gé
bī	bī	bí	bí	
	bī	bí	bī	bí
dī	dī	dí	dí	
	dī	dí	dī	dí
bū	bū	bú	bú	
	bū	bú	bū	bú
dū	dū	dú	dú	
	dū	dú	dū	dú

課外練習 Home Work

一、念熟本課的練習,特别注意 o、e、ü 的發音.

1) Learn the above exercises by heart and pay special attention to the pronunciation of "o", "e" and "ü".

二、念熟第一声、第二声,特别注意第二声的音高.

2) Learn the 1st tone and the 2nd tone by heart, and pay special attention to the pitch of the 2nd tone.

三、念熟本課字母,作到能默写.

3) Read the vowels and consonants in this lesson as many times as you can, until you are able to write them out from your memory.

四、写五遍本課字母,交給教員檢查.

4) Write the phonetic symbols in this lesson five times and hand your writing to the teacher.

第二課　Lesson 2

2.1	子音　p, t, k, m, n, ng Consonants: "p", "t" ,"k", "m", "n", "ng"
2.2	复合母音 Compound Vowels
2.3	母音帯鼻音子音 Vowels Plus Nasal Consonants
2.4	声調（二） Tones (2)

2.1　子音　p, t, k, m, n, ng

2.1 Consonants:— "p", "t", "k", "m", "n", "ng"

(1) p, t, k

这是和 b, d, g 相当的送气清塞音，所以發这三个音时要使气流尽量放出. 發音部位和 b, d, g 一样: p 是双唇音，t 是舌尖音，k 是舌根音.

(1) "p", "t", "k"

These three consonants are aspirated, corresponding to the unaspirated "b", "d", and "g", and so in pronouncing these consonants, the breath has to be puffed out strongly. The positions of pronunciation of these consonants are the same as those of "b", "d", and "g": "p" is a labial plosive, "t" an alveolar plosive and "k" a velar plosive.

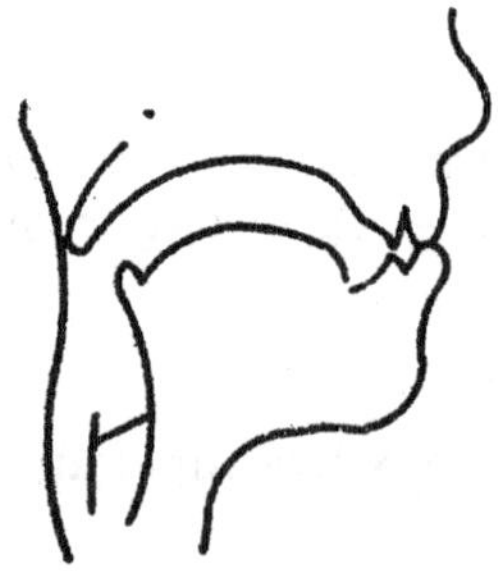

p: 在气流破唇而出时，要把气流尽量放出. 声带不振动.

"p": When the breath is about to puff out through the lips, emit as much air as possible. The vocal cords do not vibrate.

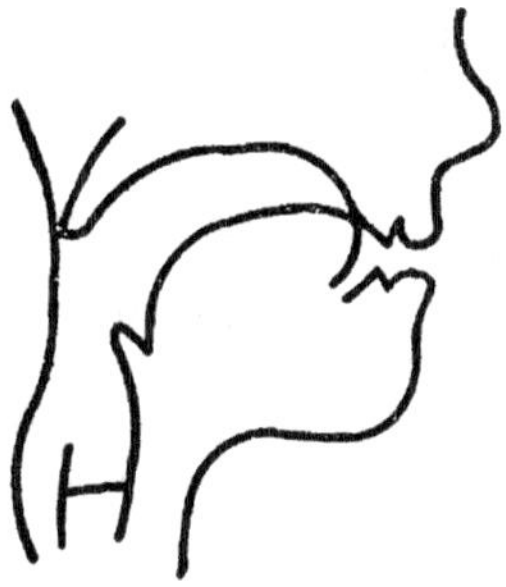

t: 在气流从口腔中爆發而出时，要把气流尽量放出. 声带不振动.

"t": When the breath is about to puff out through the mouth, emit as much air as possible. The vocal cords do not vibrate.

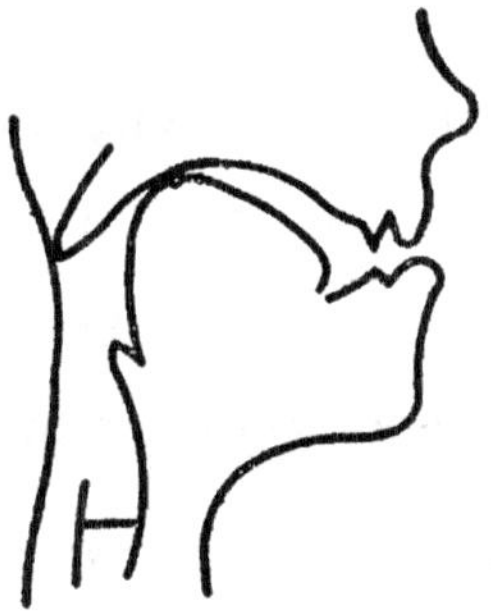

k: 在气流从口腔中爆發而出时，要把气流尽量放出. 声带不振动.

"k": When the breath is about to puff out through the mouth, emit as much air as possible. The vocal cords do not vibrate.

(2) m, n, ng

这三个是鼻音濁塞音. m 跟 b, n 跟 d, ng 跟 g 的口腔阻塞情形一样，不同的是：軟顎下垂，打开鼻腔通路，气流从鼻腔出来. m 是双唇音, n 是舌尖音, ng 是舌根音.

(2) "m", "n", "ng"

These 3 consonants are nasal, voiced, plosive sounds. The obstruction formed in the mouth in uttering "m" is like that in uttering "b", the obstruction formed in uttering "n" is like that in uttering "d", and the obstruction formed in uttering "ng" is like that in uttering "g". The difference is that in uttering "m", "n", and "ng" the soft palate must be lowered, thus opening the nasal passage and letting the breath come out from there. According to the positions of pronunciation, "m" is labial, "n" alveolar, and "ng" velar.

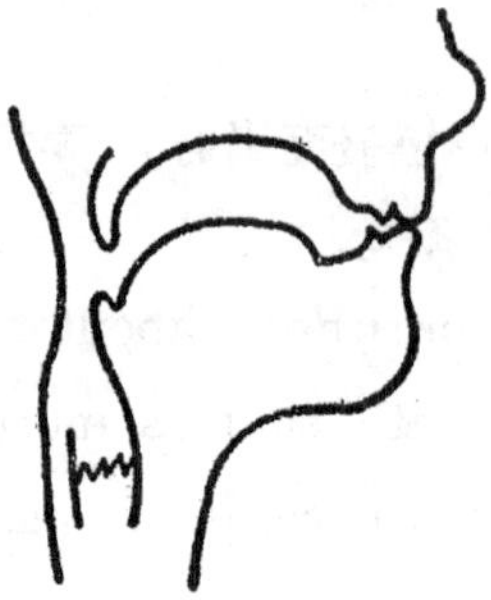

m: 紧閉双唇，气流从鼻腔通出．声带振动。

"m": It is produced by pressing the lips together, and letting the air go out through the nasal cavity. The vocal cords vibrate.

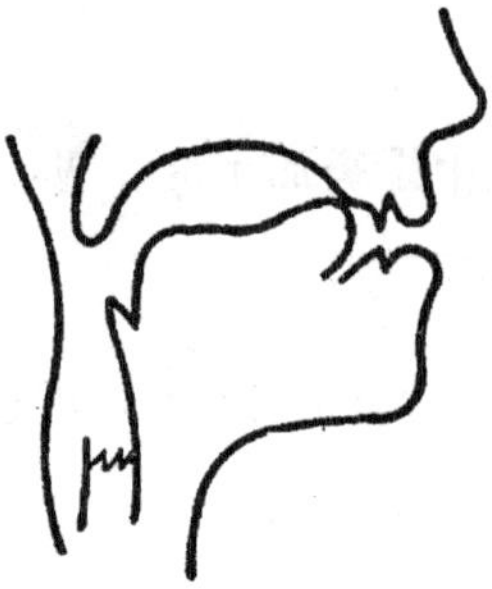

n: 舌尖頂上齿齦，气流从鼻腔通出．声带振动．

"n": It is produced by raising the tip of the tongue against the gum of the upper teeth, and letting the air come out of the nasal cavity. The vocal cords vibrate.

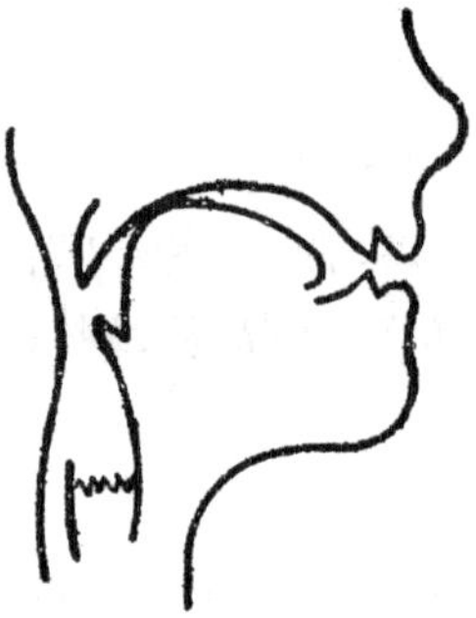

ng: 舌根貼住軟顎，气流从鼻腔通出．声带振动．（必須注意：在北京語音中 ng 只能用在音节末尾，不用在音节的开头）

"ng": It is produced by raising the back of the tongue against the soft palate, and letting the air go out through the nasal cavity. The vocal cords vibrate. (Note: In the phonetic system of Peking dialect, "ng" is only used at the end of a syllable, and never at the beginning of a syllable.)

2.2 复合母音

两个以至三个母音結合在一起，就形成一个复合母音．念复合母音时是从一个母音滑到或滑向另一个母音的地位上去，因此舌位、口腔开合、嘴唇形状都有变动．复合母音共有 13 个：

2.2 Compound Vowels (diphthongs and triphthongs):-

A compound vowel is formed by a combination of two or three vowels. The pronunciation of a compound vowel is starting from one vowel and then moving to or towards another vowel; hence there must be changes in the position of the tongue, the opening of the mouth and the shape of the lips. There are 13 compound vowels:

a:	ai	ao		
o:	ou			
e:	ei			
i:	ia	ie	iao	iou
u:	ua	uo	uai	uei
ü:	üe			

2.3 母音带鼻音子音

母音后面接上鼻音子音，可以拼成下面 16 个复合音:

2.3 Vowels Plus Nasal Consonants:-

The following 16 compound sounds are spelt by putting nasal consonants after vowels:

an	en	ang	eng	ong
ian	in	iang	ing	iong
uan	uen	uang	ueng	
üan	ün			

应該特別注意的是單独的母音和复合母音中的音值. 这里簡略地講以下几点:

The sonnd values of single vowels and compound vowels deserve special attention. A brief explanation will be given below:

1. a 和 ia, ua 中的 a 都是 [A]. ai, uai, an, uan, üan 中的 a 是前低不园唇母音 [a]. 細分起来, ai 和 üan 中的 a 近 [æ], [i] 应当是 [ɪ]. ao, iao, ang, iang, uang 中的 a 是后低不圓唇母音 [ɑ], 而 ian 中的 a 却是前半低不圓唇母音 [ɛ].

1. "a" and "a" in "ia", "ua" are [A]. "a" in "ai", "uai", "an", "uan" and "üan" is the front-low vowel [a] with the lips unrounded. Strictly speaking, "a" in "ai" and "üan" is similar to [æ], while [i] should be [ɪ]. "a" in "ao", "iao", "ang", "iang", and "uang" is the back-low unrounded vowel [ɑ], and "a" in "ian" is the front mid-low, unrounded vowel [ɛ].

2. o 和 uo, ou, iou 中的 o 都可以說是后半高母音 [o], 但略寬, 而唇又不很圓, 其不圓的程度 o, uo, ou 依次遞增. ou 中的 [u] 也略寬, iou 中的 [o], 音較輕微. ao, iao, ong, iong 中的 [o] 是較 [u] 寬的后高圓唇母音 [U].

2. "o" or "o" in "uo", "ou" and "iou" is the back-mid-high vowel [o], but a little wider, with the lips not too rounded. The rounding of the lips becomes increasingly less from "o", "uo", and "ou". [u] in "ou" is a little wider, while the sound of [o] in "iou" is rather weak. [o] in "ao", "iao", "ong" and "iong" is the back-high vowel [U] with rounded lips and wider than [u].

3. e 是后半高到半低的不圓唇母音 [ɤʌ], 也可以簡写为 [ɤ]. ie, üe 中的 e 是前半低不圓唇母音 [ɛ], 單用的 ê 也是 [ɛ]. ei, uei 中的 e 是前半高不圓唇母音 [e], 而其中的 [i] 略寬. uei 中的 [e], 音較輕微. en, uen 中的 e 是較高的中性母音 [ə]. uen 中的 [ə], 音較輕微. eng, ueng 中的 e 是后半低不圓唇母音 [ʌ].

3. "e" is the vowel [ɤʌ] uttered from back mid-high to mid-low with the lips unrounded; it may be written simply as [ɤ]. "e" in "ie", "üe" is the front mid-low vowel [ɛ] with the lips unrounded, while ê alone is also [ɛ]. "e" in "ei", "uei" is the front mid-high vowel [e] with the lips unrounded and [i] is a little wider, while the sound of [e] in "uei" is rather weak. "e" in "en" and "uen" is the high neutral vowel [ə], while the sound of [e] in "uen" is rather weak. "e" in "eng", "ueng" is the back mid-low vowel [ʌ] with the lips unrounded.

4. 在 ün 中, ü [y] 后有輕微的 [ɪ] 音.

4. In ün, ü [y] is followed by a weak [ɪ] sound.

2.4 声調 (二)

本課講第三声和第四声.

2.4 Tones (2):

In this lesson we discuss the 3rd and the 4th tones in Peking dialect.

第三声 (214) 是降升調: 由半低調降至低調, 再升至半高調. 我們用符号 "✓" 表示. 如 bǎ, nǚ.

The 3rd tone (214) is a "falling-and-rising" tone, it decends from the mid-low pitch to the low pitch and then rises up to the mid-high pitch. It is represented by the pitch-graph "✓", e. g. "bǎ" and "nǚ".

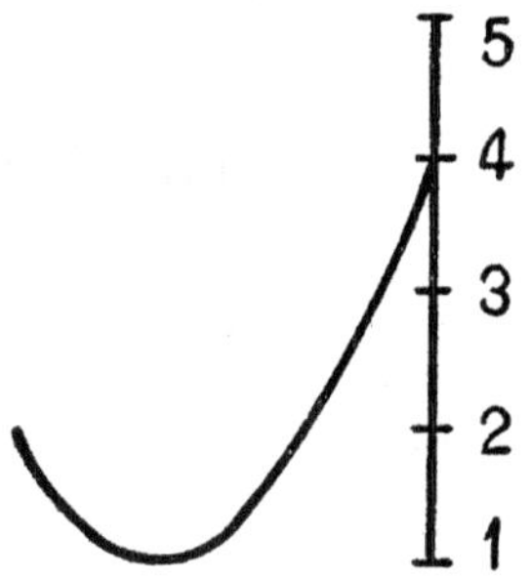

第四声 (51) 是全降调： 由高降低的调子. 我們用符号 "↘" 表示. 如 tù, pò.

The 4th tone (51) is a "falling" tone, it falls from high to low. The pitch-graph is "↘", e. g. "tù" and "pò".

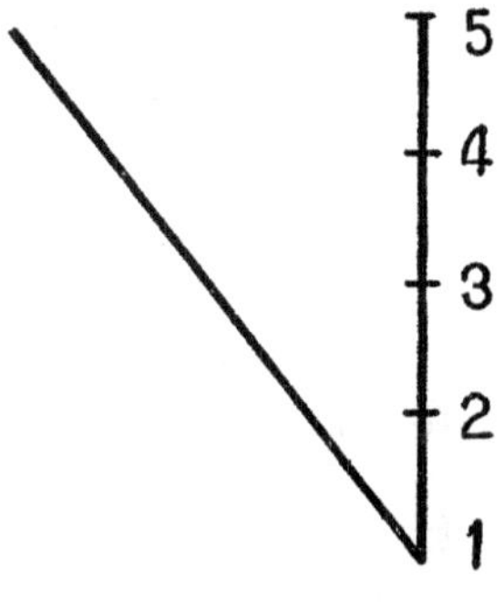

学習声調必須注意：

In learning the four tones the following points have to be noticed:

(1) 我們上面用的等分直綫圖， 只表示北京語音四个基本声調的音高变化，实际上各人所發声音的絕对音高是不同的.

(1) The above figures only indicate the pitch variation of the four tones in Peking dialect. Actually the pitch of human voice is not the same for all persons.

(2) 声調是音高变化的状态，跟音的强弱无关.

(2) The tone represents the pitch variation, it has no relation to the intensity of sound.

(3) 四个声調的音長也不尽相同，仔細分析起来是：第三声最長，第二声、第一声次之，第四声最短.

(3) The four tones are different in length, and in analysis, the 3rd tone is the longest, and the 1st and the 2nd tones are longer than the 4th tone.

練習 Exercises

一、讀下列音节，注意音节中子音的發音:

1) Read the following syllables, paying attention to the pronunciation of the consonants:

po te ke   po te ke
po te ke   po te ke
po po   te te   ke ke

po te   po te
ke po   ke po
te ke   te ke

bo bo   po po
bo po   bo po
de de   te te
de te   de te
ge ge   ke ke
ge ke   ge ke
bo de ge   po te ke

mo mo   ne ne
mo ne   mo ne

二、讀下列复合母音:

2) Read the following compound vowels:

a	i	ai		a	i	ai
a	o	ao		a	o	ao
o	u	ou		o	u	ou
e	i	ei		e	i	ei
i	a	ia		i	a	ia
i	ê	ie		i	ê	ie
i	ao	iao		i	ao	iao
i	ou	iou		i	ou	iou
u	a	ua		u	a	ua
u	o	uo		u	o	uo
u	ei	uei		u	ei	uei
u	ai	uai		u	ai	uai
ü	ê	üe		ü	ê	üe

三、讀下列复合音，注意 -n 和 -ng 的区别：

3) Read the following compound syllables and pay attention to the difference between -n and -ng:

an	an	ang	ang
en	en	eng	eng
an	en	ang	eng
in	in	ing	ing
uen	uen	ueng	ueng
uen	uen	ong	ong
in	uen	ing	ueng
ün	ün	iong	iong
uen	ün	ueng	iong

an	ang	ong	an	ang	ong
ian	iang	iong	ian	iang	iong
uan	uang		uan	uang	
üan			üan		

四、練習声調：

4) Practise the following tones:

ǔ	ǔ	ù	ù·	ǔ	ù
bǎ	bǎ	bà	bà	bǎ	bà
pǎo	pǎo	pào	pào	pǎo	pào
kǎn	kǎn	kàn	kàn	kǎn	kàn
bǎng	bǎng	bàng	bàng	bǎng	bàng

děng	děng	dèng	dèng	déng	dèng
pǐn	pǐn	pìn	pìn	pǐn	pìn

ī	í	ǐ	ì
ū	ú	ǔ	ù
mō	mó	mǒ	mò
ǖn	ǘn	ǚn	ǜn
īng	íng	ǐng	ìng

課外練習 Home Work

一、熟讀本課練習，特别注意:

1. b p, d t, g k 發音方法的不同.

2. an en, ang eng, in uen ün, ong ing ueng iong 的發音.

3. 第三声和第二声的区别.

1) Learn the above exercises and pay special attention to: 1. the different pronunciation between "b" and "p", "d" and "t", "g" and "k". 2. the pronunciation of "an, en", "ang, eng", "in, uen, ün" and "ong, ing, ueng, iong". 3. the difference between the 2nd and the 3rd tones.

二、写熟本課字母，作到能默写.

2) Learn all the phonetic symbols in this lesson by heart, until you can write them out from yonr memory.

三、写五遍本課的新字母，交給教員檢查.

3) Write the new phonetic symbols five times, and hand your writing to the teacher.

第三課 Lesson 3

3.1 子音 f, h, l, z, c, s

3.1 Consonants:— "f", "h", "l", "z", "c", "s"

(1) f, h

这两个子音是清擦音. 發音时气流通路縮小, 并不完全阻塞, 讓气流摩擦而出. f 是唇齿音, h 是舌根音.

(1) "f" and "h"

These two consonants are voiceless fricatives. In pronouncing them, the passage of the breath is small but not completely obstructed, so that the breath comes out with friction. According to their positions of pronunciation, "f" is a labio-dental fricative, and "h" a velar fricative.

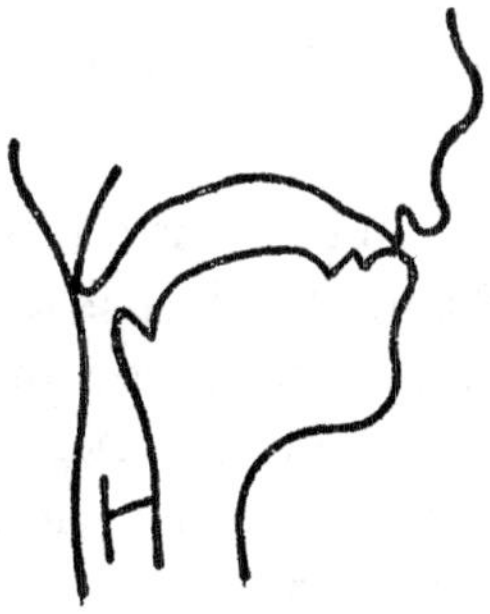

f: 上齿接触下唇, 气流从中間摩擦而出. 声带不振动.

"f"; Press the lower-lip against the upper teeth, and let the breath come out with friction. The vocal cords do not vibrate.

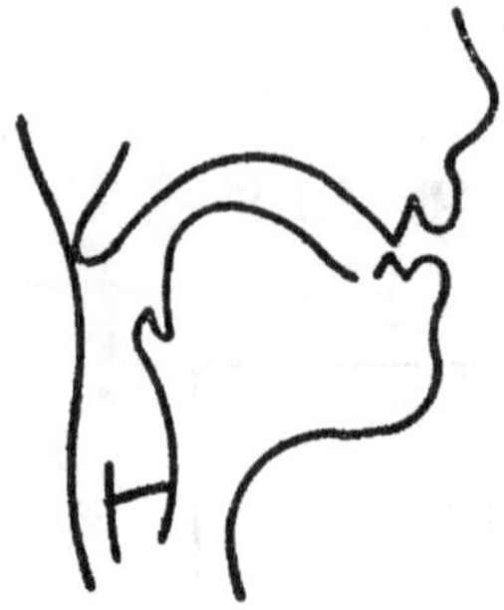

h: 舌根接近軟顎，气流从中間摩擦而出．声带不振动．

"h": Raise the back of the tongue towards the soft palate, and let the breath rub through the channel thus made. The vocal cords do not vibrate.

(2) l:

这是舌尖濁边音，發音时舌尖接触上齿齦，舌尖中間的通路阻塞，气流从舌头的两边出来．声带振动．

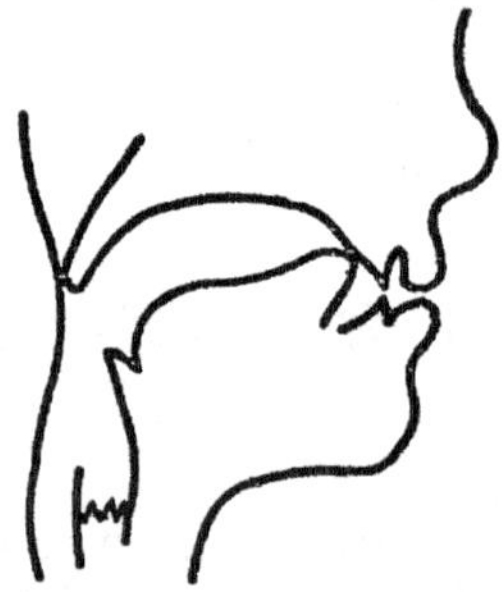

(2) "l"

It is a voiced alveolar lateral. It is produced by raising the tip of the tongue against the gum of the upper teeth to stop the air passage, and thus letting the air come out by the sides of the tongue. The vocal cords vibrate.

(3) z, c

z 是不送气清塞擦音，c 是送气清塞擦音．發音时开始气流通路完全阻塞，然后慢慢打开，讓气流从口腔中所留的空隙間摩擦出来，它的閉塞成分和摩擦成分結合得很紧．这两个子音是舌尖前音．

(3) "z" and "c"

"z" is an unaspirated voiceless affricate, and "c" is an aspirated voiceless affricate. In pronouncing them, the air passage is completely obstructed, then the passage is opened slowly and the air is let out by rubbing through the narrow channel in the mouth, and so the obstruction and the friction come close together. Both of them are blade-alveolar affricates.

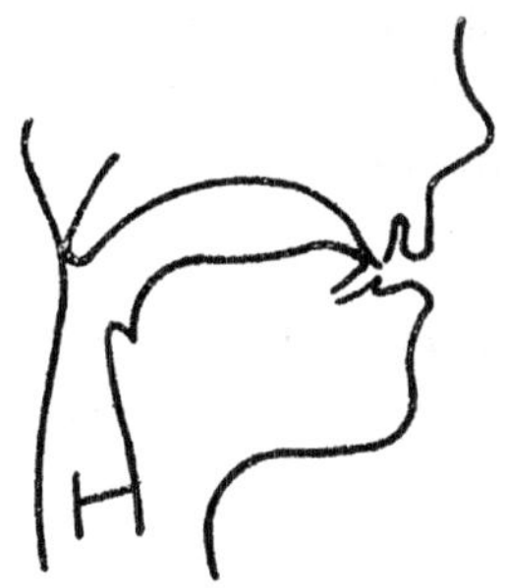

z: 舌尖頂上齿齦，气流从舌尖与齿縫間爆發摩擦而出，但不要尽量送气，声带不振动.

"z": Press the tip of the tongue against the gum of the upper teeth, and let the breath puff out and rub through the narrow channel thus made between the tip of the tongue and the teeth. Don't emit too much air. The vocal cords do not vibrate.

c: 与 z 發音不同的是要尽量送气，除此以外都相同.

"c": The pronunciation of this sound is the same as that of "z" sound. The only difference is that "c" is pronounced with a strong puff of breath.

(4) s

这是舌尖前清擦音. 發音时舌尖接近下齿背面，气流从舌面中縫跟上齿中間摩擦而出.

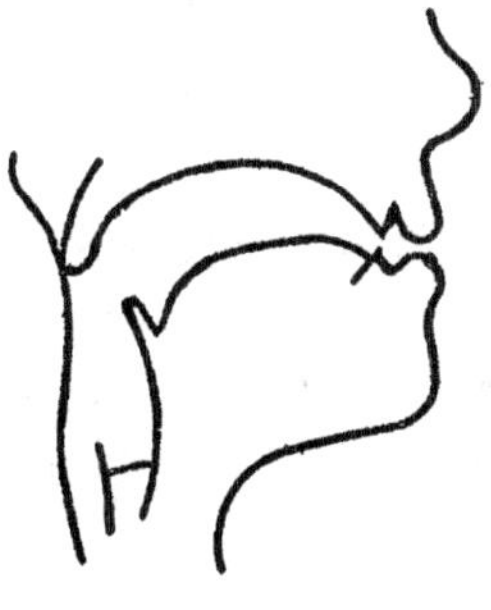

(4) "s"

It is a blade-alveolar voiceless fricative, and is produced by lowering the tip of the tongue to the back of the lower teeth, and letting the breath rub through the narrow channel between the middle of the blade and the upper teeth.

3.2 z, c, s 后面的舌尖前母音　在 z, c, s 后面的舌尖前母音 [ɿ]，我們也用 i 来表示，因为在北京語音里 i [i] 不在 z, c, s 后面出現，所以不致混淆. 这个母音只在 z, c, s 后面出現，所以听起来好像是前面子音摩擦成分的延長和減弱，而这个延長和減弱的成分是带音的.

3.2 The Blade-alveolar Vowel after "z", "c", "s":—

The blade-alveolar vowel [ɿ] after "z", "c", "s" is also represented by "i". There cannot be any confusion, because the vowel sound of "i" [i] never occurs after "z" "c", "s" in Peking dialect. This vowel [ɿ] only occurs after z, c, s, therefore it sounds like the voiced prolongation and weakening of the fricative element of the preceding consonant.

3.3 卷舌母音 er (-r)

發母音 er (-r) 时舌头的位置由央元音 e (国际音标 [ə]) 稍稍向前推动，舌尖向硬顎翘起，形成一个带有卷舌音 -r 的 e. 發音时口腔的开合情况由略开到略关.

3.3 Retroflex Vowel "er(-r)":—

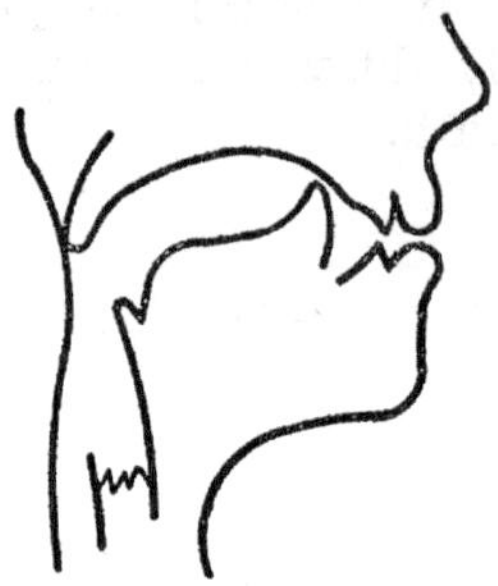

This sound is produced with the tongue a little forward from the position of the mixed vowel "e" (the international phonetic symbol is [ə]), with the tip of the tongue turned up towards the hard palate, thus producing "e" sound with a curved tongue "r". In pronouncing this sound, keep the mouth from a little open at first to a little close.

3.4 汉字字素 (一)

汉語書写符号的汉字，一般都是由几部分組成的. 把汉字的每个組成部分分析出来以后，我們叫它作"汉字字素"(有一些字素可以独立存在，这些也就是汉字). 汉字字素是由汉字的基本笔划組成的. 我們在学習时特别要注意这些基本笔划的写法和組成字素 (或汉字) 时的下笔順序等等.

3.4 Components of Chinese Characters (1):—

The Chinese characters, the written symbols of the Chinese language, are, in general, constituted of several parts. Each part of a Chinese character is called a "component of the Chinese character" (some components are also characters when they stand by themselves). The components of Chinese characters are composed of a number of basic strokes. Therefore, we should pay much attention to the ways of writing of these basic strokes and the order of the strokes in making any component (or character).

本課先講汉字的基本笔划．基本笔划最主要的有七个:

In this lesson, we only deal with the basic strokes of Chinese characters. The following seven basic strokes are the most elementary:

練習 Exercises

一、讀下列音节，注意音节中的子音發音:

1) Read the following syllables, paying attention to the pronunciation of the consonants:

fo	fo	he	he	le	le
fo	fo	he	he	le	le
le	le	he	he	fo	fo

le	fo	he	le	fo	he
zi	zi	zi	ci	ci	ci

zi	zi	ci	ci
zi	zi	ci	ci
si	si	zi	zi
si	si	zi	zi

zi	ci	si	zi	ci	si
si	ci	zi	si	ci	zi

二、讀下列拼音:

2) Read the following spellings:

fū	fú	fǔ	fù
hāo	háo	hǎo	hào
luō	luó	luǒ	luò
zāo	záo	zǎo	zào
zān	zán	zǎn	zàn
cāi	cái	cǎi	cài
sōng	sóng	sǒng	sòng
cī	cí	cǐ	cì

三、讀卷舌母音:

3) Read the following retroflex vowel "er":

er		er		er			
ēr		ér		ěr		èr	
ēr	ēr	ér	ér	ěr	ěr	èr	èr

四、練習基本笔划.

4) Practise writing the basic strokes.

課外練習 Home Work

一、讀熟本課練習的前三項，特別注意 z, c 的發音.

1) Read the first three sections of the exercises several times and pay attention to the pronunciation of "z" and "c".

二、写熟汉字基本笔划.

2) Copy the basic strokes of Chinese characters in this lesson several times.

三、写五遍本課字母及基本笔划交給教員検查.

3) Write the new phonetic symbols and basic strokes of characters five times, and then hand your exercise-book to the teacher.

第四課 Lesson 4

4.1 子音 zh, ch, sh, r, j, q, x

4.1 Consonants:— "zh", "ch", "sh", "r", "j", "q", "x"

(1) zh, ch

zh 是不送气清塞擦音，ch是送气清塞擦音．發音时开始气流通路完全阻塞，然后慢慢打开，讓气流从口腔中所留的空隙間摩擦出来，它的閉塞成分和摩擦成分結合得很紧．这两个子音是舌尖后音（又名卷舌音）．

(1) "zh" and "ch"

"zh" is an unaspirated voiceless affricate, and "ch" is an aspirated voiceless affricate. In pronouncing them, the passage of the breath is completely obstructed, then it is opened slowly and the air is let through by rubbing the narrow channel in the mouth. The obstruction and the friction come close together. These two consonants are blade-palatal sounds (or retroflex sounds).

zh: 舌尖上卷頂住硬顎，气流从舌尖与硬顎間爆發摩擦而出，但不要尽量送气．声带不振动．

"zh": Turn up the tip of the tongue against the hard palate, and then let the breath puff out and rub through the channel between the tip of the tongue and the hard palate. Don't emit too much air. The vocal cords do not vibrate.

ch: 与 zh 發音不同的是要尽量送气，除此以外都相同．

"ch": The pronunciation of this sound is the same as that of "zh" sound. The only difference is that "zh" is produced with a strong puff of breath.

(2) sh, r

sh 是清擦音，r 是濁擦音．这两个子音是舌尖后音．

(2) "sh" and "r"

These two consonants are also blade-palatal sounds. "sh" is a voiceless fricative and "r" is a voiced fricative.

sh: 舌尖上卷接近硬顎，气流从舌尖与硬顎間摩擦而出．声带不振动．

"sh": Turn up the tip of the tongue near the hard palate, and let the air rub through the channel between the tip of the tongue and the hard palate. The vocal cords do not vibrate.

r: 是和 sh 相对的濁音，發音时声带振动．（在 zh, ch, sh, r 后面的舌尖后母音 [ʅ]，我們也用 i 来表示，因为在北京語音里 i [i] 不在 zh, ch, sh, r 后面出現，所以不致混淆．这个母音只在 zh, ch, sh, r 后面出現，所以听起来像是前面子音摩擦成分的延長和減弱，而这个延長和減弱的成分是带音的．）

"r": It is the voiced sound corresponding to "sh", and so in producing this sound the vocal cords vibrate. (The blade-palatal vowel [ʅ] after zh, ch, sh, r is also represented by "i". There can be no confusion, because the vowel sound of "i" [i] never occurs after zh, ch, sh, r in Peking dialect. This vowel [ʅ] only occurs after "zh", "ch", "sh", "r", therefore it sounds like the voiced prolongation and weakening of the fricative element of the preceding consonant.

(3) j, q

j 是不送气清塞擦音，q 是送气清塞擦音. 發音时开始气流通路完全阻塞，然后慢慢打开，讓气流从口腔中所留的空隙間摩擦出来，它的閉塞成分和摩擦成分結合得很紧. 这两个子音是舌面前音.

(3) "j" and "q"

"j" is an unaspirated voiceless affricate and "q" an aspirated voiceless affricate. In producing these two sounds, the air passage is completely obstructed, then it is slowly opened and the air is let through by rubbing the narrow channel in the mouth. The obstruction and the friction come close together. These two consonants are front-palatal sounds.

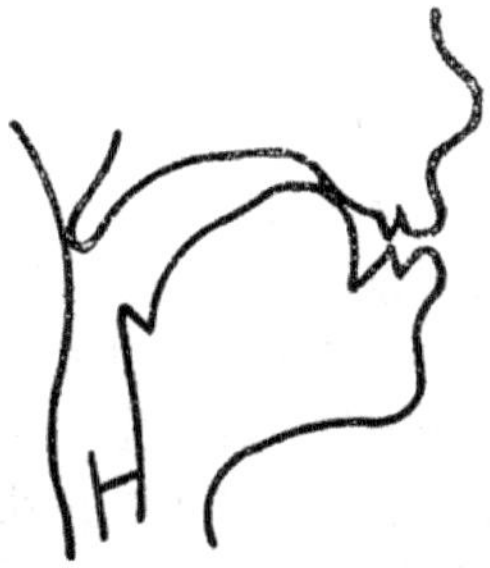

j: 舌面前部貼硬顎，舌尖頂下齿背，气流从舌面前部与硬顎間爆發摩擦而出，但不要尽量送气. 声带不振动.

"j": Raise the front of the tongue to the hard palate, place the tip of the tongue against the back of the lower teeth, and then let the air puff out and rub through the channel between the front of the tongue and the hard palate. Don't emit too much air. The vocal cords do not vibrate.

q: 与 j 發音不同的是要尽量送气. 除此以外都相同.

"q": The pronunciation of this sound is the same as that of "j" sound, except that it should be produced with a strong puff of breath.

(4) x

x 是清擦音. 發音时舌面前部与硬顎相近，气流从舌面前部与硬顎間摩擦而出. 声带不振动.

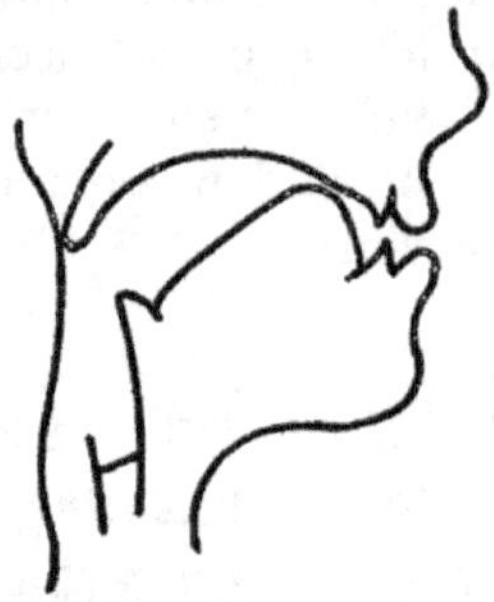

(4) "x"

"x" is a voiceless fricative. It is produced by raising the front of the tongue near the hard palate, and then letting the air rub through the channel between the front of the tongue and the hard palate. The vocal cords do not vibrate.

4.2 北京話的語音結构

4.2 The Syllable Construction of Peking Dialect:—

(1) 北京話里，單純母音，复合母音或母音結合子音（子音在母音前或后）都可以构成音节（單独的子音不能构成音节），而每一个音节都有一定的声調 (1.4). 例如:

(1) In Peking dialect, a single vowel, a compound vowel or a vowel with a consonant (whether the consonant stands before the vowel or after) may form a syllable, but a consonant cannot form a syllable by itself. Every syllable has its definite tone. e. g.

è	(餓	hungry)	ài	(愛	to love)
ēn	(恩	favour)	hé	(河	river)
bǎo	(飽	full, to eat one's fill)	shuāng	(霜	frost)

(2) 一个音节用汉語的書写符号汉字紀录下来就是一个汉字. 因此也可以用中国傳統的方法分析: 一个字音一般包含声母（音节开头的子音）和韻母（声母除外的部分），而每一个字都有一定的声調. 像上例 hé (河), shuāng (霜), h 和 sh 是声母，e uang 是韻母，hé 是第二声，shuāng 是第一声. 此外，也有一些只有韻母而沒有声母的字，就叫零声母字，例如 ēn (恩).

(2) Every syllable is a Chinese characther. Therefore, according to the Chinese traditional method of phonetic analysis, the sound of a character may be generally divided into

"shēng" 声母 (the consonant at the beginning of a syllable) and "yùn" 韻母 (the rest of the syllable after the consonant). Besides, every character has its proper tone. In "hé" and "shuāng" given in the above examples, "h" and "sh" are "shēng's" 声母, "e" and "uang" are "yùn's" 韻母; "hé" is in the second tone, and "shuāng" is in the first tone. But there are also characters which are composed of only "yùn" 韻母, such as: "ēn" in the above examples.

(3) 我們知道北京話的一个音节包含声母和韻母. 韻母可以是一个單独的(主要)母音, 如 chá (茶); 也可以是既有主要母音又有介音和韻尾的, 如 biǎo (表); 有时也可以只有介音和主要母音, 如 shuō (說); 或只有主要母音和韻尾, 如 kàn (看). 介音只有 i, u, ü 三个. 我們可以給韻母分个类: 1. 无介音或不用 i, u, ü 做主要母音的; 2. 有介音 i 或用 i 做主要母音的; 3. 有介音 u 或用 u 做主要母音的; 4. 有介音 ü 或用 ü 做主要母音的. 任何母音都可以做主要母音, 任何子音 (除了 -ng) 都可以做声母. 声母和韻母的配合关系主要由声母的發音部位和韻母的类别决定的. 哪些声母和哪些韻母相拼或不相拼, 可以看下表:

(3) Every syllable in Peking Dialect consists of a "shēng" and a "yùn". A "yùn" can be a single (main) vowel, e.g. chá (tea); it can also be a vowel plus a medial vowel and a "yùn ending", e. g. biǎo (watch); sometimes it can be a medial-vowel and a main vowel. e. g. shuō (to speak, to say); or only a vowel and a "yün ending", e.g. kàn (to see). There are only three medial vowels: "i", "u" and "ü". "yùn's" can be divided into four types: 1. those without medial vowel or without "i", "u", "ü" as the main vowel; 2. those with the medial vowel "i" or using "i" as the main vowel; 3. those with the medial vowel "u" or using "u" as the main vowel; 4. those with the medial vowel "ü" or using "ü" as the main vowel. Any vowel can be a main vowel and any consonant (except "-ng") can be a "shēng". The combinations of "shēng" and "yùn" are chiefly determined by the positions of articulation of "shēng" and the type of "yùn". The following table shows all the possible combinations of "shēng" and "yùn":

韻母 yùn / 声母 shēng	1	2	3	4
b p m	+	+	+	—
f	+	—	+	—
d t	+	+	+	—
n l	+	+	+	+
z c s	+	—	+	—
zh ch sh r	+	—	+	—
j q x	—	+	—	+
g k h	+	—	+	—
0	+	+	+	+

"+" 表示声母和韻母可以相拼，"—" 表示不能相拼.

"0" 表示零声母.

"+" indicates that "shēng" can go with "yùn", while "—" indicates that it cannot.

"0" indicates zero "shēng".

4.3 关于写法的四点注意

4.3 Four Points about the Ways of Writing:—

(1) i, u, ü 和以 i, u, ü 开头的韻母如果前面没有声母的时候，应該写作:

(1) When "i", "u", "ü" and a "yùn" 韻母 beginning with "i", "u" or "ü" are not preceded by any "shēng" 声母, they must be written as follows:

yi, ya, ye, yan, you, yao, yin,
yang, ying, yong.
wu, wa, wo, wai, wei,

wan, wen, wang, weng.

yu, yue, yuan, yun (ü 上两点省略).

(The two dots on ü are omitted.)

(2) ü 以及以 ü 开头的韻母和声母 j, q, x 相拼时写成 ju, qu, xu, ü上两点省略. 但和声母 n, l 相拼时, 仍然写成 nü, lü.

(2) When "ü" or a "yùn" 韻母 beginning with "ü" spells with "j", "q", "x", they may be written as "ju", "qu", "xu", without the two dots on "ü", but when the consonants "n", "l" are followed by "ü", the two dots cannot be omitted, e.g. "nü", "lü".

(3) iou, uei, uen 是基本式, 但前面加声母时一律写成: -iu, -ui, -un. 在 -iou, -uei 簡写作 -iu, -ui 后, 声調符号应划在音节最后的 u 或 i 上. 例如 niú, guì.

(3) "iou", "uei" and "uen" are basic forms, but they must be written as "—iu", "—ui" and "—un", when they are preceded by a consonant. The tone-graph is placed on the last vowel "u" or "i" in the simplified forms, "—iu" and "—ui", e. g. "niú", "guì".

(4) a, o, e 开头的音节連接在其他音节后面的时候, 如果音节的界限發生混淆, 用隔音符号 (') 隔开, 如:

(4) In case two syllables of which the second one begins with "a", "o", "e" should run into each other and cause confusion in pronunciation, the dividing sign "'" must be used. e. g.

{ fáng'ài 妨碍 (to hinder)
{ fāngài 翻盖 (to rebuild)

4.4 汉字字素 (二)

4.4 Components of Chinese Characters (2):—

1 去 qù to go

去

土

厶

2 唱 chàng to sing

唱

口

日

曰

練習 Exercises

一、讀下列音节，注意音节中子音的發音：

1) Read the following syllables, paying attention to the pronunciation of the consonants:

zhi	chi	shi	ri
zhi	chi	shi	ri
zhi	zhi	chi	chi
shi	shi	ri	ri
zhi	chi	zhi	chi
zhi	chi	zhi	chi
shi	ri	shi	ri
zhi	chi	zhi	chi
shi	ri	shi	ri

ji	qi	xi	ji	qi	xi
ji	ji	qi	qi	xi	xi
ji	qi	ji	qi	ji	qi
qi	xi	qi	xi	qi	xi
ji	xi	ji	xi	ji	xi
qi	ji	qi	ji	qi	ji

二、讀下列音节，注意写法.

2) Read the following syllables and pay attention to their ways of writing:

1. è, ài, ǒu, yǔ, wǎng, yǒng.
2. yōu, wán, yá, yì, yíng, wǒ, wǔ, wèng, yūan, yǔn.
3. jǔ, qù, xuǎn, qióng, lǚ, nǚ.
4. huí, wèi, guì, kuí, wěi, liū, qiú, diū, jiǔ, xiù, lún, wén, chūn, shùn, tóng, wēng.

5. { yīn àn 陰暗 (gloomy)
{ yínán 疑难 (puzzle)

{ míngē 民歌 (folk song)
{ míng'é 名額 (number)

{ fáng'ài 妨碍 (to hinder)
{ fāngài 翻盖 (to rebuild)

三、讀下列双音节詞:

3) Read the following dissyllabic words:

1. zhuānjiā 2. qīngnián 3. sīxiǎng
4. yīnsù 5. yánjiū 6. rénmín
7. niúnǎi 8. zázhì 9. diàndēng
10. wèntí 11. fùnǚ

四、注意下列汉字字素的基本笔划, 練習抄写:

4) Notice the basic strokes of the following components of Chinese characters and copy them several times:

1	土	一 十 土
2	厶	ㄥ 厶
3	口	丨 冂 口
4	日	丨 冂 冃 日
5	曰	丨 冂 冃 曰

課外練習 Home Work

一、熟讀本課練習, 特别注意 zh, ch, sh, r, j, q 的發音.

1) Learn the exercises of this lesson by heart, and pay attention to the pronunciation of "zh" "ch", "sh", "r", "j" and "q".

二、抄写一遍練習中的第二項,抄完后朗讀一遍,以后交給教員檢查.

2) Copy the second section of the exercises, read it aloud, and then hand it to the teacher.

三、抄写五遍本課汉字字素交給教員檢查.

3) Copy the components of Chinese characters five times, and hand your writing to the teacher.

第五課 Lesson 5

5.1 汉語拼音字母表

5.1 Table of the Chinese Phonetic Alphabet:—

字 母 letters			字 母 letters		
印刷体 printed form	書写体 written form	字母的名称 names	印刷体 printed form	書写体 writtten form	字母的名称 names
A a	A a	[a]	N n	N n	[nɛ]
B b	B b	[pɛ]	O o	O o	[o]
C c	C c	[tsʻɛ]	P p	P p	[pʻɛ]
D d	D d	[tɛ]	Q q	Q q	[tɕʻiou]
E e	E e	[ə]	R r	R r	[ar]
F f	F f	[ɛf]	S s	S s	[ɛs]
G g	G g	[kɛ]	T t	T t	[tʻɛ]
H h	H h	[xa]	U u	U u	[u]
I i	I i	[i]	V v	V v	[vɛ] *
J j	J j	[tɕiɛ]	W w	W w	[wa]
K k	K k	[kʻɛ]	X x	X x	[ɕi]
L l	L l	[ɛl]	Y y	Y y	[ja]
M m	M m	[ɛm]	Z z	Z z	[tsɛ]

* V [v] 只用来拼写外来語、少数民族語言和方言.

The letter "v" is used only in spelling the words adopted from foreign languages, languages of national minorities and various dialects.

5.2 母音表及子音表

5.2 Table of the Chinese Vowels and Table of the Chinese Consonants:—

(1) 母音表

(1) Table of the Chinese Vowels

	舌尖母音 tip-tongue vowels		舌面母音 palatal vowels		
	前 blade-alveolar	央或后 blade-palatal	前 front	央 central	后 back
高(关) high (close)	-i	-i	i ü		u
半高(半关) mid-high (half-close)		er		(e)	e o
半低(半开) mid-low (half-open)				ê	
低(开) low (open)				(a) a	(a)

舌尖前母音 -i 和舌尖后母音 -i，分别借用瑞典的方言字母 [ɿ]，[ʅ] 表示. er 用国际音标标記就是 [ər].

The blade-alveolar vowel and the blade-palatal vowel are represented respectively by the borrowed letters from Swedish [ɿ] and [ʅ]. "er" may be represented by the international phonetic symbol [ər].

(2) 子音表

(2) Table of the Chinese Consonants

	不送气清塞音和塞擦音 unaspirated voiceless plosives and affricates	送气清塞音和塞擦音 aspirated, voiceless plosives and affricates	浊鼻音 voiced nasals	清擦音 voiceless fricatives	浊边音、浊擦音 voiced lateral, voiced fricative
唇音 labial	b [p]	p [pʻ]	m [m]	f [f]	
舌尖音 alveolar	d [t]	t [tʻ]	n [n]		l [l]
舌尖前音 blade-alvaolar	z [ts]	c [tsʻ]		s [s]	
舌尖后音 blade-palatal	zh [tʂ]	ch [tʂʻ]		sh [ʂ]	r [ʐ]
舌面音 palatal	j [tɕ]	q [tɕʻ]		x [ɕ]	
舌根音 velar	g [k]	k [kʻ]	ng [ŋ]	h [x]	

5.3 复合母音和母音加鼻音子音表

5.3 Table of Compound Vowels and Vowels Plus Nasal Consonants:—

	a	o	e	ai	ei	ao	ou	an	en	ang	eng	ong
i	ia		ie			iao	iou	ian	in	iang	ing	iong
u	ua	uo		uai	uei			uan	uen	uang	ueng	
ü			üe					üan	ün			

5.4 汉字字素 (三)

5.4 Components of Chinese Characters (3):—

国 guó country, nation

国

口

玉

2 汉字 hànzì Chinese character

汉 字

氵 宀

又 子

練習 Exercises

一、讀汉語拼音字母表.

1) Read the Table of Chinese Phonetic Alphabet.

二、練習母音和子音.

2) Practise reading the vowels and consonants:

1. 朗讀母音 (参考母音表).

a) Read aloud the vowels (according to the Table of the Chinese Vowels).

2. 按照北京語音子音表的發音部位和發音方法順序反复朗讀.

b) Read aloud the consonants several times according to the order of the position and manner of pronunciation as shown in the Table of the Chinese Consonants.

三、熟讀复合母音及母音加鼻音子音表.

3) Read several times the Table of Compound Vowels and Vowels Plus Nasal Consonants.

四、熟悉北京語音表.

4) Learn the Table of the Speech Sounds of Peking Dialect.

五、注意下列汉字字素的基本笔划，練習抄写.

5) Pay attention to the basic strokes of the following com ponents of Chinese characters and copy them.

1	口	丨 冂 口
2	玉	一 二 干 王 玉
3	氵	丶 冫 氵
4	又	フ 又
5	宀	丶 丷 宀
6	子	乛 了 子

課外練習 Home Work

一、复習母音和子音，試与本国語音作出对比.

1) Review the Chinese vowels and consonants, and try to compare them with those of your own language.

二、抄写一遍字母（印刷体和書写体）交給教員検查.

2) Copy the alphabet (both the printed and the written), and hand your writing to the teacher.

三、抄写五遍本課汉字字素，交給教員検查.

3) Write the components of Chinese characters in this lesson five times, and hand your writing to the teacher.

第六課 Lesson 6

6.1	变調 The Change of Tones
6.2	汉字字素 (四) Components of Chinese Characters (4)

6.1 变調

在北京語音里几个音节連在一起讀的时候，它們的声調往往發生变化，跟單讀时不一样，这种現象叫做变調. 变調有下面几种:

6.1 The Change of Tones:—

In the speech sounds of Peking dialect, the tones of syllables spoken in succession are different from those of the same syllables spoken separately. This difference is called the change of tones. The important rules of the change of tones are as follows:

(1) 輕声

我們在第一、二課中說的北京語音的四个基本声調是重讀音节的調类. 汉語里每个音节單念的时候都是重讀的，因此都有自己的調类. 但是一个音节如果不是重讀的时候，它原来的声調就改变了，变得又弱又短，成为輕声. 为了教学的方便，在書写时我們用符号"∘"表示. 严格說起来輕声也有不同的音高，輕声音高的特点在于它不由这个音节原来的声調决定而由前一个音节的声調决定. 其規律大致如下:

(1) The neutral tone (or the light tone)

The four tones in the speech sounds of Peking dialect mentioned in the first two lessons, are the tones of stressed or accented syllables. In Chinese, when we read words separately, we always read it as a stressed syllable and therefore every word is given its own tone. In speaking, when a word is unstressed, it loses its original tone and becomes weak and short, that is to say, it becomes light in tone. For the convenience of teaching, the neutral tone is represented by the sign "∘" in writing. Strictly speaking, the neutral tone is much varied in pitch. The pitch of the neutral tone of a syllable is decided by the tone of the syllable preceding it and not by its original tone. The general rules are as follows:

在第一声之后为半低輕声 (2 度) .| 如:

After the 1st tone, the neutral tone is a semi-low light tone (2nd degree). e. g.

tādê 他的 (his) ˥ .|

在第二声之后为中輕声 (3 度) ·| 如:

After the 2nd tone, it is a middle light tone (3rd degree) e. g.

shéidê 誰的 (whose) ˧˥ ·|

在第三声之后为半高輕声 (4 度) ˙| 如:

After the 3rd tone, it is a semi-high light tone (4th degree). e. g.

nǐdê 你的 (your) ˨˩˦ ˙|

在第四声之后为低輕声 (1 度) .| 如:

After the 4th tone, it is a low light tone (1st degree). e. g.

dàdê 大的 (big one) ˥˩ .|

(2) 第三声后面有第一、第二、第四声或輕声时，这个第三声就由原来的先降后升的調子变成一个降調，失去了原来上升的一部分. 这个降調我們叫它半三声，它的音高是 21 (˨˩). 例如:

(2) A syllable of the 3rd tone followed by a syllable of the 1st, 2nd, 4th, or neutral tone is pronounced only with a falling tone without its final rising, that is, its pitch becomes 21 (˨˩). We call this falling tone the half-third tone. e. g.

3 + 1	˨˩˦˥ ⟶ ˨˩˥	xiǎoshuō	小說 (novel)
3 + 2	˨˩˦˧˥ ⟶ ˨˩˧˥	zǔguó	祖国 (fatherland)
3 + 4	˨˩˦˥˩ ⟶ ˨˩˥˩	qǐngzuò	請坐 (Please, sit down.)
3 + 0	˨˩˦ ˙| ⟶ ˨˩ ˙|	xǐhuân	喜欢 (like, fond of)

(3) 两个第三声相連，第一个变为第二声（書写时仍标三声）. 如：

(3) When a third tone is followed by another third tone, then the first third tone becomes a second tone (it is still marked in the third tone in writing). e. g.

3 + 3 ˨˩˦˨˩˦ ⟶ ˧˥˨˩˦ hěnlěng 很冷 (very cold)

(4) 第三声后有由第三声变来的輕声时，有时这个第三声讀为第二声，有时讀成半三声. 如：

(4) When a third tone is followed by another third tone which has become a neutral tone, the first third tone is pronounced sometimes in the second tone and sometimes in the half-third tone. e. g.

3 + 0 ˨˩˦ ˙˦ ⟶ ˧˥ ˙˧ lǎoshǔ 老鼠 (rat)

3 + 0 ˨˩˦ ˙˦ ⟶ ˨˩ ˙˦ jiějiě 姐姐 (elder sister)

(5) 两个第四声相連时，第一个由高降低得很少. 两个四声的音高成为 53 51. 例如：

(5) When a fourth tone is followed by another fourth tone, the first one does not fall so low as the 2nd one, they are pronounced as 53 51. e. g.

4 + 4 ˥˩˥˩ ⟶ ˥˧˥˩ zàijiàn 再見 (Goodbye.)

6.2 汉字字素（四）

6.2 Components of Chinese Characters (4):—

你們 nǐmen you

你 們

亻 亻

尔 門

2 油 yóu oil

油

氵

由

3 只 zhǐ only

只

口

八

練習 Exercises

一、練習輕声:

1) Practise reading the following neutral tones:

chūqů	zhūzi̊	māmå	bāngzhů
láile̊	xíngle̊	shénmo̊	péngyo̊u
míngzi̊	dǒngle̊	mǎibå	shàngwů
xièxie̊	dìfång	wàngle̊	kèqi̊

二、練習半三声:

2) Practise reading the half-third tones:

Běijīng	huǒchē	hǎijūn	zhǐhuī
zǔguó	zhǔxí	jiǎnchá	xǔanzé
zhǔyì	jiěfàng	gǎnxiè	lǐngxiù
běnzi̊	lǐzi̊	xǐhuån	

三、練習三声加三声:

3) Practise reading the third tones followed by other third tones:

biǎoyǎn	zhǎnlǎn	shǒubiǎo
xuǎnjǔ	yǐngxiǎng	

四、練習三声加輕声 (由三声变来的):

4) Practise reading the third tones followed by light tones (which are originally third tones):

xiǎngxiǎng　　kěyi　　zhǎozhǎo　　yǐzi

五、練習四声加四声:

5) Practise reading the 4th tones followed by other 4th tones:

shìjiè　　wànsuì　　sùshè
yùndòng　　zhùyì　　zhèngzhì

六、分辨难音 (一)

6) Distinguish the following difficult sounds (1):

(1) b, p

{ bǎo	飽	full, to eat one's fill
{ pǎo	跑	to run
{ bǎolê	飽了	already full
{ pǎolê	跑了	to have run away
{ bēi	背	to carry on one's back
{ pēi	披	to put over one's shoulders
{ bēizhê	背着	carrying on one's back
{ pēizhê	披着	putting over one's shoulders

(2) d, t

{ dīng	釘	to nail, a nail
{ tīng	听	to listen, to hear
{ wǒdīng	我釘	I nail.
{ wǒtīng	我听	I listen.
{ dǎng	擋	to cover, to stand in one's way
{ tǎng	躺	to lie
{ dǎngzhê	擋着	covering, standing in one's way
{ tǎngzhê	躺着	lying

(3) g, k

{ gàn	干	to do
{ kàn	看	to see, to look at
{ gànwán	干完	to have done, finished
{ kànwán	看完	to have read through

gōng	宫	palace
kōng	空	vacancy
tiāngōng	天宫	celestial palace
tiānkōng	天空	sky, heaven

(4) zh, ch

zhú	竹	bamboo
chú	厨	kitchen
zhúzi	竹子	bamboo
chúzi	厨子	cook
zhǔn	准	exact, punctual
chǔn	蠢	awkward, stupid
zhēnzhǔn	眞准	really exact, punctual
zhēnchǔn	眞蠢	really awkward

(5) j, q

jī	鷄	chicken
qī	漆	lacquer, to lacquer
yóujī	油鷄	kind of chicken
yóuqī	油漆	lacquer, resinous varnish
juàn	倦	tired
quàn	劝	to persuade, to advise
bújuàn	不倦	not tired
búquàn	不劝	not to persuade or advise

(6) q, x

qíng	晴	fine, clear
xíng	行	to walk, all right
qínglê	晴了	to have cleared up
xínglê	行了	that will do, that is right

(7) j, x

jù	剧	play
xù	序	order, preface
jùmù	剧目	program
xùmù	序幕	prelude

七、注意本課汉字字素基本笔划，練習抄写.

7) Notice the basic strokes of the components of Chinese characters in this lesson and copy them.

1	亻	ノ 亻
2	尔	⺈ (ノ ⺈)
		小 (亅 小 小)
3	門	丨 𠃌 𠃌 ... 門 門 門
4	由	丨 冂 冂 由 由
5	八	ノ 八

課外練習 Home Work

一、熟讀本課練習，特别注意:

1) Read the exercises in this lesson several times, and pay special attention to the following:

1. 第二声加輕声;
1) The second tone followed by the light tone;
2. 半三声的音高;
2) The pitch of the half-third tone;
3. 吐气音和不吐气音的区别.
3) The difference between the aspirated sounds and the unaspirated sounds.

二、抄写五遍本課汉字字素，交給敎員檢查.

2) Copy the components of Chinese characters in this lesson five times, and hand your writing to the teacher.

第七課 Lesson 7

7.1 声調总結

7.1 Summary on Tones:—

(1) 第一声到第四声：

(1) The four tones:

ā	á	ǎ	à
zhē	zhé	zhě	zhè
jū	jú	jǔ	jù
qīng	qíng	qǐng	qìng
chōng	chóng	chǒng	chòng

(2) 輕声：

(2) Neutral tones (light tones):

jīntiån	今天	(to-day)
míngtiån	明天	(to-morrow)
wǎnle̊	晚了	(late)
dìfång	地方	(place)

(3) 第三声的变讀：

(3) Changes of the 3rd tone:

3+1	˨˩˦˥ → ˨˩˥	shǒudū	首都	(capital)
3+2	˨˩˦˧˥ → ˨˩˧˥	zhěngqí	整齐	(tidiness)
3+3	˨˩˦˨˩˦ → ˧˥˨˩˦	jiǎngyǎn	講演	(to give a speech)
3+4	˨˩˦˥˩ → ˨˩˥˩	lǐngxiù	領袖	(leader)

3+0 ˨˩˦ ·˧ → ˨˩ ·˧ wǎnshȧng 晚上 (night)
3+0 ˨˩˦ ·˧ → ˨˦ ·˧ děngdėng 等等 (wait for a while)

(4) 两个四声在一起时的变讀:

(4) The pronunciation of two successive 4th tones:

4+4 ˥˩ ˥˩ ⟶ ˥˧ ˥˩ wànsuì 万岁 (Long live...)

7.2 几种应該特别注意的声調:

7.2 Tones Deserving Special Attention:—

(1) 輕声:

(1) Light tones:

míngtiȧn	wánlė	chúzi̇
shéiyȧ	wǒmėn	dǒnglė
děngdėng	kěyi̇	yǎnji̇ng
shìdė	xièxiė	zhùzi̇
duìlė		

(2) 第二声加第一声:

(2) 2nd tones plus 1st tones:

hóngjūn guójiā chénggōng Nánjīng

(3) 第二声加第二声:

(3)2nd tones plus 2nd tones:

rénmín hépíng wénxué yínháng

(4) 第四声加第二声:

(4) 4th tones,plus 2nd tones:

Lièníng èwén zhìfú liànxí

7.3 辨調:

7.3 Discrimination of Tones:—

{ Shānxī	山西	(Shansi)
{ Shǎnxī	陕西	(Shensi)
{ zhǔyì	主义	(doctrine)
{ zhùyì	注意	(notice)
{ nǔlì	努力	(endeavor, effort)
{ núlì	奴隶	(slave)
{ yànhuì	宴会	(banquet)
{ yānhuī	烟灰	(ashes, soot)

dǒnglê	懂了	(to have understood)
dònglê	冻了	(frozen)
zhòngshì	重視	(to attach importance to, to deem highly)
zhōngshí	忠实	(faithful, loyal)
zhīyuán	支援	(to aid, to give support to)
zhìyuàn	志願	(voluntary)
yǎnjing	眼睛	(eye)
yǎnjìng	眼鏡	(eye-glasses)
zhèngzhí	正直	(upright, righteous)
zhēngzhí	争执	(dispute)
zhèngzhì	政治	(politics)
tōngzhī	通知	(to notify, to inform)
tóngzhì	同志	(comrade)
tǒngzhì	統治	(control)
shíyàn	实驗	(experiment)
shíyán	食盐	(salt)
shìyàn	試驗	(test)
shìyǎn	試演	(rehearsal)
shìyán	誓言	(oath, pledge)

7.4 汉字字素(五)

7.4 Components of Chinese Characters (5):—

1 白的 báidê white (one)

白 的

白 白

勺

2 怕 pà to fear, to be afraid

怕

忄

白

3 慢 màn slow

慢

忄

曰

罒

又

4 郵票 yóupiào postage stamp

郵 票

由 西

阝 示

練習 Exercises

一、練習四声:

1) Read the following four tones:

pāng páng pǎng pàng

pīn	pín	pǐn	pìn
tān	tán	tǎn	tàn
kē	ké	kě	kè
zhōu	zhóu	zhǒu	zhòu
chēng	chéng	chěng	chèng
shē	shé	shě	shè
qiāng	qiáng	qiǎng	qiàng

Zhōngguójiěfàng
jīngshénkěpèi
shēnghuógǎishàn
fēichánggǎnxiè

二、熟讀本課課文第二項.
2) Read the 2nd section of this lesson several times.

三、熟讀本課第三項(辨調).
3) Read the 3rd section of this lesson several times (Discrimination of tones).

四、注意本課汉字字素基本笔划，練習抄写.
4) Notice the basic strokes of the components of Chinese characters in this lesson and copy them.

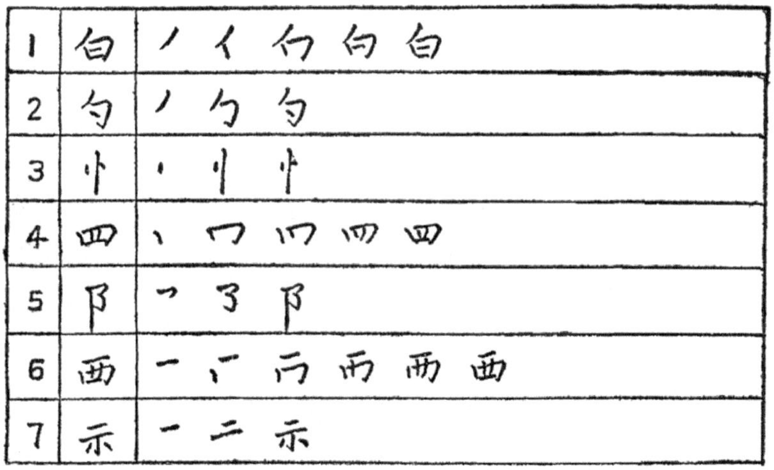

課外練習 Home Work

一、熟讀本課課文及練習，特别注意第二、三两項.

1) Read the text and exercises in this lesson as many times as you can, paying special attention to the 2nd and 3rd sections.

二、抄写五遍本課汉字字素，交給教員檢查.

2) Copy the components of the Chinese characters in this lesson five times, and hand your writing to the teacher.

第八課　Lesson 8

8.1 兒化韻

汉語里有許多后面带有 "兒" 字的 "兒化韻" 的詞. 所謂兒化韻就是这个 "兒" 音同它前面的韻母合成一个音节: 有的是原来的母音加上卷舌的 "-r", 有的是失去韻尾的母音或輔音, 而主要母音加上卷舌的 "-r". 在書写时一律在原音节后加 r.

8.1 The Retroflex Ending "-r":—

In Chinese, there are many words at the end of which the vowels are pronounced with the retroflex "r". Such vowels are called retroflex vowels, for the retroflex "r" and the vowel coming before it have been combined into one syllable. Some retroflex vowels are formed by adding the retroflex "r" to the vowels, and some are formed by dropping the final vowels or consonants out of words, and then adding the retroflex "r" to the main vowels. But in writing, only "r" is put after the original syllable.

(1) 加 -r:

(1) With "-r" added:

a. -a, -o, -e, -u 直接加 -r, 如:

(a) "-a", "-o", "-e", "-u": "-r" is added directly. e. g.

xìfǎr (xìfǎr)	戏法兒	(trick, stunt)
gēr (gēr)	歌兒	(song)
cuòr (cuòr)	錯兒	(mistake)
xiǎotùr (xiǎotùr)	小兎兒	(little rabbit)

b. -ai, -ei, -an, -en 丢掉韻尾加 -r, 如:

(b) "-ai", "-ei", "-an", "-en": "-r" is added after the final vowels or consonants have been dropped. e. g.

gàir (gàr) 盖兒 (cover)
wèir (wèr) 味兒 (smell)
pángbiānr (pángbiār) 旁边兒 (edge, margin, side)
fēnr (fēr) 分兒 (mark, work-unit)

c. -ng 变成前面母音的鼻化成分，使前面的母音成为鼻化音(即發音时气流同时由口腔鼻腔出来)．这里为了書写的方便，用 ng 代替表示鼻化成分的符号． 如：

(c) "-ng": The vowel before "-ng" must be nasalized, and is pronounced with the retroflex "r" (that is, in pronunciation, the breath is let out of the mouth and the nasal cavity at the same time). Here for the convenience of writing, "ng" is used as a symbol representing the nasalized element. e. g.

dànhuángr (dànhuángr) 蛋黃兒 (the yolk of an egg)
bǎndèngr (bǎndèngr) 板凳兒 (stool)

(2) 加 er:

(2) With "er" added:

a. -i, -ü 加 er, 如：

(a) "-i", "-ü": "er" is added after "-i" "-ü". e. g.

xiǎojīr (xiǎojiēr) 小鷄兒 (chicken)
xiǎoyúr (xiǎoyuér) 小魚兒 (little fish)

b. -in 丢掉韻尾加 er, 如：

(b) "-in": "er" is added after the final consonant has been dropped. e. g.

xìnr (xièr) 信兒 (message)

c. zh, ch, sh, r, z, c, s 后的 i 变为 er, 如：

(c) "-i": "i" after "zh", "ch", "sh", "r", "z", "c", "s" is changed into "er". e. g.

shìr (shèr) 事兒 (matter, business)

8.2 多音节連讀

8.2 Polysyllables:—

(1) 双音节：

(1) Dissyllables:

fēijī 飞机 (aeroplane)
Sūlián 苏联 (The Soviet Union)
yīngyǒng 英勇 (valiant)

yīyuàn	医院	(hospital)
nóngcūn	农村	(village)
wénxué	文学	(literature)
niúnǎi	牛奶	(milk)
shídài	时代	(times)
Běijīng	北京	(Peking)
zhǔxí	主席	(chairman)
zǒngtǒng	总統	(president)
jiěfàng	解放	(liberation)
yònggōng	用功	(studious)
dàxué	大学	(university)
zhèngfǔ	政府	(government)
jìhuà	計划	(plan)

(2) 三音节:

(2) **Trisyllables:**

gòngqīngtuán	共青团	(The Communist Youth League)
hézuòshè	合作社	(co-operative store)
bówùyuàn	博物院	(museum)

(3) 四音节:

(3) Four syllables:

chíjiǔhépíng	持久和平	(lasting peace)
guānliáozhǔyì	官僚主义	(bureaucracy)
xīnwénjìzhě	新聞記者	(journalist)

8.3 汉字字素 (六)

8.3 Components of Chinese Characters (6):—

1 分兒 fēnr mark, work-unit

分 兒

八 白

刀 儿

2 画兒 huàr drawing, picture

画 兒

一 白

田 儿

凵

3 快 kuài quick. fast

快

忄

夬

4 放 fàng to put

放

方

攵

5 照 zhào to shine

照

日

刀

口

灬

練習 Exercises

一、練習兒化韻:

1) Practise the following retroflex vowels:

wánr	yíkuàir
biānr	gāngbǐtóur
zhèr	liànxíběnr
nàr	hǎohāordė
mòshuǐr	mànmānrdė
shíhȯur	

二、分辨难音 (二):

2) Distinguish the following difficult sounds (2):

(1) o, e

luò	落	(to fall)
lè	乐	(to laugh, glad)
luòlė	落了	(to have fallen)
lèlė	乐了	(to have laughed, to have been glad)
duó	夺	(to take by force)
dé	得	(to get)
duódào	夺到	(to have taken by force)
dédào	得到	(to have got)

(2) an, en

{ pán	盘	(plate)
{ pén	盆	(basin)
{ pánzi	盘子	(plate)
{ pénzi	盆子	(basin)
{ zhān	沾	(to soil)
{ zhēn	眞	(really, real)
{ zhāndė	沾的	(soiled)
{ zhēndė	眞的	(real, genuine)

(3) ang, eng

{ bàng	磅	(pound, to weigh)
{ bèng	蹦	(to hop, to jump)
{ bàngyíbàng	磅一磅	(to weigh for once or a little while)
{ bèngyíbèng	蹦一蹦	(to jump for once or a little while)
{ fāng	方	(square)
{ fēng	風	(wind)
{ dōngfāng	东方	(the east)
{ dōngfēng	东風	(east wind)

(4) an, ang

{ mán	蛮	(wild, barbaric)
{ máng	忙	(busy)
{ mánjílė	蛮極了	(extremely wild)
{ mángjílė	忙極了	(extremely busy)
{ tān	貪	(greed)
{ tāng	湯	(soup)
{ tānduō	貪多	(greedy)
{ tāngduō	湯多	(much soup)

(5) en, eng

{ fěn	粉	(powder)
{ fěng	諷	(to ridicule)
{ fěncì	粉刺	(pimple)
{ fěngcì	諷刺	(to ridicule, ridicule)

shēn	深	(deep)
shēng	生	(to give birth to, strange)
shēnshuǐ	深水	(deep water)
shēngshuǐ	生水	(unboiled water)

(6) s, sh

sì	四	(four)
shí	十	(ten)
sìshí	四十	(forty)
shísì	十四	(fourteen)
sān	三	(three)
shān	山	(hill)
sānlǐ	三里	(three "li")
shānlǐ	山里	(among the hills)

(7) z, c

zuò	作	(to do)
cuò	錯	(mistaken)
méizuò	沒作	(did not do)
méicuò	沒錯	(not mistaken)
zǎor	棗兒	(dates)
cǎor	草兒	(grass)
xiǎozǎor	小棗兒	(little dates)
xiǎocǎor	小草兒	(little grass)

(8) c, s

cì	刺	(to sting)
sì	寺	(abbey)
yígècì	一个刺	(one sting)
yígèsì	一个寺	(one abbby)
cāi	猜	(to guess)
sāi	塞	(to stop, to fill up)
cāiyìcāi	猜一猜	(to make a guess)
sāiyìsāi	塞一塞	(to stop)

(9) i, ü

{ yìjiàn	意見	(opinion)
{ yùjiàn	遇見	(to meet)
{ méiyǒuyìjiàn	沒有意見	(no opinion)
{ méiyǒuyùjiàn	沒有遇見	(did not meet)
{ qī	期	(period)
{ qū	曲	(curved)
{ qīxiàn	期限	(limit of time)
{ qūxiàn	曲綫	(curve)

三、注意下列汉字字素的基本笔划，練習抄写.

3) Pay attention to the basic strokes of the following components of Chinese characters and copy them.

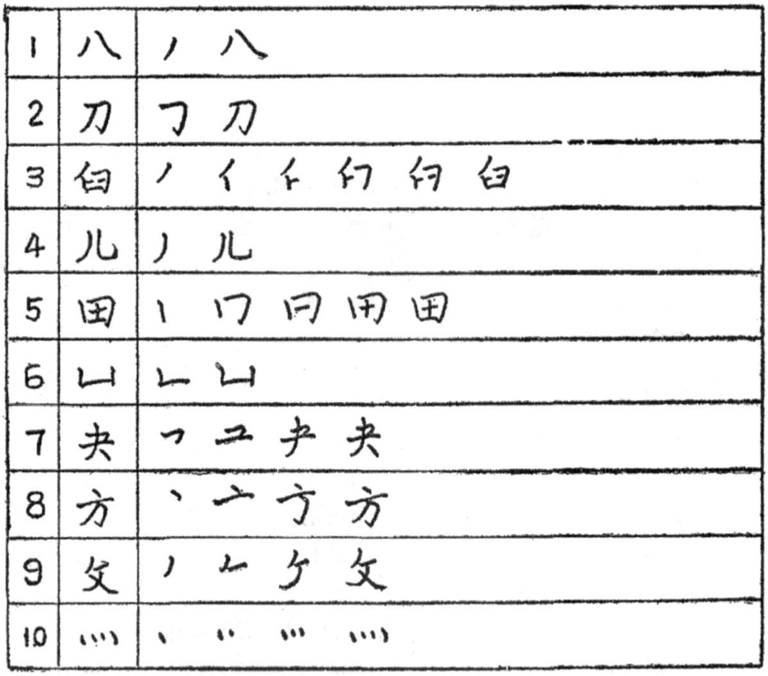

課外練習 Home Work

一、准确地讀出本課練習中带兒化韻的語詞.

1) Read correctly the words or word groups containing retroflex vowels in the exercises of this lesson.

二、熟讀本課練習中的难音对比.

2) Read as many times as possible the difficult sounds in pairs in the exercises of this lesson.

三、抄写五遍本課汉字字素，交給教員檢查.

3) Copy five times the components of Chinese characters in this lesson, and hand your writing to the teacher.

口語練習部分

Oral Exercises

第九課　Lesson 9

一、Shēngcí　生詞　New Words

1.	nǐ	你	you
2.	hǎo	好	well, good
3.	qǐng	請	please
4.	jìn	进	to come in, to enter
5.	zuò	坐	to sit (down)
6.	xièxiê	謝謝	thanks
7.	shì	是	to be
8.	něi	哪	which
9.	guó	国	country
10.	rén	人	person, man
11.	wǒ	我	I, me
12.	Yīngguó	英国	Great Britain
13.	huì	会	can
14.	shuō	說	to speak, to say
15.	zhōngwén	中文	the Chinese language
16.	mā	嗎	(an interrogative particle)
17.	bù	不	not, no
18.	yīngwén	英文	English
19.	tā	他	he, him

20. Zhōngguó 中国 China
21. jiào 叫 to call, to be called
22. shénmǒ 什么 what
23. míngzì 名字 name

二、Duǎnjù 短句 Simple Sentences

(1) Nǐ hǎo!
你 好! How are you?

(2) Nǐ hǎo.
你 好! How are you?

(3) Qǐng jìn!
請 进! Come in, please.

(4) Qǐng zuò!
請 坐! Sit down, please!

(5) Xièxiė.
謝謝. Thanks.

(6) Nǐ shì něiguó rén?
你 是 哪国 人? Where do you come from?

(7) Wǒ shì Yīngguó rén.
我 是 英国 人. I am an Englishman.

(8) Nǐ huì shuō zhōngwén mā?
你 会 說 中文 嗎? Do you speak Chinese?

(9) Bú huì, wǒ shuō yīngwén.
不 会, 我 說 英文. No, I speak English.

(10) Tā shì něiguó rén?
他 是 哪国 人? Where does he come from?

(11) Tā shì Zhōngguó rén.

他 是 中国 人. He is Chinese.

(12) Nǐ jiào shénmȯ míngzì?

你 叫 什么 名字? What is your name?

(13) Wǒ jiào ——.

我 叫 ——. My name is____.

(14) Tā jiào shénmȯ míngzì?

他 叫 什么 名字? What is his name?

(15) Tā jiào ——.

他 叫 ——. His name is____.

三、Hànzì zìsù 汉字字素
Components of Chinese Characters

1 好 hǎo good, well

好

女

子

2 請进 qǐngjìn Come in, please.

請 进

言 井

青 辶

3 是 shì yes, to be

是

日

疋

4 次 cì time

次

冫

欠

5 書店 shūdiàn bookstore

書 店

聿 广

曰 占

四、Jīběn bǐhuà　基本笔划

Basic Strokes

1	女	丿 ㄑ 夊 女
2	言	丶 亠 亠 亠 言
3	青	一 二 丰 龶 龶 青 青 青
4	井	一 二 ナ 井
5	辶	丶 ㇋ 辶
6	𤴔	一 丅 下 𤴓 𤴔
7	冫	丶 冫
8	欠	𠂊 𠂉 欠
9	𦘒	㇕ 二 ⺕ ⺕ 肀 𦘒
10	广	丶 亠 广
11	占	丨 ⺊ 占

第十課　Lesson 10

一、Shēngcí 生詞 New Words

1.	shéi	誰	who
2.	xuéshẻng	学生	student
3.	xiānshẻng	先生	teacher
4.	yǒu	有	to have, there is (are)
5.	kè	課	lesson, class
6.	méiyǒu	沒有	to have no..., to have none, not to have...
7.	xiàwǔ	下午	afternoon
8.	fǔdǎo	輔导	to help...to study
9.	zài	在	at, in, on
10.	nǎr	哪兒	where
11.	wǒmẻndẻ	我們的	our, ours
12.	jiàoshǐ	教室	classroom
13.	jǐ	几	how many
14.	diǎnzhōng	点鐘	hour
15.	kāishǐ	开始	to begin, to start
16.	sāndiǎn	三点	three o'clock
17.	bàn	半	half
18.	xuéxí	学習	to learn
19.	Běidà	北大	Peking University
20.	yě	也	also, too

二、 Duǎnjù 短句 Simple Sentences

(1)	Tā shì shéi? 他 是 誰?	Who is he?
(2)	Tā shì xuéshēng. 他 是 学生.	He is a student.
(3)	Tā shì shéi? 他 是 誰?	Who is he?
(4)	Tā shì xiānshēng. 他 是 先生.	He is a teacher.
(5)	Nǐ yǒu kè må? 你 有 課 嗎?	Do you have classes?
(6)	Yǒu kè. 有 課.	I do.
(7)	Méi yǒu. 沒 有.	I don't.
(8)	Nǐ xiàwǔ yǒu kè må? 你 下午 有 課 嗎?	Do you have classes in the afternoon.?
(9)	Méi yǒu kè, yǒu fǔdǎo. 沒 有 課, 有 輔导.	I don't, but my teacher will come to help me in my study.
(10)	Zài nǎr fǔdǎo? 在 哪兒 輔导?	Where will your teacher come to help you?
(11)	Zài wǒmėndė jiàoshì. 在 我們的 教室.	In our classroon.
(12)	Jǐ diǎnzhōng kāishǐ fǔdǎo? 几 点鐘 开始 輔导?	When will your teacher come to help you?
(13)	Sāndiǎn bàn. 三点 半.	Half past three.

(14) Nǐ zài nǎr xuéxí?

你 在 哪兒 学習? Where are you studying?

(15) Wǒ zài Běidà xuéxí.

我 在 北大 学習. I am studying in Peking University.

(16) Tā zài nǎr xuéxí?

他 在 哪兒 学習? Where is he studying?

(17) Tā yě zài Běidà xuéxí?

他也在北大学習. He is also studying in Peking University.

三、Hànzì zìsù 汉字字素

Components of Chinese Characters

1 誰 shéi who

誰

言

隹

2 沿 yán along

沿

氵

几

口

3 疼 téng painful

疼

疒

夂

冫

4 新的 xīndẻ new (one)

新 的

立

木

斤

5 草 cǎo grass

草

艹

曰

十

6 外边 wàibiān outside

外 → 夕 卜

边 → 力 辶

四、Jīběn bǐhuà 基本笔划

Basic Strokes

1	隹	亻 亻丿 亻𠂉 亻𠂉一 亻𠂉二 亻𠂉丰 隹
2	几	丿 几
3	疒	广 疒
4	夂	丿 ⺈ 夂
5	立	丶 亠 亠丶 亠丷 立
6	朩	一 十 才 朩
7	斤	丿 𠂆 斤 斤
8	癶	㇇ ㇇丶 ㇇丶丿 癶
9	十	一 十
10	夕	丿 ⺈ 夕
11	卜	丨 卜
12	力	𠃌 力

第十一課 Lesson 11

一、Shēngcí 生詞 New Words

1.	shàngkè	上課	to have classes, to go to classes
2.	lē	了	(a modal particle)
3.	hái	还	still, yet
4.	nē	呢	(a modal particle)
5.	wèntí	問題	question, problem
6.	dǒnglē	懂了	to have understood
7.	duìlē	对了	right
8.	nán	难	difficult
9.	dàshēng	大声	loudly, aloud
10.	zài	再	again, once more
11.	niàn	念	to read
12.	yíbiàn	一遍	one time, once
13.	xiě	写	to write
14.	dàjiā	大家	all (the people)
15.	yíkuàir	一塊兒	together
16.	gēn	跟	with, after, to follow
17.	tīng	听	to hear, to listen
18.	wèn	問	to ask, to inquire
19.	huídá	回答	to answer
20.	xiàkè	下課	the class is over, after class
21.	zàijiàn	再見	good-bye

二、Duǎnjù 短句 Simple Sentences

(1)	Shàng kè lê mȧ?	
	上 課 了 嗎?	Is it time for class?
(2)	Shàng kè lê.	
	上 課 了.	It is.
(3)	Hái méi yǒu nê!	
	还 沒 有 呢!	Not yet.
(4)	Nǐ yǒu wèntí mȧ?	
	你 有 問題 嗎?	Have you any question?
(5)	Yǒu.	
	有.	yes, I have.
(6)	Méi yǒu.	
	沒 有.	No, 1 have none.
(7)	Nǐ dǒng lê mȧ?	
	你 懂 了 嗎?	Do you understand?
(8)	Dǒng lê.	
	懂 了.	I do.
(9)	Bù dǒng.	
	不 懂.	I don't.
(10)	Duì lê mȧ?	
	对 了 嗎?	Is it right?
(11)	Duì lê.	
	对 了.	It is right.
(12)	Bú duì.	
	不 对.	No, it isn't.
(13)	Nán bù nán?	
	难 不 难?	Is it difficult?
(14)	Nán.	
	难。	It is.

(15) Bù nán.
不 难. No, it isn't.

(16) Qǐng nǐ niàn.
請 你 念. Please read.

(17) Qǐng nǐ dà shēng niàn.
請 你 大 声 念. Please read loudly.

(18) Qǐng nǐ zài niàn yíbiàn.
請 你 再 念 一遍. Please read it once more.

(19) Qǐng nǐ xiě.
請 你 写. Please write.

(20) Qǐng nǐ zài xiě yíbiàn.
請 你 再 写 一遍. Please write it once more.

(21) Dàjiā yíkuàir niàn.
大家 一塊兒 念. All of you read together.

(22) Dàjiā gēn wǒ niàn.
大家 跟 我 念. All of you read after me.

(23) Wǒ niàn, nǐmên tīng.
我 念, 你們 听. I'll read, and will you please listen.

(24) Wǒ shuō, nǐmên xiě.
我 説, 你們 写. I'll speak, and will you please write it down.

(25) Wǒ wèn, nǐmên huídá.
我 問, 你們 回答. I'll ask and you'll answer.

(26) Hǎo, xià kè lê, zàijiàn!
好, 下 課 了, 再見! All right, class is over, good-bye!

(27) Zàijiàn!
再見! Good-bye!

三、Hànzì zìsù 汉字字素
Components of Chinese Characters

1 呢 nē (a modal particle)

呢

口

尸

匕

2 問題 wèntí question

問 題

門 日

口 疋

頁

3 对 duì right

对

又

寸

4 找 zhǎo to find

找

扌

戈

5 知道 zhīdào to know

知 道

矢 首

口 辶

6 灶 zào kitchen stove

灶

火

土

7 跟 gēn after, to follow

跟

足

艮

8 取得 qǔdé to obtain

取 得

耳 彳

又 㝵

四、Jīběn bǐhuà 基本笔划
Basic Strokes

1	尸	フ コ 尸
2	匕	丿 匕
3	頁	一 丆 丆 丆 丙 百 百 頁
4	寸	一 丁 寸
5	才	一 丁 才
6	戈	一 弋 戈 戈
7	矢	丿 𠂉 𠂒 午 矢
8	首	丶 丷 䒑 䒑 产 肖 首 首 首
9	火	丶 丷 ⺌ 火
10	足	口 早 早 𧾷 足
11	艮	㇇ ヨ ヨ 艮 艮 艮
12	耳	一 厂 丌 丌 耳 耳
13	彳	丿 彳 彳
14	导	巳 巳 导

第十二課 Lesson 12

一、Shēngcí 生詞 New Words

1.	tóngzhì	同志	comrade
2.	dào	到	to go (to), to arrive
3.	qù	去	to go
4.	shítáng	食堂	dining hall, refectory
5.	túshūguǎn	圖書館	library
6.	hézuòshè	合作社	co-operative store
7.	yào	要	to want
8.	mǎi	买	to buy
9.	dōngxi	东西	thing
10.	běnzi	本子	note-book
11.	qiānbǐ	鉛笔	pencil
12.	shū	書	book
13.	zhǐ	紙	paper
14.	duōshǎo	多少	how many, how much
15.	qián	錢	money
16.	liǎng	两	two
17.	máo	毛	ten cents
18.	wǔ	五	five
19.	yī	一	one
20.	kuài	塊	dollar (a measure word)
21.	jìnchéng	进城	to go to the city
22.	sùshè	宿舍	dormitory
23.	xiànzài	現在	now
24.	huí	回	to return

二、 Duǎnjù 短句 Simple Sentences

(1) Tóngzhì! nǐ dào nǎr qù?
同志! 你 到 哪兒 去? Comrade! Where are you going?

(2) Wǒ dào shítáng qù.
我 到 食堂 去. I am going to the dining hall.

(3) Wǒ huí sùshè qù.
我 回 宿舍 去. I am returning to the dormitory.

(4) Tā dào nǎr qù?
他 到 哪兒 去? Where is he going?

(5) Tā dào túshūguǎn qù.
他 到 圖書館 去. He is going to the library.

(6) Nǐ qù hézuòshè mȧ?
你 去 合作社 嗎? Are you going to the co-operative store?

(7) Qù.
去. Yes, I am.

(8) Bú qù.
不 去. No, I am not.

(9) Nǐ yào mǎi shénmȯ dōngxȉ?
你 要 买 什么 东西? What do you want to buy?

(10) Wǒ yào mǎi běnzȉ.
我 要 买 本子. I want to buy note-books.

(11) Wǒ yào mǎi qiānbǐ.
我 要 买 鉛笔. I want to buy pencils.

(12) Tā yào mǎi shénmȯ dōngxȉ?
他 要 买 什么 东西? What does he want to buy?

(13) Tā yào mǎi shū hé zhǐ.
他 要 买 書 和 紙. He wants to buy books and paper.

(14) Běnzi duōshåo qián?
本子 多少 錢? — How much is the notebook?

(15) Liǎngmáo wǔ.
两毛 五. — Twenty-five cents.

(16) Shū duōshåo qián?
書 多少 錢? — How much is the book?

(17) Yíkuài qián.
一塊 錢. — One dollar.

(18) Nǐ xiànzài jìn chéng må?
你 現在 进 城 嗎? — Are you going to the city now?

(19) Jìn chéng.
进 城. — Yes, I am going to the city.

(20) Bú jìn chéng.
不 进 城. — No, I am not going to the city.

三、 Hànzì zìsù 汉字字素

Components of Chinese Characters

1 同志 tóngzhì comrade

同: 门 一 口

志: 士 心

2 計划 jìhuà plan

計 划

言 戈

十 刂

3 飯 fàn meal

飯

食

反

4 合作社 hézuòshè co-operative store

合 作 社

人 亻 礻

一 乍 土

口

5 袖子 xiùzi sleeve

袖 子

衤 子

由

6 鉛笔 qiānbǐ pencil

鉛 笔

金 ⺮

几 毛

口

7 紙 zhǐ paper

紙

糸

氏

8 雷 léi thunder

雷

雨

田

四、 Jīben bǐhuà 基本笔划

Basic Strokes

1	冂	丨 冂
2	士	十 士
3	心	丶 乚 心 心
4	刂	丨 刂
5	食	丿 𠆢 ... 食
6	反	丿 ㇀ 反
7	人	丿 人
8	乍	丿 𠂉 ... 乍
9	衤	丶 ㇇ 礻 衤
10	衤	礻 衤
11	金	𠆢 ... 金
12	⺮	丿 ... ⺮
13	毛	丿 ... 毛
14	糸	𠃋 ... 糸
15	氏	丿 ... 氏
16	雨	一 丆 ... 雨

基本語法

Basic Grammar

"生詞" 中的簡号

Abbreviations Adopted in the Words Columns

(名)	名 詞 Míngcí The Noun
(代)	代 詞 Dàicí The Pronoun
(动)	动 詞 Dòngcí The Verb
(能动)	能願动詞 néngyuàndòngcí The Optative Verb
(数)	数 詞 Shùcí The Numeral
(形)	形容詞 Xíngróngcí The Adjective
(介)	介 詞 Jièci The Preposition
(副)	副 詞 Fùcí The Adverb
(連)	連 詞 Liáncí The Conjunction
(嘆)	嘆 詞 Tàncí The Interjection
(助)	助 詞 Zhùcí The Particle
(头)	詞 头 Cítóu The Prefix
(尾)	詞 尾 Cíwěi The Suffix

第十三課 Lesson 13

13.1	体詞謂語句 (一) The Sentence with a Substantive Predicate(1)
13.2	体詞謂語句 (一) 的否定 The Negative Form of the Sentence with a Substantive Predicate (1)
13.3	疑問句 (一) The Interrogative Sentence (1)
13.4	"你" 和 "您" 你 and 您

一、生詞 Shēngcí New Words

1.	这	(代)	zhèi, zhè	this
2.	是	(动)	shì	to be
3.	書	(名)	shū	book
4.	我	(代)	wǒ	I, me
5.	学生	(名)	xuéshēng	student
6.	先生	(名)	xiānshēng	teacher
7.	中国	(名)	Zhōngguó	China, Chinese
8.	人	(名)	rén	man, person
9.	那	(代)	nèi,nà	that
10.	不	(副)	bù	not, no
11.	你	(代)	nǐ	you
12.	嗎	(助)	mā	(an interrogative particle)

13. 您	(代) nín	(the polite form of 你)
14. 报	(名) bào	newspaper
15. 他	(代) tā	he, him

二、語法 Yǔfǎ Grammar

13.1 体詞謂語句 (一) 現代汉語里的句子，可以按照謂語的构成分为四种.第一种是体詞謂語句. 現在先介紹体詞謂語句(一).

13.1 The Sentence with a Substantive Predicate (1) In modern Chinese, sentences may be divided into four kinds, according to the construction of the predicate. The first kind is the sentence with a substantive predicate. Here we will deal with the sentence with a substantive predicate (1).

以体詞构成謂語主要成分的句子，就叫体詞謂語句 (一). 体詞包括名詞、代詞和数量詞. 体詞說明主語所指的人或事物是 "什么"，而系詞可以說是一种特殊的动詞，它的功用就在于联系主語和謂語体詞. 体詞和系詞构成的謂語对主語起判断、說明的作用. 例如:

A sentence, in which the main element of the predicate is made up of a substantive, is called the sentence with a substantive predicate (1). The substantive may be a noun, a pronoun, or a numeral; it tells "what" the person or thing is as required by the subject. The copula may be looked upon as a particular verb used to connect the subject with the substantive in the predicate. The predicate which is composed of a substantive and a copula must explain the subject. e. g.

1. 这 是 書.
Zhèi shì shū.

2. 我 是 学生.
Wǒ shì xuésheng.

3. 先生 是 中国 人.
Xiānsheng shì Zhōngguó rén.

"这"、"我"、"先生" 是主語，"是書"、"是学生"、"是中国人" 是謂語. 系詞"是"后面的都是名詞.
这，我，and 先生 are subjects; 是書，是学生，and 是中国人 are predicates. All the words after the copula are nouns.

13.2 体詞謂語句（一）的否定 在体詞謂語句（一）的系詞"是"的前面加上表示否定的副詞"不"，就变成体詞謂語句(一)的否定句. 例如:

13.2 The Negative Form of the Sentence with a Substantive Predicate (1) The negative form of such kind of sentence is made by putting the negative adverb 不 before the copula 是. e. g.

4. 那 不 是 書.
Nèi bú shì shū.

5. 你 不 是 先生.
Nǐ bú shì xiānshêng.

6. 学生 不 是 中国 人.
Xuéshêng bú shì Zhōngguó rén.

副詞"不"單独用或不單独用而后面連接的音节是一声、二声或三声时，都讀作第四声；后面的音节是第四声，就讀作第二声. 因此，在上面三个例句里，"不"都是第二声.

The adverb 不 is pronounced in the 4th tone when it is used independently or followed by a syllable of the 1st, 2nd or 3rd tone; but it is pronounced in the 2nd tone when it is followed by a syllable of the 4th tone. Hence, in the above three examples, 不 is in the 2nd tone.

13.3 疑問句（一） 現代汉語里最常見的疑問句有五种. 現在先介紹第一种. 当我們把一个表示疑問的語气助詞"嗎"放在一个陈述句（肯定或否定）的句尾时，这个句子就变成了疑問句. 例如:

13.3 The Interrogative Sentence (1) In modern Chinese, there are five kinds of interrogative sentences that are frequently used. Here, we will deal with the first kind. When we put the interrogative modal particle 嗎 at the end of a declarative sentence (affirmative or negative), it is changed into an interrogative sentence. e. g.

7. 这 是 書 嗎?
Zhèi shì shū må?

8. 这 不 是 書 嗎?
Zhèi bú shì shū må?

13.4 "你"和"您" "你"和"您"都是單数第二人称代詞. 但"您"是敬称，在表示尊敬的时候才用. 例如:

13.4 你 and 您 你 and 您 are both in the second person singular. But 您 is a polite form, and used only when we wish to pay respect to the person in question. e. g.

9. 您 不 是 学生, 您 是 先生.
Nín bú shì xuéshêng, nín shì xiānshêng.

三、課文 Kèwén Text

I

1. 这 是 書.
Zhèi shì shū.

2. 那 是 报.
Nèi shì bào.

3. 他 是 先生.
Tā shì xiānshêng.

4. 我 是 学生.
Wǒ shì xuéshêng.

5. 先生 是 中国 人.
Xiānshêng shì Zhōngguó rén.

II

6. 这 不 是 書.
Zhèi bú shì shū.

7. 那 不 是 报.
Nèi bú shì bào.

8. 我 不 是 先生.
Wǒ bú shì xiānshẻng.

9. 您 不 是 学生.
Nín bú shì xuéshẻng.

10. 他 不 是 中国 人.
Tā bú shì Zhōngguó rén.

III

11. 这 是 書, 那 是 报.
Zhèi shì shū, nèi shì bào.

12. 这 是 書, 这 不 是 报.
Zhèi shì shū, zhèi bú shì bào.

13. 那 不 是 报, 那 是 書.
Nèi bú shì bào, nèi shì shū.

14. 我 是 学生, 您 是 先生.
Wǒ shì xuéshẻng, nín shì xiānshẻng.

15. 他 不 是 先生, 他 是 学生.
Tā bú shì xiānshẻng, tā shì xuéshẻng.

IV

(a_1) 这 是 書 嗎?
Zhèi shì shū må?

(b_1) 这 是 書.
Zhèi shì shū.

(a_2) 那 是 报 嗎?
Nèi shì bào må?

(b_2) 那 不 是 报, 那 是 書.
Nèi bú shì bào, nèi shì shū.

(a_3) 你 是 学生 嗎?
Nǐ shì xuéshêng må?

(b_3) 我 是 学生.
Wǒ shì xuéshêng.

(a_4) 他 是 中国 人 嗎?
Tā shì Zhōngguó rén må?

(b_4) 他 不 是 中国 人.
Tā bú shì Zhōngguó rén.

四、課外練習 Kèwài liànxí Home Work

1. 抄写生詞一遍.
   1) Copy all the new words once.
2. 用拼音（包括正确的調号）写出下面的句子来:
   2) Transcribe the following sentences by using the phonetic alphabet and give the correct tone of each syllable:
   (1) 我 是 学生.
   (2) 他 不 是 先生
   (3) 这 是 書 嗎?
3. 用汉字回答下面的問題:
   3) Answer the following questions with Chinese characters:
   (4) 你 是 中国 人 嗎?
   (5) 那 是 报 嗎?

五. 汉字表 Hànzì biǎo Chinese Characters

1	这	文（丶 亠 ナ 文）
		辶
2	是	
3	書	
4	我	ノ 二 千 手 我 我 我
5	学	⺍（丶 丶丶 丷 ⺍ ⺍）
		子
6	生	ノ 𠂉 ⺧ 牛 生
7	先	ノ 𠂉 ⺧ 生 先
8	中	丨 冂 口 中
9	国	
10	人	
11	那	冄（刀 刃 冄）
		阝
12	不	一 丆 不 不
13	你	
14	嗎	口
		馬（一 二 三 丰 耳 馬 馬）
15	您	你
		心

16	报	扌
		𠬝（㇇ 卩 𠬝）
17	他	亻
		也（𠃌 力 也）

第十四課 Lesson 14

14.1 名詞的量詞
The Nominal Measure Word

14.2 "一" 的声調
The Tones of 一

14.3 形容詞謂語句
The Sentence with an Adjectival Predicate

14.4 "多" 和 "少"
多 and 少

一、生詞 Shēngcí New Words

1.	一	(数)	yī	a, one
2.	本	(量)	běn	(a measure word)
3.	个	(量)	gè	(a measure word)
4.	三	(数)	sān	three
5.	很	(副)	hěn	very
6.	新	(形)	xīn	new
7.	好	(形)	hǎo	good, well
8.	張	(量)	zhāng	(a measure word)
9.	紙	(名)	zhǐ [張]	paper
10.	小	(形)	xiǎo	little, small
11.	大	(形)	dà	big, large
12.	多	(形)	duō	many, much
13.	少	(形)	shǎo	few, little
14.	北京	(名)	Běijīng	Peking
15.	旧	(形)	jiù	old

二、 語法 Yǔfǎ Grammar

14.1 名詞的量詞　　人、物和动作都可以有数量. 表示人、物数量單位的詞是名詞的量詞; 表示动作数量的詞是动詞的量詞. 現在先介紹名詞的量詞.

14.1 The Nominal Measure Word　Persons, things and actions may all be numbered or weighed. The words showing the numerical or quantitative units of persons or things, are called nominal measure words; and those, which indicate such units of actions are called verbal measure words. Here we will deal with the nominal measure words.

在現代汉語里, 数詞 (例如 "一") 和指示代詞 (例如 "这"、"那") 一般不能跟名詞直接联系, 而要在它們之間用上一个量詞. 例如:

In modern Chinese, generally speaking, a numeral (such as 一) or a demonstrative pronoun (such as 这 and 那) cannot be directly used with a noun; a measure word should always be used between it and the noun. e. g.

1. 这 是 一本 書.
   Zhèi shì yìběn shū.

2. 那个 学生 是 中国 人.
   Nèigê xuéshêng shì Zhōngguó rén.

我們不能說 "一書", 或 "那学生", "一" 和 "那" 后面要用量詞.

we cannot say 一書 or 那学生, for after 一 and 那 there should be a measure word.

很多名詞都有自己習慣上的特定量詞, 例如 "本" 就是 "書" 的特定量詞. "个" 是最常用的量詞, 应用范圍最广, 称人可以用 (例如 "学生" 的量詞就是 "个"), 衡量沒有特定量詞的物也可以用, 甚至有些名詞的特定量詞也可以用它來代替.

Many nouns have their specific measure words, for example, 本 is the specific measure word for 書. 个 is a very common measure word, and is most extensively used, for it may be used in connection with persons (e. g. the measure word of 学生 is 个.), and also in the case of things that have no specific measure words for themselves. It may even be substituted for other specific measure words.

用量詞时有以下四点値得注意:

The following four points should be observed in using measure words:

(一) 量詞前又有指示代詞又有数詞的时候，指示代詞在数詞之前. 例如:

(1) When there are a demonstrative pronoun and a numeral before the measure word, the demonstrative pronoun should be put before the numeral. e. g.

3. 这 三个 学生
zhèi sāngê xuéshêng

4. 那 三本 書
nèi sānběn shū

(二) 量詞是黏附在指示代詞或数詞后面的. 例如:

The measure word is directly annexed to the demonstrative pronoun or the numeral. e. g.

5. 这个 学生
zhèigê xuéshêng

6. 三本 書
sānběn shū

如果不用数詞或指示代詞就不能在名詞前面單独用量詞. 我們絕对不能說"个先生是中国人"这样的話.

If there is no numeral or demonstrative pronoun, then no measure word can be allowed to stand alone before a noun. For instance, we can never say such a thing as 个先生是中国人.

(三) 極少数名詞本身就具有量詞性質，和数詞或代詞連用时就不需要量詞，例如"一年"、"这課"等.

(3) There are a few nouns which possess in themselves the nature or function of the measure word, and hence do not require measure words when they are preceded by numerals or demonstrative pronouns. e. g. 一年 (one year) and 这課 (this lesson).

(四) 当語言环境已經明确指出名詞代表的人或物时，量詞后面的名詞就可以省略. 例如:

(4) When the person or thing denoted by the noun is already clearly defined in the context, the noun after the measure word may be omitted. e. g.

7. 这个 中国 人 是 先生,
Zhèigê Zhōngguó rén shì xiānshêng,
那个 (中国 人) 是 学生.
nèigê (Zhōngguó rén) shì xuéshêng.

"那个" 后面的 "中国人" 就可以省去.

中国人 after 那个 may be omitted.

14.2 "一" 的声調 数詞 "一" 的声調比較复杂:

14.2 The Tones of 一 The tones of the numeral 一 vary:

(一) 單用时讀第一声.

(1) When it stands alone, it is pronounced in the 1st tone.

(二) 后面的音节是一、二、三声或一、二、三声轉来的輕声时，讀第四声. 例如: "一張紙" (yìzhāng zhǐ), "一条路" (yìtiáo lù), "一本書" (yìběn shū).

(2) When it is followed by a syllable of the 1st, 2nd or 3rd tone, or by a syllable of the neutral tone that is originally in the 1st, 2nd or 3rd tone, it is pronounced in the 4th tone. e. g. 一張紙 (a sheet of paper), 一条路 (a way) and 一本書 (a book).

(三) 后边的音节是第四声或四声轉来的輕声时，讀第二声. 例如: "一个人" (yígê rén).

(3) When it is followed by a syllable of the 4th tone, or by a syllable of the neutral tone that is originally in the 4th tone, it is pronounced in the 2nd tone. e. g. 一个人 (a person).

14.3 形容詞謂語句　以形容詞构成謂語的句子，就叫形容詞謂語句．形容詞是表示人和物的性状的詞．所以在形容詞謂語句里，謂語是描写主語所指的人或物的性質、形状等等的．我們也可以說形容詞謂語句的謂語主要是描写主語所指的人或物"怎么样"的．例如：

14.3 The Sentence with an Adjectival Predicate　A sentence, of which the predicate is composed of an adjective, is called the sentence with an adjectival predicate. An adjective is a word used to show the quality or appearance of a person or thing. Therefore, in a sentence with an adjectival predicate, the predicate is used to describe the quality, appearance and so forth of the person or thing denoted by the subject. In other words, the predicate tells us chiefly "how" is the person or thing denoted by the subject. e. g.

8. 这本 书 很 新.
Zhèiběn shū hěn xīn.

9. 那个 学生 很 好.
Nèigẻ xuéshẻng hěn hǎo.

"書"、"学生"是主語，"新"、"好"是謂語．謂語里"很"是表示程度的副詞，作修飾形容詞（"新"、"好"）的状語．

書 and 学生 are subjects. 新 and 好 are predicates. In the predicates, 很 is an adverb of degree, used as adverbial modifier modifying the adjectives 新 and 好.

要作形容詞謂語句的否定句的时候，就在形容詞前用否定副詞"不"．例如：

If we wish to negate a sentence with an adjectival predicate, we simply put the negative adverb 不 before the adjective. e. g.

10. 这本 書 不 好.
Zhèiběn shū bù hǎo.

11. 那張 紙 不 小
Nèizhāng zhǐ bù xiǎo.

关于形容詞謂語句要注意以下两点：

There are two points worth noticing concerning the sentence with an adjectival predicate:

(一) 形容詞謂語前不用系詞"是", 这是汉語句法的特点.

(1) Before the adjectival predicate, the copula 是 is never used. This is a characteristic of Chinese syntax.

(二) 在肯定的陈述句里, 副詞"很"已經弱化, 完全失去了表示程度的强調意义. 如果不用这个状語, 單独用形容詞构成的謂語就带有比較的意味. 例如說"这本書新"的时候, 就意味着"那本書旧". 所以对比时常用这种表現方法. 例如:

(2) In an affirmative declarative sentence, the adverb 很 is very weak, having completely lost its significance as a word emphasizing degree. An adjectival predicate without such an adverbial modifier implies a sense of comparison, for instance, when we say 这本書新 it implies also 那本書旧. Therefore, such expressions are often used in comparisons. e. g.

12. 这張 紙 大, 那張 紙 小.
Zhèizhāng zhǐ dà, nèizhāng zhǐ xiǎo.

13. 这本 書 好, 那本 書 不 好.
Zhèiběn shū hǎo, nèiběn shū bù hǎo.

14.4 "多"和"少"　"多"和"少"是两个常用的形容詞, 可以作謂語. 作謂語的时候, 和一般形容詞一样, 可以單独构成謂語(带有比較意味), 也可以在前面加上状語. 例如:

14.4 多 and 少　多 and 少, two very common adjectives, may also be used as predicates. In such a case, either of them may be used alone as a predicate (implying comparison), and be preceded by an adverbial modifier. e. g.

14. 学生 多, 先生 少.
Xuésheng duō, xiānsheng shǎo.

15. 学生 很 多.
Xuésheng hěn duō.

16. 先生 很 少.
Xiānsheng hěn shǎo.

但在作修飾名詞的定語的时候，与一般形容詞用作定語的情形不同：一定要說“很多”或“很少”，虽然“很”这个詞的意义在这里比較空虛．我們不能說“多先生是北京人”而只能說：

But as adjective modifiers of nouns, they are different from other adjectives: we must say 很多 or 很少, though the word 很 is rather weak in meaning. We cannot say 多先生是北京人, but we must say:

17. 很 多 先生 是 北京 人.
Hěn duō xiānsheng shì Běijīng rén.

三、課文 Kèwén Text

I

1. 这 是 一本 書.
Zhèi shì yìběn shū.

2. 这 是 一張 紙, 那 是 一張 报.
Zhèi shì yìzhāng zhǐ, nèi shì yìzhāng bào.

3. 这張 紙 大, 那張 紙 小.
Zhèizhāng zhǐ dà, nèizhāng zhǐ xiǎo.

II

4. 这 是 一本 書.
Zhèi shì yìběn shū.

5. 这本 書 很 新.
Zhèiběn shū hěn xīn.

6. 这本 書 新, 那本 書 旧.
Zhèiběn shū xīn, nèiběn shū jiù.

7. 这本 書 很 好.
Zhèiběn shū hěn hǎo.

8. 这本 书 好, 那本 书 不 好.
Zhèiběn shū hǎo, nèiběn shū bù hǎo.

III

9. 这 一个 中国 人 是 学生.
Zhèi yígê Zhōngguó rén shì xuéshêng.

10. 这个 学生 很 好.
Zhèigê xuéshêng hěn hǎo.

11. 很 多 学生 是 北京 人.
Hěn duō xuéshêng shì Běijīng rén.

12. 那 一个 中国 人 是 先生.
Nèi yígê Zhōngguó rén shì xiānshêng.

13. 那个 先生 很 好.
Nèigê xiānshêng hěn hǎo.

14. 很 多 先生 是 北京 人.
Hěn duō xiānshêng shì Běijīng rén.

IV

(a_1) 这 是 書 嗎?
Zhèi shì shū må?

(b_1) 这 不 是 書, 那 是 書.
Zhèi bú shì shū, nèi shì shū.

(a_2) 那本 書 好 嗎?
Nèiběn shū hǎo må?

(b_2) 那本 書 不 好, 这本 書 好.
Nèiběn shū bù hǎo, zhèiběn shū hǎo.

(a_3) 很 多 先生 是 北京 人 嗎?
Hěn duō xiānshêng shì Běijīng rén må?

(b₃) 很 多 先生 是 北京 人.
Hěn duō xiānshêng shì Běijīng rén.

(a₄) 很 多 学生 是 北京 人 嗎?
Hěn duō xuéshêng shì Běijīng rén må?

(b₄) 很 多 学生 是 北京 人.
Hěn duō xuéshêng shì Běijīng rén.

四、課外練習 Kèwài liànxí Home Work

1. 抄写生詞一遍.
   1) Copy all the new words in this lesson once.
2. 把下面的拼音翻成汉字:
   2) Change the following phonetic spellings into Chinese characters:
   (1) Xuéshêng hěn duō.
   (2) Bào hěn shǎo.
3. 抄写并塡入适当的量詞:
   3) Copy and fill these blanks with proper measure words:
   (3) 这 是 一____ 紙.
   (4) 那____ 書 很 好.
   (5) 那____ 学生 是 中国 人 嗎?
4. 翻譯并回答下面的問題:
   4) Translate and answer the following questions:
   (6) Is that sheet of paper big ?
   (7) Is that book old ?
   (8) Is this Chinese the new teacher ?

五、汉字表 Hànzì biǎo Chinese Characters

1	一	
2	本	木 本
3	个	人 个
4	三	一 二 三
5	很	彳
		艮
6	新	
7	好	
8	張	弓（ㄱ ㄱ 弓）
		長（一 丅 F E 目 镸 镸 長）
9	紙	
10	小	
11	大	一 ナ 大
12	多	夕
		夕
13	少	小 少
14	北	丨 ⺊ 丬 北 北
15	京	丶 亠 古 京
16	旧	丨 旧

第十五課 Lesson 15

15.1 結構助詞"的"(一)
The Structural Particle 的 (1)
15.2 定語的排列
The Arrangement of Adjective Modifiers
15.3 疑問句(二)
The Interrogative Sentence (2)
15.4 "們"
The Suffix 們
15.5 "她"和"它"
她 and 它

一、生詞 Shēngcí New Words

1.	的	(助)	dē	(a structural particle)
2.	同志	(名)	tóngzhì	comrade
3.	俄文	(名)	èwén	the Russian language
4.	朋友	(名)	péngyǒu	friend
5.	干淨	(形)	gānjìng	clean
6.	我們	(代)	wǒmên	we, us
7.	你們	(代)	nǐmên	you
8.	他們	(代)	tāmên	they, them
9.	她	(代)	tā	she, her
10.	它	(代)	tā	it
11.	枝	(量)	zhī	(a measure word)
12.	鉛笔	(名)	qiānbǐ [枝]	pencil
13.	長	(形)	cháng	long

14. 短　(形) duǎn　short

15. 黑板　(名) hēibǎn　blackboard

二、語法 Yǔfǎ Grammar

15.1 結构助詞"的"(一)　我們已經知道形容詞可以修飾名詞,修飾名詞的形容詞就构成定語(14.4),而被修飾的名詞就构成中心語. 除了形容詞以外,名詞、代詞以及別类的詞或別的結构也可以作定語. 現在就先談名詞、代詞和形容詞作定語. 定語在中心語之前,它和它的中心語之間往往用一个結构助詞"的". 例如:

15.1 The Structural Particle 的 (1)　We know already that adjectives may modify nouns, an adjective modifier is an adjective modifying a noun (14.4), and the noun modified is called the central word. Besides adjectives, nouns, pronouns and words of other parts of speech and even constructions (phrases) may all be used as adjective modifiers. Here in this lesson we will consider nouns, pronouns and adjectives used as adjective modifiers. An adjective modifier must precede the central word or the word it modifies, and the structural particle 的 is often used in between. e. g.

1. 先生的 書 很 多.
   Xiānshēngdȇ shū hěn duō.
2. 这 是 他的 紙.
   Zhèi shì tādȇ zhǐ.
3. 他 是 一个 很 好的 同志.
   Tā shì yígȇ hěn hǎodȇ tóngzhì.

"書"、"紙"和"同志"是中心語,"先生"、"他"和"好"是定語,定語和中心語之間存在着領屬关系(如例1、例2)或修飾关系(如例3). 領屬性的定語只能由名詞或代詞构成,而形容詞构成的定語总是用来修飾或描写中心語的.

書, 紙, and 同志 are central words, 先生, 他 and 好 are adjective modifiers; there exists between the adjective modifier and the central word a relation of ownership (as in examples 1, 2) or a descriptive relationship (as in example 3). An adjective modifier of ownership can only be formed by a noun or a pronoun, while an adjective modifier made up of an adjective is always used to modify or describe the central word.

値得注意的是，并不是在任何定語后面都非要用一个結构助詞"的"不可；用不用这个助詞的規律大致如下：

It is not quite true that after an adjective modifier there must be a structural particle 的. From the following rules we see when it has to be used or when not.

（一）有些定語的名詞或代詞与中心語黏合得很紧，已經形成了穩固的詞組，这时候就不用助詞．例如：

(1) Some nouns and pronouns used as adjective modifiers are so integral a part of their central words that they have become stable word groups. In such cases, we do not use the particle 的. e. g.

4. 中国 人
Zhōngguó rén

5. 俄文 报
èwén bào

6. 我 朋友
wǒ péngyǒu

（二）形容詞作定語，常用的、尤其是單音的，一般地不用助詞"的"．例如：

(2) When adjectives, especially monosyllabic ones, are used as adjective modifiers, we do not use the particle 的 in general. e. g.

7. 好 学生
hǎo xuéshēng

8. 旧 書
jiù shū

9. 干净 紙
gānjìng zhǐ

但在形容詞前有状語的时候，助詞"的"一般是必要的（形容詞"多"、"少"常常可以例外）。例如：

But, when there is an adverbial modifier before the adjective, the particle 的 is generally indispensable (the adjectives 多 and 少 are exceptions). e. g.

10. 很 旧的 报
hěn jiùdě bào

11. 不 好的 書
bù hǎodě shū

12. 很 干淨的 紙
hěn gānjìngdě zhǐ

（三）如果語言环境足够清楚的时候，例如上文已經交代了中心語，下文的中心語就可以省略。这时候定語后面的助詞"的"是絕对必要的。例如：

(3) When it is clear from the context what the central word should be, the central word may be omitted, but the particle 的 must on no account be left out after the adjective modifier. e. g.

13. 这本 新 書 干淨，那本 旧的 不 干淨.
Zhèiběn xīn shū gānjìng, nèiběn jiùdě bù gānjìng.

我們不說"旧書"而說"旧的"，就因为"新書"已經把"書"点明了的緣故。

We say 旧的 instead of 旧書, because the idea of 書 is already expressed by 新書.

15.2 定語的排列　数量詞用在名詞前边（如"一本書"）和指示代詞連带量詞或数量詞用在名詞前边（如"这本書"、"这三本書"），也都是定語（除了由名詞借来的量詞以外，量詞后面总是不要結构助詞"的"）。数量詞和指示代詞作定語并用的时候，指示代詞在前，

数量詞在后(14.1). 指示代詞和数量詞跟人称代詞、名詞或形容詞形成并列定語的时候，其排列次序如下:

15.2 The Arrangement of Adjective Modifiers　Numerals in conjunction with measure words used before nouns (such as 一本書) and demonstrative pronouns in conjunction with measure words or with numerals and measure words used before nouns (such as 这本書 and 这三本書) are also adjective modifiers (with the exception of nouns used as measure words, all measure words are used without 的). When an adjective modifier is composed of a demonstrative pronoun, a numeral and a measure word, the demonstrative pronoun stands first, then the numeral and the measure word (14.1). When the modifier contains not only the three elements mentioned above, but also a personal pronoun, a noun or an adjective, the word order is as follows:

(一) 形容詞构成的定語靠近中心語. 例如:

(1) In an adj. modifier, the adjective should be near the central word. e. g.

14. 那 一本 新 書
nèi yìběn xīn shū

15. 这 一張 旧 报
zhèi yìzhāng jiù bào

(二) 人称代詞总是在指示代詞前面，所以人称代詞或名詞构成的領属性的定語，都是在最前面. 例如:

(2) The personal pronoun must always stand before the demonstrative pronoun, therefore an adjective modifier of ownership composed of a personal pronoun or a noun must always come first. e. g.

16. 他的 那 一張 旧 报
tādė nèi yìzhāng jiù bào

17. 先生的 这 一本 新 書
xiānshėngdė zhèi yìběn xīn shū

15.3 疑問句(二)　第二种提問的方法是用选擇式. 选擇的項目包括一件事情的肯定方面和否定方面，因此选擇式就是并列謂語的肯定形式和否定形式. 回答的人可以任擇其一. 如果是体詞謂語句(一) 就用"是不是". 例如.

15.3 The Interrogative Sentence (2) The second kind of the interrogative sentence is alternative in form, including both the affirmative and the negative sides of a thing set side by side; in other words, the alternative form includes both the affirmative and the negative forms of the predicate. The person trying to answer the question is expected to choose between the two. In the sentence with a substantive predicate (1), the alternative form is 是不是. e. g.

18. 他 是 不 是 先生?
Tā shì bú shì xiānshěng?

19. 这 是 不 是 报?
Zhèi shì bú shì bào?

"不是" 也可以用在句尾. 例如:

不是 may also stand at the end of a sentence .e. g.

20. 他 是 先生 不 是?
Tā shì xiānshěng bú shì?

21. 这 是 报 不 是?
Zhèi shì bào bú shì?

如果是形容詞謂語句, 就是并列形容詞构成的謂語的肯定形式和否定形式. 例如:

In the sentence with an adjectival predicate, the alternative form includes both the affirmative and the negative forms of the predicative adjective. e. g.

22. 这本 書 好 不 好?
Zhèiběn shū hǎo bù hǎo?

23. 那張 紙 干淨 不 干淨?
Nèizhāng zhǐ gānjìng bù gānjìng?

15.4 "們" "們" 是一个表示复数的詞尾. 單数人称代詞后面加上"們", 就形成了复数. 例如:

15.4 們 們 is a suffix indicating plural number. All singular personal pronouns with 們 are plural in number. e. g.

24. 我—我們
wǒ —wǒmėn

25. 你—你們
nǐ —nǐmėn

("您"不能加"們"表示复数.)
(們 is never used after 您 to indicate plural number.)

26. 他—他們
tā —tāmėn

"們"也可以用在名詞后面表示复数. 但是有两点要注意:

"們" may also be used after nouns indicating plural number, but attention should be paid to the following two points:

(一) 只能用在指人的名詞后面, 例如"先生們"、"学生們"等等. 其余的名詞都不能加"們", 所以不能說"書們"、"报們"等等.

(1) 們 is only used after nouns denoting persons, such as 先生們, 学生們 etc. The other nouns cannot take such a suffix. We cannot say 書們, 报們 etc.

(二) 名詞加"們"的一定是复数, 不加的不一定是單数. 如果語言环境已經明确指出了它的复数时, 这个名詞后面就不再用詞尾"們". 例如:

(2) A noun followed by the suffix 們 is always plural, but a noun without such a suffix may be either singular or plural. When it is clearly shown by context that the noun is in the plural, it is no longer necessary to use the suffix. e. g.

27. 我們 是 学生.
Wǒmėn shì xuéshėng.

28. 很多先生是北京人.
Hěn duō xiānshêng shì Běijīng rén.

因为"我們"和"很多"指出了复数,"学生"、"先生"和"北京人"的后面就不用"們". 因此, 我們也可以說"們"虽然是表示名詞复数的詞尾, 但是只是在沒有其他条件而又絕对需要的时候才用.

Because 我們 and 很多 already imply that 学生, 先生 and 北京人 are in the plural, we no longer use the suffix 們. According to the above, 們 is used only when there is absolute necessity and when there is no other indication of plurality.

15.5 "她"和"它" 这两个詞讀音和"他"完全一样, 也都是單数的第三人称代詞. 在書面語里, 可以用"他"指所有第三身單数的人或事物. 但是我們現在常用"他"代表男人, "她"代表女人, "它"代表人以外的事物. "她"的用法完全和"他"一样, 而"它"一般地不用在句首. 所以我們可以說"她是先生", 但是不能說"它是紙". "它"也沒有复数形态, 我們不能用"它們"代表复数事物.

15.5 她 and 它 These two words have the same pronunciation as 他, and are also pronouns of the third person singular. In writing, 他 may be used to indicate any person or thing of the third person singular. But now we always use 他 to denote the male, 她 the female and 它 all things or matters exclusive of human beings. 她 is the same as 他 in use, but 它 should never be used at the beginning of a sentence. We can say 她是先生, but we must never say 它是紙. Moreover, the word 它 has no plural form, so we cannot use 它們 to represent things in the plural number.

三、課文 Kèwén Text

I

1. 我朋友的書很多.
Wǒ péngyôudê shū hěn duō.

2. 她的書很新.
Tādê shū hěn xīn.

II

3. 这 是 一枝 新 鉛笔.
Zhèi shì yìzhī xīn qiānbǐ.

4. 这枝 鉛笔 很 長.
Zhèizhī qiānbǐ hěn cháng.

5. 新 鉛笔 長, 旧 鉛笔 短.
Xīn qiānbǐ cháng, jiù qiānbǐ duǎn.

III

(a_1) 这 是 黑板 不 是?
Zhèi shì hēibǎn bú shì?

(b_1) 这 是 黑板.
Zhèi shì hēibǎn.

(a_2) 这个 黑板 干淨 不 干淨?
Zhèigẻ hēibǎn gānjỉng bù gānjỉng?

(b_2) 很 干淨, 这 是 一个 新 黑板.
Hěn gānjỉng, zhèi shì yígẻ xīn hēibǎn.
新的 干淨, 旧的 不 干淨.
Xīndẻ gānjỉng, jiùdẻ bù gānjỉng.

(a_3) 你們的 先生 是 中国 人 嗎?
Nǐmẻndẻ xiānshẻng shì Zhōngguó rén mả?

(b_3) 是 中国 人.
Shì Zhōngguó rén.

(a_4) 你們的 先生 多 不 多?
Nǐmẻndẻ xiānshẻng duō bù duō?

(b_4) 很 多.
Hěn duō.

(a_5) 那个 同志 是 不 是 你們的 先生?
Nèigẻ tóngzhì shì bú shì nǐmẻndẻ xiānshẻng?

(b₆) 是, 她 是 我們的 先生 她 很
Shì, tā shì wǒmêndê xiānshêng. Tā hěn

好, 她 是 一个 很 好的 先生.
hǎo, tā shì yígê hěn hǎodê xiānshêng.

四、課外練習 Kèwài liànxí Home Work

1. 抄写生詞一遍.

1) Copy all the new words once:

2. 下面这些詞語都可以作名詞的定語,請把适当的名詞写出来(注意助詞"的"的应用和省略):

2) The following words and word groups can all be used as adjective modifiers of nouns, so please fill the blanks with proper nouns (pay attention to the use and omission of the particle 的):

(1) 她們____ (2) 朋友____ (3) 旧 ____

(4) 干淨____ (5) 很 長____ (6) 不 好____

3. 先把下面的問題改成选擇式的疑問句,再回答:

3) Change the following questions into alternative interrogative sentences, and write answers to all of them:

(7) 这个 黑板 大 嗎?

(8) 那 是 先生的 紙 嗎?

(9) 他 那枝 鉛笔 長 嗎?

(10) 您的 那个 朋友 是 一个 新 学生 嗎?

五、汉字表 Hànzì biǎo Chinese Characters

1	的	
2	同	
3	志	
4	俄	亻
		我
5	文	
6	朋	月（丿 ⺆ 月 月）
		月
7	友	一 ナ 友
8	干	一 干
9	淨	氵
		爭（ノ ㄑ ⺈ 爫 𠬤 𠬤 𠬤 爭）
10	們	
11	她	女
		也

12	它	宀
		匕
13	枝	木
		支（十 支）
14	鉛	
15	笔	
16	長	
17	短	矢
		豆（一 戸 戸 豆 豆）
18	黑	丨 冂 冂 冂 四 四 罒 里 黑
19	板	木
		反

第十六課 Lesson 16

16.1	动詞謂語句 The Sentence with a Verbal Predicate
16.2	动詞謂語句的否定 The Negative Form of the Sentence with a Verbal Predicate
16.3	"有" 的否定 The Negative Form of 有
16.4	动詞謂語句的提問 How to Change a Sentence with a Verbal Predicate into an Interrogative Sentence

一、生詞 Shēngcí New Words

1.	工作	(动、名)	gōngzuò	to work, work
2.	学習	(动)	xuéxí	to study
3.	教	(动)	jiāo	to teach
4.	中文	(名)	zhōngwén	the Chinese language
5.	給	(动)	gěi	to give
6.	看	(动)	kàn	to see, to look at
7.	来	(动)	lái	to come
8.	有	(动)	yǒu	to have
9.	沒	(副)	méi	not
10.	只	(副)	zhǐ	only
11.	本子	(名)	běnzi [本]	note-book

二、 語法 Yǔfǎ Grammar

16.1 动詞謂語句 以动詞构成謂語的句子，就叫动詞謂語句．动詞是表示动作、行为、变化的詞．在动詞謂語句里，謂語叙述主語所指的人或事物的动作、行为或变化．动詞謂語句可以分为以下三种：

16.1 The Sentence with a Verbal Predicate A sentence in which the predicate is composed of a verb is called the sentence with a verbal predicate. A verb is a word that describes some action, behaviour or change. In the sentence with a verbal predicate, the predicate tells about the action, behaviour or change of the person or thing denoted by the subject. The sentence with a verbal predicate may be divided into three kinds:

（一）簡單的动詞謂語句 謂語里只有动詞而沒有宾語，即是动詞單独构成謂語的句子．例如：

(1) The simple verbal sentence This is the kind of sentence where there is only a verb and no object, that is to say, the predicate of such a sentence is formed by the verb itself. e. g.

1. 先生 工作.
   Xiānshêng gōngzuò.

2. 我們 学習.
   Wǒmên xuéxí.

（二）單宾語动詞謂語句 謂語由动詞和宾語构成，动詞在前，宾語在后．例如：

(2) The verbal sentence with a single object This is the kind of sentence where the predicate is made up of a verb and its object. The verb precedes the object. e. g.

3. 先生 教 我.
   Xiānshêng jiāo wǒ.

4. 我們 学習 中文.
   Wǒmên xuéxí zhōngwén.

"先生"和"我們"是主語，"教"和"学習"是动詞，"我"和"中文"是宾語．主語在前，謂語在后．这个詞序可以說是汉語动詞謂語句的基本形式：

主語——动詞——宾語

先生 and 我們 are subjects, 教 and 学習 are verbs, and 我 and 中文 are objects. The subject precedes the predicate. The following word order is recognized as the basic construction of the verbal sentence:

Subject — Verb — Object

(三) 双宾語动詞謂語句 謂語里一个动詞也可以带两个宾語. 这样的句子就是双宾語动詞謂語句. 在这种句子里, 动詞仍然在宾語之前, 而間接宾語 (一般是指人的) 又在直接宾語 (一般是指物的) 之前. 例如:

(3) The verbal sentence with double object This is the kind of sentence where there may be one verb and two objects in the predicate. Such a sentence is called the verbal sentence with double object. The verb precedes the objects, and the indirect object (which in general denotes some person) precedes the dircet object (which in general denotes some thing).e. g.

5. 先生 教 我 中文.
Xiānshêng jiāo wǒ zhōngwén.

6. 他 給 朋友 一枝 鉛笔.
Tā gěi péngyǒu yìzhī qiānbǐ.

"先生"和"他"是主語, "教"、"給"是动詞, "中文"和"鉛笔"是直接宾語, 而"我"和"朋友"就是間接宾語. 双宾語动詞謂語句的詞序是:

主語——动詞——間接宾語——直接宾語

先生 and 他 are subjects, 教 and 給 are verbs. 中文 and 鉛笔 are direct objects, while 我 and 朋友 are indirect objects. Therefore, the word order of the verbal sentence with double object is as follows:

Subject — Verb — Indirect Object — Direct Object

例 6 的宾語 (名詞"鉛笔") 前有数量詞构成的定語"一枝". 其

实，不但宾語可以有定語，主語也可以有. 下面是主語和宾語都带有定語的例子:

In example 6, the object (or the noun 鉛笔) is preceded by an adjective modifier made up of a numeral and a measure word 一枝. In fact, all the subjects and objects in such sentences can be preceded by adjective modifiers. In the following example, the subject and the objects all have adjective modifiers:

7. 我們 先生 給 那个 学生 一本
Wǒmėn xiānshėng gěi nèigė xuéshėng yìběn

很 新的 書.
hěn xīndė shū.

16.2 动詞謂語句的否定 和体詞謂語句、形容詞謂語句一样,我們也用否定副詞"不"来构成动詞謂語句的否定句. 当我們把"不"放在动詞前面的时候, 可以表达这样的意思: "經常不这样"、"将要不这样"或者是"不願意这样". 例如:

16.2 The Negative Form of the Sentence with a Verbal Predicate Just like the negative forms of the sentence with a substantive predicate and the sentence with an adjectival predicate, we use the negative adverb 不 to form the negative of the sentence with a verbal predicate. When we put the adverb 不 before the verb, it means "used not to do so", "shall or will not do so" or "to be not willing to do so". e. g.

8. 我 不 看 俄文 报.
Wǒ bú kàn èwén bào.

9. 我的 朋友 不 来.
Wǒdė péngyǒu bù lái.

10. 她 不 給 我 那張 紙.
Tā bù gěi wǒ nèizhāng zhǐ.

16.3 "有"的否定 "有"是一个比較特殊的动詞，否定的时候一定不能說"不有"而要說"沒有". 例如:

16.3 The Negative Form of 有 The word 有 is a rather special verb, its negative form is 沒有 and not 不有. e. g.

11. 我 沒 有 鉛笔.
Wǒ méi yǒu qiānbǐ.

12. 先生 沒 有 俄文 报.
Xiānshêng méi yǒu èwén bào.

"沒有"后面如果有其他成分，可以省为"沒"。但是在句尾，必須用"沒有"。例如：

When there is some other element following 沒有, 沒有 can be simplified as 沒 only. But at the end of a sentence, we must say 沒有. e. g.

13. 你們 有 書 嗎?
Nǐmên yǒu shū må?

14. 他 有 書, 我 沒 書.
Tā yǒu shū, wǒ méi shū.

(或: 我 沒 有.)
Wǒ méi yǒu.

16.4 动詞謂語句的提問　动詞謂語句的提問可以用在句尾加"嗎"或选擇式两种方法。例如：

16.4 How to Change a Sentence with a Verbal Predicate into an Interrogative Sentence　Such a sentence is changed into an interrogative sentence either by adding the particle 嗎, or by using the alternative form e. g.

15. 你 来 嗎?
Nǐ lái må?

16. 你 不 来 嗎?
Nǐ bù lái må?

17. 你 来 不 来?
Nǐ lái bù lái?

有賓語的时候，在选擇式的疑問句里就有两种可能的詞序：賓語在动詞之后或在肯定的与否定的动詞之間（比較体詞謂語句（一）的选擇式疑問句）。例如：

When there is an object, this is the word order of the alternative interrogative sentence: the object may stand after the verbs or between the affirmative verb and the negative verb (refer to the alternative interrogative form of the sentence with a substantive predicate (1)). e. g.

18. 你們 学習 不 学習 俄文?
Nǐmen xuéxí bù xuéxí èwén?

19. 你們 学習 俄文 不 学習?
Nǐmen xuéxí èwén bù xuéxí?

20. 那个 同志 教 不 教 你們 中文?
Nèigê tóngzhì jiāo bù jiāo nǐmen zhōngwén?

21. 那个 同志 教 你們 中文 不 教?
Nèigê tóngzhì jiāo nǐmen zhōngwén bù jiāo?

如果动詞是"有",就用"有沒有…"或"有…沒有"的形式.例如:

If the verb is 有, we have to use the form 有沒有 ... or the form 有 ...沒有. e. g.

22. 他 有 沒 有 鉛笔?
Tā yǒu méi yǒu qiānbǐ?

23. 他 有 鉛笔 沒 有?
Tā yǒu qiānbǐ méi yǒu?

三、課文 Kèwén Text

I

(a_1) 您 来 不 来?
Nín lái bù lái?

(b_1) 我 来, 您 来 嗎?
Wǒ lái, nín lái mâ?

(a_2) 我 不 来.
Wǒ bù lái.

II

(a_3) 他 看 俄文 書 嗎?
Tā kàn èwén shū mả?

(b_3) 他 不 看, 他 只 看 中文 書.
Tā bú kàn, tā zhǐ kàn zhōngwén shū.

(a_4) 您 看 俄文 書 不 看?
Nín kàn èwén shū bú kàn?

(b_4) 我 看, 我 学習 俄文, 我 有 很 多 俄文 書.
Wǒ kàn, wǒ xuéxí èwén, wǒ yǒu hěn duō èwén shū.

III

(a_5) 这个 先生 教 不 教 你?
Zhèigẻ xiānshẻng jiāo bù jiāo nỉ?

(b_5) 教 我, 她 教 我們 中文.
Jiāo wỏ, tā jiāo wǒmẻn zhōngwén.

(a_6) 他 教 俄文 不 教?
Tā jiāo èwén bù jiāo?

(b_6) 她 不 教 俄文, 只 教 中文.
Tā bù jiāo èwén, zhǐ jiāo zhōngwén.

(a_7) 她 教 他們 不 教?
Tā jiāo tāmẻn bù jiāo?

(b_7) 不 教, 她 只 教 新 学生.
Bù jiāo, tā zhǐ jiāo xīn xuéshẻng.

(a_8) 您的 朋友 有 本子 嗎?
Níndẻ péngyỏu yǒu běnzỉ mả?

(b_8) 有 本子, 他的 本子 很 多.
Yǒu běnzỉ, tādẻ běnzỉ hěn duō.

(a₉) 那个 学生 有 本子 沒 有?
Nèigě xuéshēng yǒu běnzi méi yǒu?

(b₉) 沒 有, 他 只 有 一張 紙.
Méi yǒu, tā zhǐ yǒu yìzhāng zhǐ.

四、課外練習 Kèwài liànxí Home Work

1. 把生詞抄写一遍.
1) Copy all the new words in this lesson once.

2. 用下面的动詞各作一个句子:
2) Make sentences with each of the following verbs:

(1) 工作 (2) 有 (3) 給

3. 抄写下面的句子, 并用符号标出主語、定語、动詞、直接宾語和間接宾語来:
3) Copy the following sentences and underline the subjects, the adjective modifiers, the verbs, and the direct objects and indirect objects:

例如:
For example:

那个 先生 教 我 中文.

(4) 这个 先生 来, 那个 先生 不 来.

(5) 您的 朋友 看 中文 报, 我的 朋友 看 俄文 报.

(6) 先生 給 学生 一本 新 書.

4. 用否定句子回答下面的問題:
4) Answer the questions in the negative:

(7) 你 有 干淨的 紙 嗎?

(8) 那个 学生 看 俄文 書 不 看?

五、 汉字表 Hànzì biǎo Chinese Characrters

1	工	一 丅 工
2	作	
3	習	羽（ㄱ ㄱ 习 羽 ）
		白
4	教	孝（土 耂 孝 ）
		攵
5	給	糸
		合
6	看	手（丿 二 三 手 ）
		目（丨 冂 月 月 目 ）
7	来	一 ㇀ ㇀ 立 平 来 来
8	有	一 ナ 有
9	沒	氵 氵 沒 沒
10	只	
11	子	

第十七課 Lesson 17

一、生詞 Shēngcí New Words

1.	鋼笔	(名)	gāngbǐ	pen
2.	都	(副)	dōu	all
3.	也	(副)	yě	also, too
4.	桌子	(名)	zhuōzi [張]	table
5.	和	(連)	hé	and
6.	把	(量)	bǎ	(a measure word)
7.	椅子	(名)	yǐzi [把]	chair
8.	杂誌	(名)	zázhì [本]	magazine
9.	画报	(名)	huàbào [本]	pictorial
10.	北京大学	(名)	Běijīngdàxué	Peking University
11.	会	(动)	huì	to know how to do
12.	对了		duìlê	yes, that is right
13.	有意思		yǒuyìsi	interesting

二、 語法 Yǔfǎ Grammar

17.1 体詞謂語句(二) 名詞可以有名詞、代詞或形容詞构成的定語 (15.1). 所以体詞謂語句(一)里的名詞謂語也可以带这种定語. 例如:

17.1 The Sentence with a Substantive Predicate (2) Nouns, pronouns and adjectives may all be used as adjective modifiers to modify nouns (15.1), therefore in the sentence with a substantive predicate (1), when the predicate is made up of a noun, it may carry any of these adjective modifiers. e. g.

1. 这本 書 是 先生的 書.
   Zhèiběn shū shì xiānshēngdê shū.
2. 那枝 鋼笔 是 我的 鋼笔.
   Nèizhī gāngbǐ shì wǒdê gāngbǐ.
3. 这个 本子 是 新 本子.
   Zhèigê běnzi shì xīn běnzi.

在語言环境足够清楚的时候, 我們可以把中心語省去 (15.1), 上边这种体詞謂語句(一)式的句子就常常可以說成:

We have already learned that the central word (or the word modified) may be omitted, if the context is clear without it (15.1), so all the above sentences may be recast as follows:

4. 这本 書 是 先生的.
   Zhèiběn shū shì xiānshēngdê.
5. 那枝 鋼笔 是 我的.
   Nèizhī gāngbǐ shì wǒdê.
6. 这个 本子 是 新的.
   Zhèigê běnzi shì xīndê.

这里, 作中心語的体詞 (都是名詞: "書" "鋼笔" "本子") 是省略了, 但是构成定語的名詞、代詞或形容詞与結构助詞 "的" 結合起來("先生的""我的""新的")起体詞作用，它就是体詞結构．以这种体詞結构为謂語主要成分的句子，就叫体詞謂語句(二)．

Here, all the substantives used as central words (all of them being nouns: 書, 鋼笔, and 本子) have been omitted, but the noun, pronoun or adjective in the adjective modifiers may, together with the structural particle 的, assume the function of a substantive (先生的, 我的 or 新的). This is called the substantive construction. A sentence, in which the main element of the predicate is composed of such a substantive construction, is called the sentence with a substantive predicate (2).

体詞謂語句(二)除了謂語的主要成分是結构助詞"的"所形成的体詞結构以外，在結构上，它和体詞謂語句(一)基本上还是相同的：体詞謂語句(二)也需要系詞"是"联系主語和謂語的主要成分．在用途和意义上，体詞謂語句(二)跟体詞謂語句(一)一样，它的謂語都是判断、說明主語所指的人或事物"是什么"的．但是具体地說来，体詞謂語句(二)的謂語是說明主語所指的人或事物是"具有什么屬性"或"屬於哪个类别"的．

With the exception of the chief element of the predicate which is composed of a substantive construction, the sentence with a substantive predicate (2) is essentially the same as the sentence with a substantive predicate (1). So far as the sentence structure is concerned, in the sentence of the second kind, the copula 是 is also required to connect the subject with the chief element of the predicate. As for its function, the predicate of the second kind is to explain the person or thing denoted by the subject. But speaking more in detail, the predicate of the second kind describes the quality of the person or thing denoted by the subject, or the kind of person or thing.

17.2 体詞謂語句(二)的否定　我們在系詞"是"前加否定副詞"不"造成体詞謂語句(一)的否定句，也用同样的方法造成体詞謂語句(二)的否定句．例如：

17.2 The Negative Form of the Sentence with a Substantive Predicate (2)　We put the negative adverb 不 before the copula 是 to negate the sentence with a substantive predicate

(1) as has been explained before. Here we do the same to negate the sentence with a substantive predicate (2). e. g.

7. 这本 書 是 先生的 嗎?
Zhèiběn shū shì xiānshêngdê mȧ?

8. 这本 書 不 是 先生的.
Zhèiběn shū bú shì xiānshêngdê.

9. 那張 紙 是 不 是 你的?
Nèizhāng zhǐ shì bú shì nǐdê?

10. 不 是, 那張 紙 不 是 我的.
Bú shì, nèizhāng zhǐ bú shì wǒdê.

11. 那个 本子 是 不 是 新的?
Nèigê běnzi shì bú shì xīndê?

12. 不 是 新的.
Bú shì xīndê.

同时可以注意: 提問的方法也和体詞謂語句(一)一样.

Note: The method of asking questions is the same as explained under the sentence with a substantive predicate (1).

17.3 "都"和"也" 我們知道"不"是表示否定的副詞, "很"是表示程度的副詞, "只"是表示范圍的副詞. 現在要学的"都"也是一个表示范圍的副詞. 在意义上它所总括的人或事物都是在它的前面提到过的, 在句法上它的位置一般在主語之后, 謂語之前. 例如:

17.3 都 and 也 We know that 不 is an adverb of negation, 很 is an adverb of degree and 只 is an adverb of extent. Now, 都 is also an adverb of extent. As far as the meaning is concerned, it refers to the persons and things that have already appeared in the same sentence; its place in the syntax is after the subject and before the predicate. e. g.

13. 先生 都 是 中国 人.
Xiānshêng dōu shì Zhōngguó rén.

14. 她的 書 都 是 俄文的.

Tādė shū dōu shì èwéndė.

值得注意的是汉語里当名詞作主語是复数的时候，这个复数常用副詞“都”来表示. 例 13 虽然也可以說成“先生們都是中国人”，但要說成“先生們是中国人”就不合乎汉語習慣. 例 14 里“書”的复数当然更是非由“都”来表示不可了.

Note: In Chinese, when a plural noun is used as subject, the plural number is always expressed by the adverb 都. Although example 13 may be changed into 先生們都是中国人, yet it would be not idiomatic if we say 先生們是中国人. In example 14, the plural number of 書 is of course expressed by the adverb 都.

“也”也是副詞, 和“都”一样, 要用在謂語之前. 例如:

“也” is also an adverb, and like the adverb “都” it has to be put before the predicate. e. g.

15. 这本 書 好, 那本 書 也 好.

Zhèiběn shū hǎo, nèiběn shū yě hǎo.

16. 我 看 报, 他 也 看 报.

Wǒ kàn bào, tā yě kàn bào.

我們不能說“也那本書”“也他”, 就和不能說“都先生”“都她的書”一样.

We must not say 也那本書 or 也他. Similarly, it is not correct to say 都先生 and 都她的書.

一般副詞，特別是單音副詞不能作謂語，因之也不能單独回答問題(否定副詞“不”比較特殊，是个例外).必須帶着动詞或形容詞构成的謂語. “都”和“也”也是如此. 例如:

In general, adverbs, especially when monosyllabic, are not used as predicates, therefore they cannot be used to answer questions by themselves (the negative adverb 不 is an exception), for they must be affixed to verbs or adjectives. 都 and 也 come under the same rule. e. g.

17. 你的 朋友 都 来 嗎?
Nǐdė péngyǒu dōu lái må?

18. 都 来.
Dōu lái.

19. 黑板 很 干淨, 桌子 也 很 干淨 嗎?
Hēibǎn hěn gānjìng, zhuōzi yě hěn gānjìng må?

20. 也 很 干淨.
Yě hěn gānjìng.

"都"和"也"并用的时候,一般是"也"在前、"都"在后. 例如:
When 都 and 也 are used together, the general rule is that 也 precedes 都. e. g.

21. 我們 是 学生, 他們 也 都 是 学生.
Wǒmėn shì xuéshėng, tāmėn yě dōu shì xuéshėng.

17.4 "和" 这个連詞的主要功用是連接名詞和代詞. 例如:
17.4 和 The chief function of this conjunction is to connect nouns and pronouns. e. g.

22. 这本 書 和 那本 書 都 好.
Zhèiběn shū hé nèiběn shū duō hǎo.

23. 她 和 那个 同志 都 是 我的 朋友.
Tā hé nèigė tóngzhì dōu shì wǒdė péngyǒu.

24. 我 和 他 都 不 是 先生.
Wǒ hé tā dōu bú shì xiānshėng.

不过, 汉語里并非所有的并列成分都要用連詞来連接, 特别是名詞和名詞并列的时候, 我們常常用語气停頓来代替連詞. 例如:
But in Chinese, not all nouns and pronouns are connected by conjunctions, particularly when two nouns stand together. There, we often use a pause instead of a conjunction. e. g,

25. 这本 书、那本 书 都 好.
Zhèiběn shū、nèiběn shū dōu hǎo.

26. 先生、学生 都 来.
Xiānshėng、xuéshėng dōu lái.

二、 課文 Kèwén Text

I

(a_1) 这張 桌子 是 您的 嗎?
Zhèizhāng zhuōzi shì níndė må?

(b_1) 不 是, 这張 桌子 是 我 朋友的.
Bú shì, zhèizhāng zhuōzi shì wǒ péngyǒu-dė.

(a_2) 这把 椅子 是 您的 不 是?
Zhèibǎ yǐzi shì níndė bú shì?

(b_2) 也 不 是, 这把 椅子 也 是 她的.
Yě bú shì, zhèibǎ yǐzi yě shì tādė.

(a_3) 她 这本 杂誌 和 这本 画报 都 是 新的 嗎?
Tā zhèiběn zázhì hé zhèiběn huàbào dōu shì xīndė må?

(b_3) 都 是 新的, 她的 杂誌、画报 都 是 新的.
Dōu shì xīndė, tādė zázhì、huàbào dōu shì xīndė.

(a_4) 那个 先生 和 那个 学生 都 是
Nèigẻ xiānshẻng hé nèigẻ xuéshẻng dōu shì

北京 大学的 嗎?
Běijīng Dàxuédẻ mẻ?

(b_4) 都 是 北京 大学的.
Dōu shì Běijīng Dàxuédẻ.

(a_5) 你們 也 都 是 北京 大学的 嗎?
Nǐmẻn yě dōu shì Běijīng Dàxuédẻ mẻ?

(b_5) 不 都 是, 我 是, 他 不 是.
Bù dōu shì, wǒ shì, tā bú shì.

II

(a_6) 这本 杂誌 是 中文的 嗎?
Zhèiběn zázhì shì zhōngwéndẻ mẻ?

(b_6) 不 是 中文的, 是 俄文的.
Bú shì zhōngwéndẻ, shì èwéndẻ.

我 不 会 中文.
Wǒ bú huì zhōngwén.

(a_7) 那本 画报 也 是 俄文的 嗎?
Nèiběn huàbào yě shì èwéndẻ mẻ?

(b_7) 不 是 俄文的, 是 中文的.
Bú shì èwéndẻ, shì zhōngwéndẻ.

(a_8) 你 看 中文 画报 嗎?
Nǐ kàn zhōngwén huàbào mẻ?

(b_8) 对 了, 我 看 中文 画报.
Duì lẻ, wǒ kàn zhōngwén huàbào.

(a$_9$) 你的 朋友 也 都 看 中文 画报
Nǐdȇ péngyȍu yě dōu kàn zhōngwén huàbào

嗎?
mȁ?

(b$_9$) 他們 也 都 看 中文 画报.
Tāmȇn yě dōu kàn zhōngwén huàbào.

中文 画报 很 有意思.
Zhōngwén huàbào hěn yǒuyìsȋ.

(a$_{10}$) 你們 只 看 中文 画报 嗎?
Nǐmȇn zhǐ kàn zhōngwén huàbào mȁ?

(b$_{10}$) 不, 我們 也 看 俄文 画报.
Bù, wǒmȇn yě kàn èwén huàbào.

四、課外練習 Kèwài liànxí Home Work

1. 把下面問題翻成中文以后再回答:

   1) Translate and answer the following questions:—

   (1) Are all your books and magazines new?
   (2) Do these three students belong to Peking University?
   (3) Are this magazine and that pictorial yours?
   (4) Does that new pencil belong to your friend or not?

2. 把下面的拼音翻成汉字, 再写出回答來:

   2) Change the following phonetic spellings into Chinese characters and write down the answers:

   (5) Xiānshȇngdȇ huàbào yǒuyìsȋ méi yǒu?
   (6) Zhèibǎ yǐzȋ shì bú shì jiùdȇ?
   (7) Nǐmȇndȇ xiānshȇng huì bú huì èwén?

五、汉字表 Hànzì biǎo Chinese Characters

1	鋼	金	
		岡（冂 冂 冂 冈 罓 罔 岡）	
2	都	者（土 耂 者）	
		阝	
3	也		
4	桌	丨 ⺊ 占 桌	
5	和	禾（ノ 禾）	
		口	
6	把	扌	
		巴（乛 コ 巳 巴）	
7	椅	木	
		奇	大
			可（一 口 可）

8	杂	九（丿 九）
		朩
9	誌	言
		志
10	画	
11	会	人
		云（ˉ 二 云）
12	对	
13	了	㇇ 了
14	意	立
		曰
		心
15	思	田
		心

第十八課 Lesson 18

18.1 体詞謂語句（一）和体詞謂語句（二）
The Sentence with a Substantive Predicate (1) and the Sentence with a Substantive Predicate (2)

18.2 形容詞謂語句和体詞謂語句（二）
The Sentence with an Adjectival Predicate and the Sentence with a Substantive Predicate (2)

一、語法复習 Yŭfă fùxí Review

18.1 体詞謂語句（一）和体詞謂語句（二） 我們学了体詞謂語句（一）(13.1). 这种句子的公式是:

主語——"是"——体詞

18.1 The Sentence with a Substantive Predicate (1) and the Sentence with a Substantive Predicate (2). We have already learned the sentence with a substantive predicate (1) (13.1). The syntax of the sentence is as follows:

Subject——Copula——Substantive.

例如像:

For examples:

1. 他 是 先生.
   Tā shì xiānshēng.

2. 这 是 报.
   Zhèi shì bào.

"是" 后面是一个簡單的体詞，所以例 1，例 2 都是簡單的体詞謂語句（一）. 带定語以后，句子就比較复杂了. 例如:

Examples 1 and 2 are all simple sentences with substantive predicate (1), for after each 是, there is only a simple substantive. We know that nouns may take adjective modifiers, such sentences are rather complicated. e. g.

3. 那个 中国 学生 是 新 学生.
Nèigẻ Zhōngguó xuéshẻng shì xīn xuéshẻng.

4. 很多 中国 学生 是 我們的 好 朋友.
Hěnduō Zhōngguó xuéshẻng shì wǒmẻndẻ hǎo péngyǒu.

体詞既包括名詞、代詞和数量詞，当然代詞和数量詞也可以作"是"后面的成分. 指示代詞和数量詞結合起來作謂語里的主要成分，也可以使句子比較复杂. 例如:

Since substantives include nouns, pronouns, numerals and measure words, it is beyond question that pronouns, numerals and measure words may be used after 是. When a demonstrative pronoun, a numeral and a measure word make up the chief element of the predicate of a sentence, the whole sentence will also appear more or less complicated. e. g.

5. 我的 書 是 这 一本，你的 是 那 一本.
Wǒdẻ shū shì zhèi yìběn, nǐdẻ shì nèi yìběn.

"是"后面的是一个詞組：例 3 和例 4 里的是名詞带有定語，例 5 里的是代詞和数量詞的結合. 这样的句子都还是体詞謂語句 (一). 所以无論是單詞还是詞組，只要符合上面的公式，就都是体詞謂語句 (一). 再从用途和意义方面看，謂語都是說明主語所指的人或事物"是什么"的.

In examples 3,4 and 5, the elements after 是 are word groups: the first two are made up of nouns and their adjective modifiers, and the last one is a combination of a pronoun, a numeral and a measure word. Such sentences are still sentences with substantive predicates (1). Therefore whether the substantive after 是 is a single word or a word group does not make it a different kind of sentence. So long as the sentence is in agreement with the word order given above, it is called the sentence with a substantive predicate (1). So far as the function of such kind of sentence is concerned, the predicate is used to describe the person or thing denoted by the subject.

我們也学了体詞謂語句 (二) (17.1), 这种句子的公式是:

主語——"是"——体詞結构 (名詞、代詞或形容詞+"的")

We have also learned the sentence with a substantive predicate (2) (17.1). The word order of this kind of sentence is as follows:

Subject — Copula — Substantive Construction (a noun, pro noun or adjective + "的")

"是" 后面的名詞、代詞、形容詞带 "的" 形成了体詞結构, 說明主語所指的人或事物是具有 "什么屬性" 或屬於 "哪个类别" 的. 例如:

In the sentence with a substantive predicate (2), the noun, pronoun or adjective and 的 after the copula form a substantive construction or its equivalent describing the quality of the person or thing denoted by the subject, or the kind of the person or thing. e. g.

6. 他的 杂誌 是 中文的.
Tādė zázhì shì zhōngwéndė.

7. 那本 新 書 是 他的.
Nèiběn xīn shū shì tādė.

8. 这張 紙 是 干净的.
Zhèizhāng zhǐ shì gānjìngdė.

作体詞謂語句的时候, 要注意两点:

Two points have to be noticed, when we use the sentence with a substantive predicate:

(一) 謂語里一定要用系詞, 不能說 "我学生" 或 "这張桌子干净的" 之类的話.

(1) In the predicate, the copula has to be used. We cannot say 我学生 or 这張桌子干净的.

(二) 作体詞謂語句 (二) 的句子, 一定要用 "…是…的" 結构, 不能把 "的" 忘掉. 我們必須說: "这本杂誌是旧的", 不能說 "这本杂誌是旧".

(2) In the sentence with a substantive predicate (2), we should use …是…的 and the word 的 should never be omitted. We must say 这本杂誌是旧的, and we never say 这本杂誌是旧.

18.2 形容詞謂語句和体詞謂語句 (二) 我們学了形容詞謂語句 (14.3). 現在先看以下的例句:

18.2 The Sentence with an Adjectival Predicate and the Sentence with a Substantive Predicate (2) We have already learned the sentence with an adjectival predicate (14.3), let us look at the following examples:

9. 这个 黑板 很 大.
Zhèigê hēibǎn hěn dà.

10. 这个 黑板 很 干淨.
Zhèigê hēibǎn hěn gānjìng.

上面两个例句的謂語 "大" "干净" 就是由形容詞构成的. 这就是以形容詞为謂語的形容詞謂語句. 再看下面的例句:
The predicates of the above examples, 大 and 干淨, are made up of adjectives. Such sentences are called sentences with adjectival predicates, because the predicates are made up of adjectives. Now let us look at more examples:

11. 这个 黑板 是 大的.
Zhèigê hēibǎn shì dàdê.

12. 这个 黑板 是 干淨的.
Zhèigê hēibǎn shì gānjìngdê.

"大" 和 "干净" 虽然是形容詞, 但是带 "的" 以后, 就变成了体詞結构. 这两个句子当然就是体詞謂語句 (二).
Although the words 大 and 干淨 are adjectives, with the use of 的, they have become substantive constructions. Therefore, the two sentences given above are sentences with substantive prèdicates (2).

形容詞謂語句和体詞謂語句 (二) 显然是不同的:

(一) 形容詞謂語句的謂語形容詞前一定不用系詞 "是" (14.3), 而体詞謂語句的謂語里一定要用系詞 "是" (13.1, 17.1, 18.1).

There are marked difference between the sentence with an adjectival predicate and the sentence with a substantive predicate (2):

(1) The copula 是 can never be used before the predicate in the sentence with an adjectival predicate (14.3), should always be used in the predicate of the sentence with a substantive predicate (13.1, 17.1, 18.1).

(二) 形容詞謂語句里的形容詞起描写作用，而体詞謂語句里的形容詞带"的"以后就变成体詞結构，跟系詞結合成謂語起判断、說明作用.

(2) The adjective in the sentence with an adjectival predicate is descriptive in function; while in the sentence with a substantive predicate, the adjective with 的 is a substantive construction, which in conjunction with the copula, becomes a complete predicate, assuming the function of judgement or explanation.

根据以上所說，形容詞謂語句起描写作用，当我們要描写一件事物怎么样的时候，就用形容詞謂語句. 要是我們問"这个黑板怎么样"，就可以回答:

According to the above, the sentence with an adjectival predicate is used for the purpose of description. When we wish to describe something or tell what it is like, we use the sentence with an adjectival predicate. When we ask "how is this blackboard" (这个黑板怎么样), we may answer:

13. 这个 黑板 很 大.
Zhèigê hēibǎn hěn dà.

14. 这个 黑板 不 大.
Zhèigê hēibǎn bú dà.

或用其他形容詞如"新""旧""長""短""小"等来描述黑板的性質和形状. 体詞謂語句 (二) 起判断、說明的作用. 当我們問这个黑板是"什么黑板"，"誰的黑板"，"哪种黑板"，"什么样的黑板"等等的时候，回答这些問題，就必須用体詞謂語句 (二).

Or we may use other adjectives, such as 新，旧，長，短，小 and so on to describe the quality or shape of the blackboard.

On the other hand, the sentence with a substantive predicate (2) is used to judge of or explain something. When we ask "what blackboard" (什么黑板), "whose blackboard" (誰的黑板), "what kind of blackboard" (哪种黑板), "of what shape is the blackboard" (什么样的黑板) and so forth, then we have to use the sentence with a substantive predicate (2) in our answers.

因此，我們可以概括地說，要描写主語所指的人或物"怎么样"的时候，我們就用形容詞謂語句；要判断、說明主語所指的是"怎么样"的人或事物的时候，我們就用体詞謂語句（二）.

Therefore, we may reach the conclusion that whenever we wish to describe the person or thing denoted by the subject, we use the sentence with an adjectival predicate, and whenever we wish to tell the kind of person or thing denoted by the subject, we use the sentence with a substantive predicate (2).

二、課文 Kèwén Text

I

(a_1) 先生、学生 都 有 椅子 嗎？
Xiānshe̊ng、xuéshe̊ng dōu yǒu yǐzi̊ må?

(b_1) 不，学生 有 椅子，先生 沒 有 椅子. 先生 只 有 一張 桌子.
Bù, xuéshe̊ng yǒu yǐzi̊, xiānshe̊ng méi yǒu yǐzi̊. Xiānshe̊ng zhǐ yǒu yìzhāng zhuōzi̊.

(a_2) 桌子、椅子 都 是 新的 嗎？
Zhuōzi̊、yǐzi̊ dōu shì xīnde̊ må?

(b_2) 是，桌子、椅子 都 是 新的.
Shì, zhuōzi̊、yǐzi̊ dōu shì xīnde̊.

II

(a_3) 这 是 不 是 鉛笔？
Zhèi shì bú shì qiānbǐ?

(b_3) 这 是 鉛笔.
Zhèi shì qiānbǐ.

(a$_4$) 那 也 是 鉛笔 嗎?
Nèi yě shì qiānbǐ må?

(b$_4$) 对 了, 那 也 是 鉛笔.
Duì lẻ, nèi yě shì qiānbǐ.

(a$_5$) 这枝 鉛笔 和 那枝 鉛笔 都 是
Zhèizhī qiānbǐ hé nèizhī qiānbǐ dōu shì
你的 嗎?
nǐdẻ må?

(b$_5$) 不, 短的 是 我的, 長的 是 我
Bù, duǎndẻ shì wǒdẻ, chángdẻ shì wǒ
朋友的.
péngyỏudẻ.

III

(a$_6$) 您 工作 不 工作?
Nín gōngzuò bù gōngzuò?

(b$_6$) 不 工作, 我 学習. 您 也 学習 嗎?
Bù gōngzuò, wǒ xuéxí. Nín yě xuéxí må?

(a$_7$) 我 不 学習, 我 工作. 我 教 中文.
Wǒ bù xuéxí, wǒ gōngzuò. Wǒ jiāo zhōngwén.

(b$_7$) 您的 学生 多 不 多?
Níndẻ xuéshẻng duō bù duō?

(a$_8$) 我的 学生 不 少.
Wǒdẻ xuéshẻng bù shǎo.

(b$_8$) 您 教 俄文 不 教?
Nín jiāo èwén bù jiāo?

(a$_9$) 不 教, 我 不 会 俄文.
Bù jiāo, wǒ bú huì èwén

IV

(a_{10}) 你 有 本子 沒 有?
Nǐ yǒu běnzi méi yǒu?

(b_{10}) 沒 有, 我 有 紙, 沒 有 本子.
Méi yǒu, wǒ yǒu zhǐ, méi yǒu běnzi.

(a_{11}) 你 只 有 一張 紙 嗎?
Nǐ zhǐ yǒu yìzhāng zhǐ må?

(b_{11}) 对 了, 只 有 这 一張.
Duì lẻ, zhǐ yǒu zhèi yìzhāng.

(a_{12}) 这張 紙 是 干淨的 不 是?
Zhèizhāng zhǐ shì gānjìngdẻ bú shì?

(b_{12}) 是 干淨的, 这張 紙 很 干淨.
Shì gānjìngdẻ, zhèizhāng zhǐ hěn gānjìng.

第十九课　Lesson 19

19.1	疑問句 (三) The Interrogative Sentence (3)
19.2	用“叫”的体詞謂語句 The Substantive Sentence with the Verb 叫
19.3	“一些” The Expression 一些

一、生詞　Shēngcí　New Words

1.	誰	(代)	shéi	who
2.	什么	(代)	shénmȯ	what
3.	哪	(代)	něi	which
4.	怎么样	(代)	zěnmȯyàng	how (is it)
5.	叫	(动)	jiào	to call, to be called
6.	名字	(名)	míngzi	name
7.	些	(量)	xiē	some
8.	懂	(动)	dǒng	to understand
9.	学	(动)	xué	to learn, to study
10.	国	(名)	guó	country
11.	苏联	(名)	Sūlián	the Soviet Union
12.	知道	(动)	zhīdȧo	to know
13.	人民	(名)	rénmín	people
14.	同屋	(名)	tóngwū	roommate

二、語法　Yǔfǎ　Grammar

19.1　疑問句(三)　我們已經学習了两种形式的疑問句(13.3, 15.3).另外的一种常用的疑問句就是在句中用疑問代詞提問的.例如:

19.1 The Interrogative Sentence (3) In the previous lessons, we have learned two kinds of interrogative sentences (13.3, 15.3). Here, we will deal with the third kind of interrogative sentence, made by using interrogative pronouns. e. g.

1. 他 是 誰?
   Tā shì shéi?

2. 他 是 先生.
   Tā shì xiānshêng.

3. 这 是 什么?
   Zhèi shì shénmo̊?

4. 这 是 画报.
   Zhèi shì huàbào.

5. 哪枝 鉛笔 短?
   Něizhī qiānbǐ duǎn?

6. 这枝 鉛笔 短.
   Zhèizhī qiānbǐ duǎn.

7. 那本 杂誌 怎么样?
   Nèiběn zázhì zěnmo̊yàng?

8. 那本 杂誌 很 好.
   Nèiběn zázhì hěn hǎo.

在上面这些句子里，"誰" "什么" "哪" "怎么样" 都是疑問代詞.

In the above, 誰, 什么, 哪, and 怎么样, are all interrogative pronouns.

关于这种疑問句，有两点值得特别注意:

There are two points to be noticed, when we use this kind of interrogative sentence:

(一) 我們在这种疑問句里用疑問代詞表示疑問所在. 因此必須把疑問詞放在要求答案的位置上. 例如:

(1) The question is asked by using the interrogative pro-

noun in the sentence, so the interrogative pronoun has to be placed where an answer is expected. e. g.

9. 誰 教 你們 中文?
Shéi jiāo nǐmen zhōngwén?

10. 那个 先生 教 我們 中文.
Nèigè xiānsheng jiāo wǒmen zhōngwén.

11. 他 教 誰 中文?
Tā jiāo shéi zhōngwén?

12. 他 教 我們 中文.
Tā jiāo wǒmen zhōngwén.

同是一个"誰",因为疑問所在不同,在句子里的位置也就不一样:一个在主語的位置上,一个在宾語的位置上. 又如:

The questions appear in different places in the above two examples, and the same word 誰 is used in two different positions; in the first sentence, it is used as subject, and in the second, it is used as object. Other examples are:

13. 你 看 哪本 画报?
Nǐ kàn něiběn huàbào?

14. 我 看 这本 画报.
Wǒ kàn zhèiběn huàbào.

15. 哪本 画报 有意思?
Něiběn huàbào yǒuyìsi?

16. 这本 画报 有意思.
Zhèiběn huàbào yǒuyìsi.

同是一个"哪",因为疑問所在不同,在句子里位置也就不一样:一个在宾語的定語位置上,一个在主語的定語位置上.

For the same reasons, the same word 哪 is used as adjective modifier of the object and then as adjective modifier of the subject.

（二）疑問詞本身就足以构成疑問句，用了疑問詞就不需要再在句尾用"嗎"来表示疑問.

(2) The interrogative word itself forms an interrogative sentence; so there is no need to put the word 嗎 at the end of the sentence in which an interrogative pronoun has already been used.

19.2 用"叫"的体詞謂語句　有一种句子，謂語里的动詞是"叫". 这种句子的謂語主要是說明主語所指的人或事物是叫什么名称的. 例如:

19.2 The Substantive Sentence with the Verb 叫　There is one kind of sentence in which the verb of the predicate is 叫. The predicate of such kind of sentence is used mainly to tell the name of the person or thing denoted by the subject. e. g.

17. 这　叫　什么?
Zhèi　jiào　shénmô?

18. 这　叫　椅子.
Zhèi　jiào　yǐzǐ.

19. 他　叫　什么　名字?
Tā　jiào　shénmô　míngzì?

20. 他　叫　張友文.
Tā　jiào　Zhāngyǒuwén.

这种句子也是一种体詞謂語句. 在这里"叫"也是一个比較特殊的动詞，可以說跟系詞"是"的性質和功用相似. 因之"叫"后面的成分并不是宾語，而是体詞謂語.

This kind of sentence is also called the sentence with a substantive predicate. Here the verb 叫 is a special verb, the same in nature and function as the copula 是. Hence, the element following 叫 is not an object, but a substantive predicate.

应当注意，例 19 里的"什么"是在定語的位置上，与例 17 里的"什么"用法不同. 这种用法也是很常見的.

Note: 什么 in example 19 is used as adjective modifier,

and so different in use from 什么 in example 17. It is very common to use it as an adjective modifier.

19.3 "一些" "些"是个量詞，表示不定量复数. 例如:

19.3 一些 些 is a measure word used to express some quantity or number. e. g.

21. 我 有 一些 杂誌.
Wǒ yǒu yìxiē zázhì.

22. 他 懂 一些 中文.
Tā dǒng yìxiē zhōngwén.

"一些"后边的名詞，可以是表示能計数的事物的(如"杂誌")，也可以是表示不能計数的事物的(如"中文").

The nouns following 一些 may be nouns denoting countable things (such as 杂誌), or nouns denoting uncountable things (such as 中文).

"一些"除了在句首或在句尾作宾語的时候，永远可以省去"一". 例如:

Except when 一些 is used at the beginning of a sentence, or as an object at the end of a sentence, 一 may always be omitted. e. g.

23. 他 有 (一)些 中国 朋友.
Tā yǒu (yì)xiē Zhōngguó péngyǒu.

24. 先生 給 我 (一)些 杂誌.
Xiānshêng gěi wǒ (yì)xiē zázhì.

当它和"这""那""哪"連用的时候，"一"更是經常省去，我們甚至可以說"这些""那些""哪些"是"这""那""哪"的复数. 例如:

When it is used together with 这, 那 and 哪, 一 is always omitted. Indeed we may say 这些, 那些, and 哪些 are the plural forms of 这, 那 and 哪. e. g.

25. 这些 鉛笔 都 是 短的.
Zhèixiē qiānbǐ dōu shì duǎndê.

26. 哪些 桌子 干淨?
Něixiē zhuōzỉ gānjỉng?

27. 那些 桌子 干淨.
Nèixiē zhuōzỉ gānjỉng.

三、課文 Kèwén Text

I

(a_1) 那个 同志 是 誰?
Nèigê tóngzhì shì shéi?

(b_1) 她 是 我的 朋友.
Tā shì wǒdê péngyǒu.

(a_2) 哪个 先生 教 她?
Něigê xiānshêng jiāo tå?

(b_2) 張 先生 教 她.
Zhāng xiānshêng jiāo tå.

(a_3) 她 学 什么?
Tā xué shénmỏ?

(b_3) 她 学 中文.
Tā xué zhōngwén.

(a_4) 她 是 哪国 人?
Tā shì něiguó rén?

(b_4) 她 是 苏联 人.
Tā shì Sūlián rén.

(a_5) 她 叫 什么 名字?
Tā jiào shénmỏ míngzỉ?

(b_5) 我 不 知道.
Wǒ bù zhīdào.

(a_6) 她的 中文 怎么样?
Tādė zhōngwén zěnmȯyàng?

(b_6) 不 很 好, 懂 一些.
Bù hěn hǎo, dǒng yìxiē.

II

(a_7) 这本 書 是 誰的?
Zhèiběn shū shì shéidė?

(b_7) 这本 書 是 我的.
Zhèiběn shū shì wǒdė.

(a_8) 这 是 一本 什么 書?
Zhèi shì yìběn shénmȯ shū?

(b_8) 这 是 一本 中文 書.
Zhèi shì yìběn zhōngwén shū.

(a_9) 这 叫 什么?
Zhèi jiào shénmȯ?

(b_9) 这 叫 画报.
Zhèi jiào huàbào.

(a_{10}) 这 是 什么 画报?
Zhèi shì shénmȯ? huàbào?

(b_{10}) 这 是 "人民 画报".
Zhèi shì "Rénmín Huàbào".

(a_{11}) "人民 画报" 怎么样?
"Rénmín Huàbào" zěnmȯyàng?

(b_{11}) 很 有意思.
Hěn yǒuyìsi.

(a_{12}) 那些 是 什么?
Nèixiē shì shénmǒ?

(b_{12}) 哪些? 这些 都 是 旧 杂誌.
Něixiē? Zhèixiē dōu shì jiù zázhì.

(a_{13}) 那些 旧 杂誌 都 怎么样?
Nèixiē jiù zázhì dōu zénmǒyàng?

(b_{13}) 我 也 不 知道. 这些 杂誌 都 不 是 我的. 都 是 我 同屋 的.
Wǒ yě bù zhīdào. Zhèixiē zázhì dōu bú shì wǒdě. Dōu shì wǒ tóngwū-dě.

四、課外練習 Kèwài liànxí Home Work

1. 回答下面的問題 (人名和国名可以用拼音写出):
1) Answer the following questions (Names of persons and countries may be written in phonetic spellings.):

(1) 你的 同屋 叫 什么 名字?
(2) 你 知道 他的 中国 名字 嗎?
(3) 这个 同志 是 哪国 人?
(4) 他 懂 不 懂 俄文?

2. 用下面的詞語各作一个句子:
2) Make sentences with each of the following words and word combinations:

(5) 誰的
(6) 哪些
(7) 什么
(8) 怎么样

五、汉字表 Hànzì biǎo Chinese Characters

1	誰		
2	什	亻	
		十	
3	么	丿 么	
4	哪	口	
		那	
5	怎	乍	
		心	
6	样	木	
		羊（丶 丷 兰 羊）	
7	叫	口	
		丩（乚 丩）	
8	名	夕	
		口	
9	字		
10	些	丨 ⺊ 𣥂 止 此 此 些 些	
11	懂	忄	
		董	艹
			重（丿 𠂉 台 亩 重 重）

12	苏	艹
		办（力 力 办）
13	联	耳
		关（丶 丷 䒑 兰 龹 关）
14	知	
15	道	
16	民	乛 コ 巳 巳 民
17	屋	尸
		至（一 𠫔 至）

第二十課　Lesson 20

20.1	狀語 The Adverbial Modifier
20.2	形容詞重叠 The Repetition of Adjectives

一、生詞　Shēngcí　New Words

1. 积極	(形)	jījí	enthusiastic, active
2. 努力	(形)	nǔlì	diligent, strenuous
3. 跟	(介)	gēn	with, after
4. 从	(介)	cóng	from
5. 学校	(名)	xuéxiào	school
6. 一起	(副)	yìqǐ	together
7. 那兒(那里)	(代)	nàr (nàli)	there
8. 这兒(这里)	(代)	zhèr(zhèli)	here
9. 去	(动)	qù	to go
10. 地	(助)	dē	(a structural particle)
11. 高兴	(形)	gāoxìng	glad, happy
12. 喜欢	(动)	xǐhuān	to like, to be fond of
13. 电影	(名)	diànyǐng	film, moving picture
14. 哪兒(哪里)	(代)	nǎr (nǎli)	where

二、 語法 Yǔfǎ Grammar

20.1 状語　状語就是修飾动詞或形容詞的成分. 除了副詞以外,别类詞或别的結构也有可以作状語的. 現在只談形容詞作状語和介詞結构作状語.

20.1 The Adverbial Modifier The adverbial modifier is an element used to modify the verb or the adjective. Besides adverbs, there are many words of other parts of speech and constructions that can function as adverbial modifiers. In this lesson, only adjectives and prepositional constructions are introduced as adverbial modifiers.

(一) 形容詞作状語　形容詞除了作定語、謂語以外, 也可以作状語. 例如:

(1) Adjectives Used as Adverbial Modifiers Adjectives are not only used as adjective modifiers and predicates, but also as adverbial modifiers. e. g.

1. 这个 同志 积極 工作.
   Zhèigê tóngzhì jījí gōngzuò.
2. 他的 同屋 努力 学習.
   Tādê tóngwū nǔlì xuéxí.

在这里形容詞"积極""努力"就是修飾动詞"工作""学習"的状語. 状語經常出現於它的中心語之前.

Here, the adjectives 积極 and 努力 are used as adverbial modifiers to 工作 and 学習. Adverbial modifiers are always put before the central words or the words modified.

(二) 介詞結构作状語　介詞經常帶着自己的宾語形成介詞結构, 可以作定語, 更常作状語. 作状語的时候, 也是在中心語之前. 例如:

(2) The Prepositional Construction (Phrase) Used as Adverbial Modifier A preposition always carries its own object in a prepositional construction. It can be used either as adjective modifier or as adverbial modifier. When it is used as adverbial modifier, it has to be placed before the central word. e. g.

3. 我 朋友 跟 我 很 好.
Wǒ péngyǒu gēn wǒ hěn hǎo.

4. 那个 同志 从 学校 来.
Nèigê tóngzhì cóng xuéxiào lái.

"跟"、"从"是介詞,"跟我"、"从学校"就是介詞結构."跟我"是修飾形容詞"好"的,"从学校"是修飾动詞"来"的.

跟 and 从 are prepositions, and 跟我 and 从学校 are prepositional constructions. 跟我 modifies the adjective 好, and 从学校 modifies the verb 来.

汉語里有不少介詞,有的比較难用,現在就特别談一下"跟"和"从"这两个介詞.

In Chinese, there are some prepositions that are rather difficult to use properly. For the present, let us discuss only the following two prepositions 跟 and 从:

(一) "跟" 最常見的有两种用法:一种是有"对"的意思,这时后面的宾語就是由表示"跟"的对象的詞語构成的.例 3 就是如此.另外一种有"和…一起"的意思.例如;

(1) 跟 It is commonly used in two ways. It may be used with the meaning of "to" or "with" (对), pointing out the object to which action or feeling is directed. See example 3. It may also be used with the meaning of "和…一起" (together…with). e. g.

5. 她 跟 我 看 一張 报.
Tā gēn wǒ kàn yìzhāng bào.

因此副詞"一起"就常常和"跟…"的介詞結构連用.例如:

The adverb 一起 is often used together with the prepositional construction composed of 跟. e. g.

6. 我 朋友 跟 我 一起 学習.
Wǒ péngyǒu gēn wǒ yìqǐ xuéxí.

(二)"从"　这个詞是表示出發点的．它的宾語可以是表示时間或空間的詞語．例 4 里的"学校"就是表示空間的(表示时間的以后要談到)．表示空間的时候，宾語必須是由指地点的名詞或代詞构成的．例如:

(2) 从　从 denotes a starting point, its object may be a word or word group of time or of place. 学校 in example 4 is a word denoting place. (The words expressing time will be introduced afterwards.) When such a construction is used to represent place, the object must be a noun or pronoun denoting place. e. g.

7. 先生　从　学校　来.
Xiānshêng cóng xuéxiào lái.

8. 他　从　那兒　来.
Tā cóng nàr lái.

如果动作的出發点是和人相联系的，我們就要把指人的名詞或代詞变为指地点的．常用的方法是在指人名詞或代詞之后加上"这兒"或"那兒"．例如:

When the starting point of an action is represented by a person or persons, we have to change the noun or pronoun denoting persons into a word for place by adding 这兒 or 那兒. e. g.

9. 他　从　朋友　那兒　来.
Tā cóng péngyǒu nàr lái.

10. 我　从　你　这兒　去.
Wǒ cóng nǐ zhèr qù.

20.2 形容詞重叠　汉語里的形容詞可以重叠起来．重叠的时候，以音节为單位:

20.2 The Repetition of Adjectives　In Chinese, adjectives can be repeated by reduplicating the syllable:

11. 好 ⟶ 好好兒
hǎo ⟶ hǎohāor

12. 干淨 ——→ 干干淨淨

gānjìng ——→ gāngånjìngjìng

單音詞重叠，第二个音节常常变为第一声并加兒化；双音詞重叠，重音落在最后一个音节上.

When a monosyllabic adjective is reduplicated, the second syllable is always pronounced in the 1st tone with the retroflex "兒". When a dissyllabic adjective is reduplicated, the final syllable is always stressed.

形容詞重叠起强調它所表示的性状的作用，可以作定語，也可以作状語. 作状語的时候，后面常常需要結构助詞"地"（也可以写作"的"）联系中心語. 例如：

The reduplicated adjective has the function of emphasizing the quality expressed by that adjective. It can be used either as adjective modifier or as adverbial modifier. As adverbial modifier, it is in general followed by the structural particle 地 (also written as 的) to join it with the central word. e. g.

13. 我們 都 好好兒地 学習.

Wǒmên dōu hǎohāordê xuéxí.

14. 同志們 都 高高兴兴地 工作.

Tóngzhìmên dōu gāogåoxìngxìngdê gōngzuò.

三、課文 Kèwén Text

I

(a₁) 那个 新 同志 是 誰？

Nèigê xīn tóngzhì shì shéi?

(b₁) 那个 新 同志 是 我的 朋友.

Nèigê xīn tóngzhì shì wǒdê péngyǒu.

他的 名字 叫 張友文.

Tādê míngzì jiào Zhāngyǒuwén.

(a₂) 那个 新 同志 怎么样？

Nèigê xīn tóngzhì zěnmôyàng?

(b_2) 很 好，很 积極．他 会 中文，也
Hěn hǎo, hěn jījí. Tā huì zhōngwén, yě
懂 俄文．他 积極地 工作，我們
dǒng èwén. Tā jījídė gōngzuò, wǒmėn
都 喜欢 他．
dōu xǐhuȧn tȧ.

II

(a_3) 这个 学生 学 什么？
Zhèigė xuéshėng xué shénmȯ?

(b_3) 他 学 中文．
Tā xué zhōngwén.

(a_4) 他 跟 你 一起 学习 嗎？
Tā gēn nǐ yìqǐ xuéxí mȧ?

(b_4) 对了，我們 一起 学习，我們 很
Duìlė, wǒmėn yìqǐ xuéxí, wǒmėn hěn
努力地 学习，我們 都 高高兴兴
nǔlìdė xuéxí, wǒmėn dōu gāogȧoxìngxìng-
地 学习．
dė xuéxí.

III

(a_5) 您 看 电影 不 看？
Nín kàn diànyǐng bú kàn?

(b_5) 看．
Kàn.

(a_6) 您 从 哪兒 去？
Nín cóng nǎr qù?

(b_6) 我 从 学校 去，你 也 从 学校
Wǒ cóng xuéxiào qù, nǐ yě cóng xuéxiào

去 嗎?
qù må?

(a7) 不, 我 从 朋友 那兒 去.
Bù, wǒ cóng péngyǒu nàr qù.

四、課外練習 Kèwài liànxí Home Work

把下面的句子翻成中文:

Translate the following English into Chinese:

1) Where have you been?
I have been at teacher Chang's place.
2) With whom do you study?
I study with him.
3) What do you study together?
We study Chinese and Russian together.
4) Will you see the film (or the moving picture)?
Yes. we will. It is very interesting.

五、汉字表 Hànzì biǎo Chinese Characters

1	积	禾	
		只	
2	極	木	
		亟(一 了 了 可 亟 亟)	
3	努	奴	女
			又
		力	
4	力		
5	跟		

6	从	人	
		人	
7	校	木	
		交（丶 亠 六 亣 交）	
8	起	走（土 丰 丰 走 走）	
		巳（㇆ コ 巳）	
9	兒		
10	里	日 旦 甲 里	
11	去		
12	地	土	
		也	
13	高	丶 亠 古 古 高 高	
14	兴	丶 丷 ⺍ 业 兴	
15	喜	士 吉 壴 壴 喜 喜	
16	欢	又	
		欠	
17	电	日 电	
18	影	景	日
			京
		彡（丿 彡 彡）	

第二十一課 Lesson 21

21.1	动宾結构 The Verb-Object Construction
21.2	程度补語 The Complement of Degree
21.3	关于程度补語的注意事項 Rules of the Complement of Degree

一、生詞 Shēngcí New Words

1.	念	(动)	niàn	to read
2.	得	(助)	dē	(a structural particle)
3.	早	(形)	zǎo	early
4.	快	(形)	kuài	quick, fast
5.	写	(动)	xiě	to write
6.	汉字	(名)	hànzì	Chinese character
7.	晚	(形)	wǎn	late
8.	慢	(形)	màn	slow
9.	常常	(副)	chángcháng	often
10.	説(話)	(动)	shuō (huà)	to speak
11.	話	(名)	huà	words, speech
12.	太	(副)	tài	too
13.	跳(舞)	(动)	tiào (wǔ)	to dance
14.	一定	(副)	yídìng	certainly
15.	唱(歌兒)	(动)	chàng (gēr)	to sing (song)
16.	歌兒	(名)	gēr	song

二、 語法 Yǔfǎ Grammar

21.1 动宾結构　由动詞和宾語組成的詞組叫动宾結构. 今天要談的是一种特殊的动宾結构. 这种动宾結构有两个特点:

21.1 The Verb-Object Construction　The construction composed of a verb and an object is termed a verb-object construction. Today we shall learn a special kind of verb-object construction. It has two characteristic features:

(一) 从意义上看, 它只代表一个單一的概念, 相当於英語里的一个动詞. 例如:

(1) So far as its meaning is concerned, it represents a single idea equivalent to a verb without object in English. e.g.

1. 我 念 書.
Wǒ niàn shū.

2. 先生 教 書.
Xiānshēng jiāo shū.

"念書" "教書" 都可以从結构上分析为动詞和宾語, 但是就它的意义說只相当於 "学習" 和 "教" 两个簡單的动詞. "書" 在这里是宾語, 但是只是一个極概括的、習慣常用的宾語, 本身已經失去了 "一本書" 的 "書" 的具体意义了. "書" 在这里是必需的, 就是因为在汉語里我們不說 "我念" "先生教", 一定要用上宾語才覺得意思完全.

Structurally speaking, 念書 and 教書 are two verb-object constructions, they are equivalent to two simple verbs "to study" and "to teach" in English. Here 書 is the object, but it is so habitually used that it has already lost the concrete meaning of "book". Yet, in the above examples, the word 書 is necessary, because in Chinese we are not accustomed to say 我念 and 先生教. Without 書 the meaning of the sentence is incomplete.

(二) 从結构上看, 这是一个动詞和宾語的組合, 用法上和一般的动宾結构还是一样. 这个結构之后, 不能另有宾語, 如果另有宾語, 原來的宾語就必須取消. 例如:

(2) So far as its construction is concerned, it is a combination of a verb and its object. It is the same in use as the general verb-object constructions. We must never use another object after such a construction. If another object is required, the habitually used object has to be omitted. e. g.

3. 我 念 中文.
Wǒ niàn zhōngwén.

4. 先生 教 中文.
Xiānshêng jiāo zhōngwén.

这时候就决不能說"念書中文"或"教書中文".

Then, we can't say 念書中文 or 教書中文.

21.2 程度补語　动詞或者形容詞的补充成分就是补語. 被补充的动詞或形容詞就是中心語. 定語和状語在中心語之前, 而补語是在中心語之后的. 补語也有几种, 現在只談动詞的程度补語. 当我們要着重地說明一个动作达到的程度(或結果)的时候, 就在动詞后面用程度补語. 这个动作常常是已經完成(或假設已經完成), 或經常發生并且达到某种程度或結果的. 例如:

21.2 The Complement of Degree　A word or words placed after a verb or adjective to tell something more about the action of the verb or the quality of the adjective are called a complementary element, and the verb or adjective is called the central word. The adjective modifier or the adverbial modifier is placed before the central word, while the complementary element is placed after the central word. There are several kinds of complementary element, here let us take a look at the complement of degree. Whenever we wish to describe emphatically the degree or extent (or result) an action has reached, we use the complement of degree. The action is often already completed (or taken for granted that it is completed), or it is habitually frequent, or has gained a certain level or result. e. g.

5. 他 来得 早.
Tā láidê zǎo.

6. 我 念得 快.
Wǒ niàndê kuài.

"早"是补充"来"的,"快"是补充"念"的.

早 is used to complete 来, and 快 is used to complete 念.

21.3 关于程度补語的注意事項:

21.3 Rules Concerning the Complement of Degree:

(一) 程度补語的主要标誌就是它与中心語之間要用一个結构助詞"得"来联系("得"与"的"同音,也有人写作"的").

(1) The main feature of the complement of degree is that between the verb and the complement there is a structural particle 得 used as connective. (得 and 的 have the same pronunciation, may be used interchangeably.)

(二) 程度补語主要地是由形容詞来担任.但是句子复杂的时候,用复杂結构作程度补語的情况也非常普遍.这种复杂的句子,以后要遇到的.

(2) The complement of degree is generally composed of an adjective. But in a complicated sentence, it is very common to use a complicated construction as the complement of degree. Such complicated sentences will appear in the coming lessons.

(三) 在有程度补語的句子里,如果动詞有宾語,必須在重复动詞之后再加助詞"得"和补語.例如:

(3) If there is an object after the verb, we have to reduplicate the verb and place the complement after the second verb. e. g.

7. 他 学 中文 学得 快.
Tā xué zhōngwén xuédê kuài.

8. 先生 教 中文 教得 好.
Xiānshêng jiāo zhōngwén jiāodê hǎo.

因此,遇見上面談到的那种特殊的动宾結构时,也要重复动詞。例如:

Hence, in the special kind of verb-object constructions mentioned above, we have to reduplicate the verb too. e. g.

9. 他 念 書 念得 快.
Tā niàn shū niàndê kuài.

10. 先生 教 書 教得 好.
Xiānshêng jiāo shū jiāodê hǎo.

(四) 在用程度补語的句子里, 补語很重要, 它前面的动詞或动宾結构好像只是一个話題. 因此:

(4) In the sentence containing a complement of degree, the complement is very important. The verb or verbal construction standing before it seems merely the subject of the sentence. Therefore:

(1) 否定的时候, "不" 这个否定詞用在补語之前, 不用在动詞(或形容詞)之前. 例如:

(a) In the negative sentence, the negative adverb 不 is not placed before the verb (or adjective) but before the complement. e. g.

11. 他 来得 不 早.
Tā láidê bù zǎo.

12. 我 写 汉字 写得 不 快.
Wǒ xiě hànzì xiědê bú kuài.

也常常不用补語的否定形式而用一个反义詞作补語. 例如:
We do not often use a word in the negative form as complement; instead, we use its antonym. e. g.

13. 他 来得 晚.
Tā láidê wǎn.

14. 我 写 汉字 写得 慢.
Wǒ xiě hànzì xiědê màn.

(2) 在选擇式的疑問句里，我們并列补語的肯定和否定形式，而不是动詞的肯定和否定形式. 例如:

(b) In the alternative interrogative sentence, we give both the affirmative and the negative forms of the complement but not those of the verb. e. g.

15. 他 来得 晚 不 晚?
Tā láidẻ wǎn bù wǎn?

16. 他 学 中文 学得 快 不 快?
Tā xué zhōngwén xuédẻ kuài bú kuài?

三、課文 Kèwén Text

I

1. 先生 常常 来得 很 早.
Xiānshẻng chángcháng láidẻ hěn zǎo.

2. 学生 也 来得 很 早.
Xuéshẻng yě láidẻ hěn zǎo.

3. 先生 說 話 說得 不 太 快.
Xiānshẻng shuō huà shuōdẻ bú tài kuài.

4. 那些 学生 跳 舞 跳得 很 高兴.
Nèixiē xuéshẻng tiào wǔ tiàodẻ hěn gāoxìng.

5. 張 同志 看 中文 报 一定 看得 很 快.
Zhāng tóngzhì kàn zhōngwén bào yídìng kàndẻ hěn kuài.

6. 他 懂 俄文, 他 說 俄文 說得 很 好.
Tā dǒng èwén, tā shuō èwén shuōdẻ hěn hǎo.

II

(a_1) 你們 学習得 怎么样?
Nǐmėn xuéxídė zěnmȯyàng?

(b_1) 我 学習得 不 太 好, 張 同志
Wǒ xuéxídė bú tài hǎo, Zhāng tóngzhì
学習得 很 好.
xuéxídė hěn hǎo.

(a_2) 你們 写 汉字 嗎?
Nǐmėn xiě hànzì mȧ?

(b_2) 写 汉字. 我們 都 写得 很 慢.
Xiě hànzì. Wǒmėn dōu xiědė hěn màn.

(a_3) 張 同志 也 写得 很 慢 嗎?
Zhāng tóngzhì yě xiědė hěn màn mȧ?

(b_3) 不, 張 同志 写得 很 快.
Bù, Zhāng tóngzhì xiědė hěn kuài.

(a_4) 你們 喜欢 唱 歌兒 不 喜欢?
Nǐmėn xǐhuȧn chàng gēr bù xǐhuȧn?

(b_4) 喜欢. 我們 常常 跟 中国 朋友
Xǐhuȧn. Wǒmėn chángcháng gēn Zhōngguó péngyȯu
一起 唱 歌兒. 中国 朋友 教
yìqǐ chàng gēr. Zhōngguó péngyȯu jiāo
我們 中国 歌兒. 我們 跟 中国
wǒmėn Zhōngguó gēr. Wǒmėn gēn Zhōngguó
朋友 一起 唱得 很 高兴.
péngyȯu yìqǐ chàngdė hěn gāoxìng.

四、 課外練習 Kèwài liànxí Home Work

1\. 把下面的句子翻成中文:

1) Translate the following into Chinese:
   (1) This comrade always comes very early.
   (2) The students in our school learn Russian very rapidly.
   (3) I read Chinese books very slowly.

2\. 用程度补語完成下面的句子:

2) Complete the following sentences with complements of degree:

(4) 她 跳 舞 ______________________.

(5) 那些 中国 学生 説 俄文 ________

(6) 先生 写 我的 名字 ____________

______________________________________.

(7) 努力的 学生 一定 学習 ________

______________________________________.

(8) 我的 同屋 唱 中国 歌兒 ____

______________________________________.

五、汉字表 Hànzì biǎo Chinese Characters

1	念	今(人 亼 今)	
		心	
2	得		
3	早	日	
		十	
4	快		
5	写	冖(丶 冖)	
		与(一 丂 与)	
6	汉		
7	晚	日(丨 冂 冃 日)	
		免(丿 ⺈ ⺈ 㑒 㑒 㑒 免)	
8	慢		
9	常	尚	龸(丨 丨 ⺌ 龸)
			口
		巾(丨 冂 巾)	
10	説	言	
		兑(丶 丷 㕣 兑)	
11	話	言	
		舌(丿 二 千 舌)	

12	太	大 太	
13	跳	𧾷	
		兆（丿 丬 丬 兆 兆 兆）	
14	舞	無（丿 𠂉 𠂉 午 㐃 無 無 無）	
		舛（夕 夕 舛 舛 舛）	
15	定	宀	
		𤴓	
16	唱		
17	歌	哥	可
			可
		欠	

第二十二課 Lesson 22

22.1 一百以下的称数法
The Enumeration of Cardinal Numerals from One to Ninety-nine
22.2 "二"和"两"
二 and 两
22.3 "几"和"多少"
几 and 多少
22.4 "半"
The Numeral 半

一、生詞 Shēngcí New Words

1.	二	(数)	èr	two
2.	四	(数)	sì	four
3.	五	(数)	wǔ	five
4.	六	(数)	liù	six
5.	七	(数)	qī	seven
6.	八	(数)	bā	eight
7.	九	(数)	jiǔ	nine
8.	十	(数)	shí	ten
9.	两	(数)	liǎng	two
10.	几	(数)	jǐ	several, how many
11.	多少	(数)	duōshǎo	how many
12.	半	(数)	bàn	half
13.	年	(名)	nián	year
14.	練習	(名、动)	liànxí	exercise, to exercise, to practise

二、語法 Yǔfǎ Grammar

22.1 一百以下的称数法　在汉語里是用"十进法"来称数

的. "一" "二" "三" "四" "五" "六" "七" "八" "九" "十" 之后就是 "十一" "十二".... 从 "十一" 到 "九十九" 的数字是用以下三种方法組成的:

22.1 The Enumeration of Cardinal Numerals from One to Ninety-nine In Chinese, the decimal system is used for counting numbers. Besides the numerals 一, 二, 三, 四, 五, 六, 七, 八, 九 and 十, are the numerals 十一, 十二 etc. The numerals from 11 to 99 are formed by the following three methods:

(一) 从 "11" 到 "19" 用加法. 例如: "11" 是 "10" 加 "1", "19" 就是 "10" 加 "9".

(1) From eleven to nineteen the numerals are formed by addition. For example: 11 is 10 plus 1; 19 is 10 plus 9.

(二) "20" "30" "40" "50" "60" "70" "80" "90" 用乘法. 例如: "30" 是 "3" 乘 "10", "50" 是 "5" 乘 "10".

(2) 20, 30, 40, 50, 60, 70, 80, 90 are formed by multiplication. For example: 30 is 10 multiplied by 3, 50 is 10 multiplied by 5.

(三) 上面以外的数字用先乘后加法. 例如: "22" 是 "2" 乘 "10" 加 "2", "78" 是 "7" 乘 "10" 加 "8".

(3) The numerals between the tens are formed first by multiplication, then by addition. For example: 22 is two tens plus 2, 78 is seven tens plus 8.

22.2 "二" 和 "两" 汉語里除了 "二" 以外, 还有一个代表 "2" 的数詞 "两". 虽然 "二" 和 "两" 代表同一个数字, 但是用法不同:

22.2 二 and 两 In Chinese, the numerals 二 and 两 denote the same number "two", but they are different in use:

(一) 在量詞前面, 一般用 "两" 不用 "二". 例如:

(1) Before measure words we prefer 两 to 二. e. g.

1. 两个 朋友
liǎnggê péngyǒu

2. 两張 桌子
liǎngzhāng zhuōzi

只有極少数的例外，例如：我們可以說："二年""二斤糖"，但在这种情况下，用"两"依然是可以的.

There are a few exceptions, such as 二斤糖 (two catties of sugar) and 二年 (two years). Yet, even in such cases, we may use 两 instead of 二.

(二) 在多位数中，"2"是最后一位时，一定用"二"，不能用"两". 例如:

(2) If 2 comes at the end of a big number, we have to use 二 and never 两. e. g.

3. 十二个 学生
shíèrgè xuéshēng

4. 四十二把 椅子
sìshíèrbǎ yǐzi

(三) "20"只能說"二十"不能說"两十".

(3) "20" is only read as 二十, never as 两十.

22.3 "几"和"多少" 問数目的时候我們用"几"或者"多少"，但这两个詞并非在任何情况下都可以互换的:

22.3 几 and 多少 In asking about numbers or figures we use 几 and 多少; however, they are not always used interchangeably:

(一) "多少"代表的数目范圍很广，可大可小. 而"几"只代表从"1"到"9"这几个数目. 例如:

(1) 多少 may be used to ask about any number, big or small; while 几 is used only for the numbers from one to nine. For example:

5. 你 有 几本 "人民 画报"?
Nǐ yǒu jǐběn "Rénmín Huàbào"?

6. 你 有 多少本 "人民 画报"?
Nǐ yǒu duōshǎoběn "Rénmín Huàbào"?

两句都是問人民画报的本数. 当我們估計画报数目在十本以內的时候，我們用例 5; 我們对画报数目毫無估計的时候，用例 6. "几" 也常和 "十" 連用. 例如:

Both sentences are questions about the number of pictorials. When the number of pictorials is less than ten, it is example 5; when the number of pictorials is indefinite, it is example 6. 几 is often used before 十. e. g.

7. 你 有 几十本 杂誌?
Nǐ yǒu jǐshíběn zázhì?

这时，我們要求的答案就是 20, 30…或 90.

The expected answer will be 20, 30 …… or 90.

(二) "多少" 可以和名詞直接联系，而 "几" 的后面必須用量詞. 例如:

(2) 多少 can be directly connected with a noun, while 几 must be followed by a measure word. e. g.

8. 这个 学校 有 多少(个) 先生?
Zhèigê xuéxiào yǒu duōshǎo(gê) xiānshêng?

9. 那个 同志 有 几本 杂誌?
Nèigê tóngzhì yǒu jǐběn zázhì?

22.4 "半" 这是一个数詞. 与量詞連用时要注意它的位置:

22.4 半 It is a numeral. Be careful of the position of this numeral when it is used together with a measure word:

(一) 如果它不和别的数詞連用的时候，就和一般的数詞完全一样，用在量詞的前面. 例如:

(1) When there is no numeral used together with 半, it can be directly placed before the measure word like the general numerals. e. g.

10. 半張 紙
bànzhāng zhǐ

11. 半年
bànnián

(二) 如果“半”和别的数詞連用的时候，就把表示整数的数詞用在量詞之前，而把“半”用在量詞之后。例如：

(2) When the word 半 is used together with numerals, the integral numerals are put before the measure word, while the word 半 follows the measure word. e. g.

12. 两張半 紙
liǎngzhāngbàn zhǐ

13. 两年半
liǎngniánbàn

三、課文 Kèwén Text

I

(a₁) 你 有 画报 嗎？
Nǐ yǒu huàbào må?

(b₁) 有，我 有 中文 画报，也 有 俄文 画报.
Yǒu, wǒ yǒu zhōngwén huàbào, yě yǒu èwén huàbào.

(a₂) 你 有 多少本 中文 画报？
Nǐ yǒu duōshåoběn zhōngwén huàbào?

(b₂) 我 有 十二本 中文 画报.
Wǒ yǒu shíèrběn zhōngwén huàbào.

(a₃) 你 有 多少本 俄文 画报？
Nǐ yǒu duōshåoběn èwén huàbào?

(b₃) 我的 俄文 画报 不 多，只 有 三本.
Wǒdė èwén huàbào bù duō, zhǐ yǒu sānběn.

II

(a_4) 这个 学校 有 多少(个) 苏联 学生?
Zhèigê xuéxiào yǒu duōshảo(gê) Sūlián xuéshêng?

(b_4) 有 二十二个 苏联 学生.
Yǒu èrshíèrgê Sūlián xuéshêng.

(a_5) 他們 都 学 中文 嗎?
Tāmên dōu xué zhōngwén? må?

(b_5) 他們 都 学 中文.
Tāmên dōu xué zhōngwén.

(a_6) 几个 先生 教 这些 学生?
Jǐgê xiānshêng jiāo zhèixiē xuéshêng?

(b_6) 两个 先生.
Liǎnggê xiānshêng.

(a_7) 一个 先生 教 多少 学生?
Yígê xiānshêng jiāo duōshảo xuéshêng?

(b_7) 一个 先生 教 十一个 学生.
Yígê xiānshêng jiāo shíyīgê xuéshêng.

III

(a_8) 你 有 几个 中国 朋友?
Nǐ yǒu jǐgê Zhōngguó péngyǒu?

(b_8) 我 有 三个.
Wǒ yǒu sāngê.

(a_9) 他們 唱 不 唱 苏联 歌兒?
Tāmên chàng bú chàng Sūlián gēr?

(b_9) 唱, 他們 唱 苏联 歌兒.
Chàng, tāmên chàng Sūlián gēr.

(a_{10}) 他們 会 多少 苏联 歌兒?
Tāmên huì duōshảo Sūlián gēr?

(b₁₀) 他們 会 很 多.
Tāmen huì hěn duō.

(a₁₁) 你 会 中国 歌兒 嗎?
Nǐ huì Zhōngguó gēr ma?

(b₁₁) 会, 我 只 会 两个.
Huì, wǒ zhǐ huì liǎngge.

(a₁₂) 誰 教 你 中国 歌兒?
Shéi jiāo ni Zhōngguó gēr?

(b₁₂) 我的 中国 朋友.
Wǒde Zhōngguó péngyou.

(a₁₃) 你 常常 練習 嗎?
Nǐ chángcháng liànxí ma?

(b₁₃) 我 常常 練習.
Wǒ chángcháng liànxí.

四、課外練習 Kèwài liànxí Home Work

1. 用汉字和拼音（包括調号）写出下面的数目来:
1) Write out the following numbers in Chinese and phonetic spellings and give the tone-marks:

(1) 16　(2) 32　(3) 95　(4) 40
(5) 22　(6) 81　(7) 53　(8) 77

2. 抄写下面的句子并把括弧內的数目改为汉字:
2) Copy the following sentences and change the numbers within parentheses into Chinese numerals:

(9) 那 (2)枝 短 鉛笔 是 誰的?
(10) 他 有 (52)本 杂誌.

3. 用"几"或"多少"塡进下面的句子，并注意量詞的用与不用:
3) Fill the blanks with 几 or 多少 and pay attention to the use of the measure word:

(11) 他 会 ____ 汉字?

不 知道, 他 一定 会 很 多.

(12) 那个 学生 有 ____ 鋼笔?

只 有 一枝.

五、汉字表 Hànzì biǎo Chinese Characters

1	二	一 二
2	四	丨 冂 冂 四 四
3	五	一 丆 万 五
4	六	丶 亠 六
5	七	一 七
6	八	
7	九	
8	十	
9	两	一 丆 丙 两
10	几	
11	半	丶 丷 兰 半
12	年	丿 𠂉 𠂒 乍 乍 年
13	練	糹
		柬(一 丆 冂 冂 冂 亘 亘 亘 柬)

第二十三課 Lesson 23

一、生詞 Shēngcí New Words

1.	在	(动)	zài	to be, on, in, at
2.	里边兒	(名)	lǐbiānr	inside
3.	外边兒	(名)	wàibiānr	outside
4.	上边兒	(名)	shàngbiānr	above
5.	下边兒	(名)	xiàbiānr	below, the following
6.	中間兒	(名)	zhōngjiànr	middle
7.	前边兒	(名)	qiánbiānr	front
8.	工厂	(名)	gōngchǎng	factory
9.	后边兒	(名)	hòubiānr	back, the following
10.	宿舍	(名)	sùshè	dormitory, hostel
11.	作	(动)	zuò	to do, to make, to work, to be
12.	地方	(名)	dìfāng	place
13.	圖書館	(名)	túshūguǎn	library
14.	礼堂	(名)	lǐtáng	auditorium (hall)
15.	旁边兒	(名)	pángbiānr	side, beside

二、語法 Yǔfǎ Grammar

23.1 "在" "在"是一个动詞，可以作謂語的主要成分. 例如:

23.1 在 在 is a verb and can be used as the chief element of a predicate. e. g.

1. 你 在 哪兒?
   Nǐ zài nǎr?

2. 我 在 学校.
   Wǒ zài xuéxiào.

但是，它也可以是一个介詞. 它的宾語如果是由表示空間的詞語构成的，这时介詞"在"連同自己的宾語所形成的介詞結构，就常常作处所状語. 例如:

It can also be used as a preposition. If the object of 在 is composed of a word or word group of place, then this preposition and its object form a prepositional construction which is often used as adverbial modifier of place. e. g.

3. 我們 在 中国 学習.
   Wǒmen zài Zhōngguó xuéxí.

4. 先生 在 这兒 工作.
   Xiānshêng zài zhèr gōngzuò.

动詞"在"或介詞"在"的宾語一般是表示空間的名詞或代詞. 如果这个名詞或代詞是指人的，和在介詞"从"的后面一样，必須在名詞或代詞后面加上"这兒"或"那兒"把宾語变为指地点的. 例如:

Whether the word 在 is used as a verb or a preposition, its object is in general a noun or pronoun denoting place. If the noun or pronoun denotes a person, then just as in the case of 从, 这兒 and 那兒 must be used to change this object into one denoting place. e. g.

5. 我的 練習 本子 在 先生 那兒.
   Wǒdê liànxí běnzǐ zài xiānshêng nàr.

6. 中国 朋友 在 我們 这兒 看 画报.
Zhōngguó péngyǒu zài wǒmên zhèr kàn huàbào.

此外"在"后面也可以有表示时間的名詞，这等以后再談.

Of course, the word 在 may be followed by a noun denoting time. This we shall discuss later.

23.2 表示方位的名詞　有些名詞是專門表示方位的，例如："里边兒""外边兒""上边兒""下边兒""中間兒"等. 这些詞和一般名詞一样，可以作主語. 例如:

23.2 Nouns of Locality　Some nouns are used exclusively to indicate locality, e. g. 里边兒，外边兒，上边兒，下边兒，中間兒 etc. Like other nouns, a noun of locality can be used as subject. e. g.

7. 里边兒 很 干淨.
Lǐbiânr hěn gānjìng.

可以作宾語. 例如:

It can be used as object. e. g.

8. 我 在 外边兒.
Wǒ zài wàibiânr.

可以作定語. 例如:

It can also be used as adjective modifier. e. g.

9. 上边兒的 杂誌 是 新的.
Shàngbiânrdê zázhì shì xīndê.

10. 我 不 看 下边兒的 旧 杂誌.
Wǒ bú kàn xiàbiânrdê jiù zázhì.

也可以作中心語，它的定語一般是名詞或代詞. 例如:

As a central word, it can also be modified by a noun or a pronoun. e. g.

11. 那張 桌子 在 两把 椅子 中間兒.
Nèizhāng zhuōzi zài liǎngbǎ yǐzi zhōngjiànr.

12. 先生 在 我們 前边兒.
Xiānshêng zài wǒmên qiánbiānr.

"两把椅子中間兒"和"我們前边兒"这种結构，常常不用結构助詞"的".

In the word combinations of 两把椅子中間兒 and of 我們前边兒, the word 的 is often understood and omitted.

"上边兒"和"里边兒"用在名詞之后时，常常省去"边兒". 例如:

When 上边兒 and 里边兒 are used after nouns, we often omit the word 边兒. e. g.

13. 練習 本子 在 桌子上.
Liànxí běnzi zài zhuōzishâng.

14. 我的 同屋 在 学校里.
Wǒdê tóngwū zài xuéxiàoli.

但也可以用"边兒"，而且其他表示方位的名詞不能如此省略，或者省略之后，意思有所改变.

In such cases, we may use the word 边兒 as well. But the other nouns of locality should not be shortened in this way, for their meanings will be different when 边兒 is omitted.

在"我們前边兒"这种結构里用"的"不是絕对不可以，但是"里边兒""上边兒"已經省为單音节詞"里"和"上"的时候，一定不能用"的". 也就是說"桌子上""学校里"不能說成"桌子的上""学校的里".

We have mentioned above that particle 的 in such a word combination as 我們前边兒 may be omitted; but when 里边兒 and 上边兒 are already shortened into monosyllabic words 里 and 上, the particle 的 should not be used. That is to say: 桌子上 and 学校里 are correct, but not 桌子的上 and 学校的里.

23.3 方位詞"里边兒"的用法　方位詞"里边兒"比較特殊，在某些名詞后一定用，某些名詞后一定不用，在某些名詞后可用可不用，其大致規律如下:

23.3 The Noun of Locality 里边兒　The noun of locality 里边兒 is rather peculiar in use. Some nouns require it, some don't, and still some others may or may not require it at all. The general rules are as follows:

(一) 地理名詞后面不用"里边兒". 例如:

(1) After geographical terms, we do not use 里边兒. e. g.

15. 我們　在　中国.
Wǒmên　zài　Zhōngguó.

16. 他的　朋友　在　北京　学习.
Tādê　péngyôu　zài　Běijīng　xuéxí.

一定不能說"中国里边兒""北京里边兒".

We must remember that in such cases, we never say 中国里边兒 or 北京里边兒.

(二) 一些名詞（如表示建筑物、机关、团体所在地等的）用在"在"的后面的时候，如果意思是"在…里边兒"，这个"里边兒"可有可无. 例如:

(2) When the word 在 is followed by nouns such as names of buildings, organizations and so on, and if the meaning of 里边兒 is understood, then 里边兒 may or may not be omitted. e. g.

17. 他們　都　在　工厂　(里边兒)　工作.
Tāmên　dōu　zài gōngchǎng　(lǐbiânr)　gōngzuò.

因为不在"里边兒"的时候必須标明（如"外边兒""旁边兒"等等），沒有标明的就照例理解为"在…里边兒".

If the persons are not inside the factory, we must use other nouns of locality, such as 外边兒 and 旁边兒 to indicate that they are outside or by the side of the factory etc. When there is no noun of locality following the object of 在, 里边兒 is understood as a rule.

（三）一般名詞（如表示物件名称的）可能有各种方位，便需要用方位詞．因此，"里边兒"不能省．例如：

(3) Some nouns, such as the nouns denoting implements, must take nouns of locality, because there are many sides of a thing and it is difficult to ascertain where without a noun of locality. Therefore 里边兒 cannot be omitted. e. g.

18. 那 半張 紙 在 書 里(边兒).
Nèi bànzhāng zhǐ zài shū lǐ(biånr).

其他的方位詞也都不能省略．
We cannot omit the other nouns of locality.

三、課文 Kèwén Text

I

1. 椅子 在 桌子 后边兒.
Yǐzi zài zhuōzi hòubiånr.

2. 桌子 在 椅子 前边兒.
Zhuōzi zài yǐzi qiánbiånr.

3. 人民 画报 在 杂誌 下边兒.
Rénmín Huàbào zài zázhì xiàbiånr.

4. 杂誌 在 画报 上边兒.
Zázhì zài huàbào shàngbiånr.

5. 我 同屋 在 宿舍(里) 唱 歌兒.
Wǒ tóngwū zài sùshè(li) chàng gēr.

6. 他 朋友 在 書上 写 名字.
Tā péngyou zài shūshang xiě míngzi.

7. 我 在 本子里 作 練習.
Wǒ zài běnzili zuò liànxí.

8. 他 在 紙上 練習 汉字.
Tā zài zhǐshang liànxí hànzì.

II

(a₁) 你們的 宿舍 在 哪兒?
Nǐmendė sùshè zài nǎr?

(b₁) 在 北京 大学 里边兒.
Zài Běijīng、Dàxué lǐbiānr.

(a₂) 你 在 什么 地方 学習?
Nǐ zài shénmȯ dìfȧng xuéxí?

常常 在 宿舍(里) 学習 嗎?
Chángcháng zài sùshè(lǐ) xuéxí mȧ?

(b₂) 我 在 圖書館(里) 学習.
Wǒ zài túshūguǎn(lǐ) xuéxí.

我 同屋 在 宿舍(里) 学習.
Wǒ tóngwū zài sùshè(lǐ) xuéxí.

III

(a₃) 你們 圖書館 在 什么 地方?
Nǐmen túshūguǎn zài shénmȯ dìfȧng?

(b₃) 在 礼堂 旁边兒.
Zài lǐtáng pángbiānr.

(a₄) 你 在 圖書館(里) 都 作 什么?
Nǐ zài túshūguǎn(lǐ) dōu zuò shénmȯ?

(b₄) 念 書, 作 練習. 我 也 看 报.
Niàn shū, zuò liànxí. Wǒ yě kàn bào.

圖書館的 报 很 多.
Túshūguǎndė bào hěn duō.

(a₅) 这本 杂誌 也 是 圖書館的 嗎?
Zhèiběn zázhì yě shì túshūguǎndė mȧ?

(b₅) 不 是. 是 我的. 你 看, 这 是
Bú shì. Shì wǒdė. Nǐ kàn, zhèi shì

我的　名字.
wǒdê　míngzì.

四、課外練習　Kèwài liànxí　Home Work

1. 用下面的詞語各作一个句子:
1) Make sentences with each of the following word combinations:

(1) 什么　地方

(2) 在…旁边兒

2. 把下面的句子翻成中文:
2) Translate the following into Chinese:

(3) The teachers' dormitories are outside the school, the students' dormitories are inside the school.

(4) The chairs in the front of the auditorium are new ones and those at the back are old ones.

3. 根据本課語法点完成下面的句子:
3) Complete the following sentences according to the grammar rules given in this lesson:

(5) 学生　都　在　圖書館　＿＿.

(6) 我　同屋　在　張　同志　＿＿.

(7) 杂誌　在　書　上边兒,　画报　在　書　下边兒,　書　在　杂誌　和　画报　＿＿.

五、汉字表 Hànzì biǎo Chinese Characters

1	在	一 ナ 才 在
2	边	
3	外	
4	上	丨 ⺊ 上
5	下	一 丅 下
6	間	門
		日
7	前	䒑（丶 丷 䒑）
		月
		刂
8	厂	一 厂
9	后	丿 𠂆 ⺁ 后

10	宿	宀	
		佰	亻
			百（一 百）
11	舍	人 今 全 舍	
12	方		
13	圖	冂 冋 冐 冐 冐 冐 啚 圖 圖	
14	館	食	
		官（宀 宀 宀 宀 官 官）	
15	礼	礻	
		乚	
16	堂	尚	
		土	
17	旁	丶 亠 亠 方 产 旁	

第二十四課 Lesson 24

一、 語法复習 Yǔfǎ fùxí Review

24.1 状語和程度补語　我們知道，形容詞可以放在动詞或形容詞前边作状語 (20.1)，也可以放在动詞或形容詞后边作程度补語 (21.2). 形容詞作状語，有的时候用結构助詞"地"，有的时候不用；但是形容詞作程度补語必須要用結构助詞"得". 形容詞作状語或程度补語都是对中心語有所說明的. 因此有必要把这种状語和程度补語区别一下:

24.1 The Adverbial Modifier and the Complement of Degree

We know that an adjective may be used as an adverbial modifier before a verb or an adjective (20.1). It may also be used as a complement of degree after a verb or an adjective (21.2). As an adverbial modifier, the adjective is sometimes followed by the structural particle 地 and sometimes not; but as a complement of degree, it must be preceded by the structural particle 得. Whether as an adverbial modifier or as a complement or degree, the adjective always says something about the central word. Hence it is necessary here to get a clear idea of their different uses:

(一) 形容詞作动詞的程度补語是常見的. 用程度补語的句子，动作一般是完成了的或是經常發生的. 例如:

(1) It is very common to use an adjective as the complement of degree to a verb. In a sentence containing a complement of degree, the verb generally denotes an action in the past, or customary tenses. e.g.

1. 他　来得　很　早.
Tā　láidê　hěn　zǎo.

2. 他　学　中文　学得　很　快.
Tā　xué　zhōngwén　xuédê　hěn　kuài.

"来"和"学"这两个动作是已經完成了或进行了一段时間的，我們才能說"他来得很早"或"他学得很快"．这里主要地不在於說明"他来沒来"或"他学不学"，因为說这种句子的时候，"来"或"学"这个动作是已經肯定了的．現在要說明的是动作"怎么样"．所以这种带程度补語的动詞謂語句，具有描写性．至於用程度补語的形容詞謂語句，自然更是描写性的句子了．

Here 来 and 学 are two completed actions or actions that have continued for some time, meaning "he comes early" or "he is quick in learning". Here what we wish to express is not "whether he has come or not" or "whether he is studying or not"; because in such sentences, the actions of 来 and 学 have already happened. Now what we wish to make clear is only "how" have the actions proceeded. Therefore, a verbal sentence with a complement of degree possesses the nature of a descriptive sentence. And a sentence with an adjectival predicate followed by a complement of degree is of course a pure descriptive sentence.

(二) 形容詞作动詞的状語也是常見的．在有这种状語的句子里，动作不受时間的限制．因为状語是說明动作的方式或状态的，而不是描写动作所达到的程度或結果的．因此这种动詞謂語句当然还是叙述性的．

(2) It is also common to use an adjective as adverbial modifier of a verb. In a sentence containing such an adverbial modifier, the action is not restricted by time, because in this kind of sentence the adverbial modifier is used to describe the way or manner of the action, and not to describe the extent or result of the action. Therefore, this kind of sentence with a verbal predicate is more narrative in nature.

24.2 状語后結构助詞"地"的应用　状語后面的結构助詞"地"有时候用，有时候不用．現在把用不用"地"的情形大致归納如下:

24.2 The Use of the Structural Particle 地 after the Adverbial Modifier The adverbial modifier is sometimes followed by the structural particle 地, and sometimes not. The following rules show when this particle 地 is needed:

(一) 絕对不用"地" 有两种情况:

(1) 地 should never be used under the following conditions:

(1) 如果状語是由單音节的詞构成的(无論是副詞或形容詞)都不能用"地". 例如:

a) If the adverbial modifier is a monosyllabic word (it may be an adverb or an adjective), the particle 地 is not used. e.g.

3. 他 不 去.
Tā bú qù.

4. 我 一定 早 来.
Wǒ yídìng zǎo lái.

(2) 如果状語是一个介詞結构, 也不用"地". 例如:

b) If the adverbial modifier is a prepositional construction, the particle 地 is not used. e. g.

5. 他們 从 礼堂 来.
Tāmen cóng lǐtáng lái.

6. 我 跟 張 同志 跳 舞.
Wǒ gēn Zhāng tóngzhì tiào wǔ.

(二) 多半不用"地" 如果状語是一个双音节的副詞, 一般不用"地". 例如:

(2) 地 is often not used. If the adverbial modifier is a dissyllabic adverb, 地 is generally not used. e. g.

7. 我們 一起 学習.
Wǒmen yìqǐ xuéxí.

个别的双音节副詞也可以用 "地", 但以不用"地"更合習慣. 例如:

There are a few dissyllabic adverbs that can be followed by the particle, but it is more idiomatic not to use it. e. g.

8. 他 常常(地) 唱 歌兒.
Tā chángcháng(dê) chàng gēr.

(三) 多半用"地" 如果状語是由双音节形容詞或重叠的形容詞构成的，虽然可以不用"地"，但用"地"更常見. 例如:

(3) 地 is often used. If the adverbial modifier is made up of a dissyllabic adjective or a reduplicated adjective, the particle 地 is more often used than not. e. g.

9. 他們 都 积極地 工作.
Tāmên dōu jījídê gōngzuò.

10. 我 一定 好好兒地 学習 中文.
Wǒ yídìng hǎohāordê xuéxí zhōngwén.

11. 朋友 都 高高兴兴地 唱 歌兒.
Péngyǒu dōu gāogåoxìngxìngdê chàng gēr.

(四) 必須用"地" 一般形容詞作状語而本身又带有状語的，必須用"地". 例如:

(4) 地 must be used. In general, when an adjective used as an adverbial modifier is modified by another adverbial modifier, the particle must be used. e. g.

12. 他 很 努力地 学習.
Tā hěn nǔlìdê xuéxí.

二、課文 Kèwén Text

I

(a_1) 你 从 哪兒 来?
Nǐ cóng nǎr lái?

(b_1) 我 从 圖書館 来.
Wǒ cóng túshūguǎn lái.

(a_2) 你　在　圖書館　作　什么?
Nǐ　zài　túshūguǎn　zuò　shénmȯ?

(b_2) 学習　中文，我　在　那兒　看　書，
Xuéxí　zhōngwén,　wǒ　zài　nàr　kàn　shū,

写　汉字，作　練習.
xiě　hànzì,　zuò　liànxí.

(a_3) 你　不　看　电影　嗎?
Nǐ　bú　kàn　diànyǐng　må?

(b_3) 什么　电影? 是　苏联　电影　嗎?
Shénmȯ　diànyǐng? Shì　Sūlián　diànyǐng　må?

(a_4) 不　是，是　中国的. 你　喜欢　不　喜
Bú　shì,　shì　Zhōngguódė.　Nǐ　xǐhuån　bù　xǐ-

欢　中国　电影?
huån　Zhōngguó　diànyǐng?

(b_4) 喜欢，很　多　中国　电影　都　很
Xǐhuån,　hěn　duō　Zhōngguó　diànyǐng　dōu　hěn

好，都　很　有意思.
hǎo,　dōu　hěn　yǒuyìsi.

II

(a_5) 張　先生　在　哪兒?
Zhāng　xiānshêng　zài　nǎr?

(b_5) 他　在　学生　宿舍(里).
Tā　zài　xuéshêng　sùshè(lǐ).

(a_6) 他　在　学生　宿舍(里)　作　什么?
Tā　zài　xuéshêng　sùshè(lǐ)　zuò　shénmȯ?

(b_6) 他 在 那兒 跟 学生 説 話.
Tā zài nàr gēn xuéshėng shuō huà.

(a_7) 他們 説 哪国 話?
Tāmėn shuō něiguó huà?

(b_7) 説 中国 話. 張 先生 是 中文
Shuō Zhōngguó huà. Zhāng xiānshėng shì zhōngwén

先生. 他 跟 学生 只説 中文.
xiānshėng. Tā gēn xuéshėng zhǐ shuō zhōngwén.

(a_8) 学生 都 懂 嗎?
Xuéshėng dōu dǒng mȧ?

(b_8) 張 先生 説 中文, 学生 都 懂.
Zhāng xiānshėng shuō zhōngwén, xuéshėng dōu dǒng.

他 説 中文 説得 很 慢, 他
Tā shuō zhōngwén shuōdė hěn màn, Tā

常常 跟 学生 説 話, 学生 都
chángcháng gēn xuéshėng shuō huà, xuéshėng dōu

懂 他的 話.
dǒng tādė huà.

第二十五課　Lesson 25

25.1	表示时間的名詞 Nouns of Time
25.2	年、月、日、时的表示法 The Expressions of Year, Month, Day and Hour
25.3	表示时間的詞語作状語 Words or Word Groups of Time Used as Adverbial Modifiers
25.4	"有" The Verb 有

一、生詞　Shēngcí　New Words

1.	月	(名)	yuè	month
2.	今天	(名)	jīntiān	today
3.	日	(名)	rì	day
4.	号	(名)	hào	day, number
5.	星期	(名)	xīngqī	week
6.	天	(名)	tiān	day
7.	点(鐘)	(名)	diǎn(zhōng)	o'clock
8.	过	(动)	guò	to pass, past
9.	分	(名)	fēn	minute
10.	刻	(名)	kè	a quarter
11.	差	(动)	chà	less (to differ)
12.	忙	(形)	máng	busy
13.	今年	(名)	jīnnián	this year
14.	現在	(名)	xiànzài	now, at present
15.	时候兒	(名)	shíhòur	time

二、 語法 Yǔfǎ Grammar

25. 1 表示时間的名詞 有一些名詞是專門表示时間的. 这些名詞具有一般名詞的功能:在句子里作主語、宾語、定語等等.例如:

25.1 Nouns of Time In Chinese, some nouns are exclusively used to indicate time. So far as their functions are concerned, they are just the same as other nouns. They may all be used as subject, object, adjective modifier etc. in a sentence.

1. 一年 有 十二个 月.
   Yìnián yǒu shíèrgê yuè.

2. 这 是 今天的 报.
   Zhèi shì jīntiåndê bào.

"一年"是主語, "十二个月" 是宾語, 而 "今天" 就是 "报" 的定語.

一年 is subject, 十二个月 is object, and 今天 is the adjective modifier of 报.

25.2 年、月、日、时的表示法 汉語里表示时間的順序是从大到小的:

年——月——日——时

25.2 The Expressions of Year, Month, Day and Hour In Chinese, indication of time begins from the biggest unit to the smallest unit, that is to say: 年 stands first, 月 second, 日 third, and then 时.

年代是經常用簡縮的形式来表示的. 例如 "1957年" 經常讀为 "一九五七年", 而很少讀作 "一千九百五十七年". 在問題中, 我們用 "哪" 或 "几", 例如 "哪年" 或 "一九五几年".

The year is always expressed in a simple way, e.g. "1957" is always read as 一九五七年, only very occasionally read as 一千九百五十七年 (one thousand nine hundred fifty seven). In a question, we use 哪 or 几, such as 哪年 or 一九五几年.

"月" 的称謂很簡單，一年十二个月只要按照次第把数詞放在"月" 前边就可以了. 例如: "一月" "二月"... "十月" "十一月" "十二月". 在問題中我們問 "几月".

The designation of "months" in Chinese is very simple; the names of the twelve months in a year are formed by putting the numerals 1 — 12 before the word 月. Such as: 一月 (January) 二月(February)... 十月 (October), 十一月 (November) and 十二月 (December). In a question, we say 几月.

"日" 的称謂也很簡單. 把数詞放在 "日" 或 "号"的 "前边". "...日" 比較正式, 多半用於書面語中. "...号" 是口語里常用的形式. 例如: "二日 (号)" "十日 (号)" "三十日 (号)". 在問題中, 我們問 "几号" "十几号" "二十几号".

The designation of "days" is also very simple. We have only to place the numerals 1 — 31 before 日 or 号. 日 is formal and often used in the written language, while 号 is always used in the spoken language. e. g. 二日 (号), 十日 (号) and 三十日 (号). In asking questions, we use 几号, 十几号, 二十几号.

一个星期內前六天的称謂是按照次序把数詞 "一"... "六" 放在 "星期" 的后边. 例如: "星期一" "星期二"... "星期五" "星期六"; 第七天叫 "星期日", 也可以省略为 "星期". 在問題里, 我們問 "星期几".

In naming the seven days of the week, we place the numerals one, two, ...six after the word 星期. For example: 星期一 (Monday), 星期二 (Tuesday)... 星期五 (Friday) and 星期六 (Saturday); the seventh day in a week is called 星期日 (Sunday), it can also be shortened as 星期. In a question, we say 星期几.

有一点应当注意: 我們只能說 "一个月有三十天(或三十一天)", 或 "一个星期有七天", 而不能說 "一个月有三十号 (或三十一号)", 或 "一个星期有七号".

Note: We can only say 一个月有三十天 (or 三十一天) and 一个星期有七天, but we cannot say 一个月有三十号 (or 三十一号), and 一个星期有七号.

一天的时間如何表示，可由下面的实例中看出来：

Time of the day is shown in the following:

3. 12:00 十二点(鐘)
shíèrdiǎn (zhōng)

4. 12:05 十二点 (过) 五分
shíèrdiǎn (guò) wǔfēn

5. 12:15 十二点 十五分
shíèrdiǎn shíwǔfēn

十二点 一刻
shíèrdiǎn yíkè

6. 12:30 十二点 半(鐘)
shíèrdiǎn bàn(zhōng)

十二点 三十分
shíèrdiǎn sānshífēn

7. 12:45 十二点 三刻
shíèrdiǎn sānkè

十二点 四十五分
shíèrdiǎn sìshíwǔfēn

差 一刻 一点
chà yíkè yìdiǎn

8. 12:55 十二点 五十五分
shíèrdiǎn wǔshíwǔfēn

差 五分 一点
chà wǔfēn yìdiǎn

因此，年、月、日、时連在一起的时候，是下面这个形式：

Therefore in a date, when the year, the month, the day and the hour are given at the same time, the word order is as follows:

9. 一九五七年 十月 一日（星期二） 十点
yījiǔwǔqīnián shíyuè yírì (xīngqīèr) shídiǎn

25.3 表示时間的詞語作状語　时間詞語除了作主語、宾語和定語以外,还常常作状語.当我們要說明在什么时間或哪段时間里發生什么动作或存在什么情况的时候,就用表示时間的詞語作状語.例如:

25.3 Words and Word Groups of Time Used as Adverbial Modifiers　Words of time are not only used as subjects, objects and adjective modifiers, but also frequently as adverbial modifiers. When we wish to tell the time or period of a certain action, we use a word or word group of time as adverbial modifier. e. g.

10. 我 七点半 去.
Wǒ qīdiǎnbàn qù.

11. 他 星期二 很 忙.
Tā xīngqièr hěn máng.

"七点半"和"星期二"都是表示某个时間的,在这里"七点半"是"去"这个动作發生的时間,"星期二"是"忙"的情况存在的时間.又如:

七点半 and 星期二 are both words of time. The adverbial modifier, 七点半, gives the time of 去, and 星期二 tells when he is busy. More examples are:

12. 我們 一天 学 十八个 汉字.
Wǒmen yìtiān xué shíbāgè hànzì.

13. 我的 朋友 这个 月 很 忙.
Wǒdè péngyǒu zhèigè yuè hěn máng.

"一天""这个月"都表示一段时間,在这里"一天"是"学汉字"这个动作的时間,而"这个月"是"忙"这个情况存在的时間.

一天 and 这个月 both represent certain periods of time. Here 天 indicates the time of the action 学汉字, and 这个月 tells when the state of 忙 (being busy) takes place.

当我們要特別强調时間的时候,表示时間的詞語也可以提到句首.例如:

When we wish to emphasize the time, we may put the word or word group of time at the beginning of a sentence. e. g.

14. 星期二 他 很 忙.
Xīngqīèr tā hěn máng.

15. 一天 我們 学 十八个 汉字.
Yìtiān wǒmên xué shíbāgê hànzì.

25.4 "有" "有"是个动詞，但并不表示什么动作.它可以表示領屬关系，它的主語常常是指人的名詞或代詞. 但我們要說明一个空間容納多少人或物，或一个时間內包含多少更小單位的时候，也用"有". 这时候，表示空間或时間的詞語就是主語. 例如:

25.4 有 有 is a verb, but it does not express any action. It shows a relation of ownership, and its subject is always a noun or pronoun denoting a person or persons. But if we wish to tell how many persons or things there are in a certain place, or how many smaller units there are in a definite period of time, we also use the verb 有. In such a case, the word or word group denoting place or time is the subject. e. g.

16. 一年 有 十二个 月.
Yìnián yǒu shíèrgê yuè.

17. 北京 大学 有 很 多 学生.
Běijīng Dàxué yǒu hěn duō xuéshêng.

18. 圖書館里 有 很 多 書.
Túshūguǎnlî yǒu hěn duō shū.

这种句子的結构和"我有書""你有报"一样，"一年""北京大学""圖書館里"就是主語. 因此，習慣上，特別是口語里，我們不在这种表示时間或空間的詞語前边用介詞，例如說"在一年有十二个月"或"在北京大学有很多学生".

The above-mentioned sentences are by structure similar to the sentences 我有書 and 你有报. 一年，北京大学 and 圖書館里 are subjects. Therefore, it is idiomatic, especially in the spoken language, not to use the preposition 在 before the word or word group expressing place or time. We never say 在一年有十二个月 or 在北京大学有很多学生.

三、 課文 Kèwén Text

(a₁) 今年 是 一九五几年?
Jīnnián shì yījiǔwǔjǐnián?

(b₁) 今年 是 一九五八年.
Jīnnián shì yījiǔwǔbānián.

(a₂) 这个 月 是 几月?
Zhèigê yuè shì jǐyuè?

(b₂) 这个 月 是 十月.
Zhèigê yuè shì shíyuè.

(a₃) 今天 是 几月 几号?
Jīntiân shì jǐyuè jǐhào?

(b₃) 今天 是 十月 十六号.
Jīntiân shì shíyuè shíliùhào.

(a₄) 今天 是 星期几?
Jīntiân shì xīngqījǐ?

(b₄) 今天 是 星期三.
Jīntiân shì xīngqīsān.

(a₅) 一个 星期 有 几天?
Yígê xīngqī yǒu jǐtiān?

(b₅) 一个 星期 有 七天.
Yígê xīngqī yǒu qītiān.

(a₆) 这 七天的 名字 都 叫 什么?
Zhèi qītiāndê míngzî dōu jiào shénmô?

(b_6) 这 七天 叫: 星期一、星期二、星期三、星期四、星期五、星期六、星期日.
Zhèi qītiān jiào: xīngqīyī、xīngqīèr、xīngqīsān、xīngqīsì、xīngqīwǔ、xīngqīliù、xīngqīrì.

(a_7) 現在 是 几点 几分?
Xiànzài shì jǐdiǎn jǐfēn?

(b_7) 現在 是 两点 过 一刻.
Xiànzài shì liǎngdiǎn guò yíkè.

(a_8) 先生 什么 时候兒 来?
Xiānshêng shénmô shíhôur lái?

(b_8) 先生 两点半 来.
Xiānshêng liǎngdiǎnbàn lái.

(a_9) 这个 星期 你們 忙 不 忙?
Zhèigê xīngqī nǐmên máng bù máng?

(b_9) 很 忙, 我們 这个 星期 有 很 多 工作.
Hěn máng, wǒmên zhèigê xīngqī yǒu hěn duō gōngzuò.

(a_{10}) 这个 星期六 你 看 电影 嗎?
Zhèigê xīngqīliù nǐ kàn diànyǐng mâ?

(b_{10}) 不 看, 这个 星期六 我 不 看 电影.
Bú kàn, zhèigê xīngqīliù wǒ bú kàn diànyǐng.

四、課外練習 Kèwài liànxí Home Work

1. 用汉字把下边的时間表示出来:

1) Put the following units of time in Chinese:

(1) 7:05 (2) 4:50 (3) 8:30 (4) 11:00
(5) May first (1st of May) — Wednesday
(6) 8th of March 1958

2. 給下面的句子写出相应的問題來:

2) Write out appropriate questions for the following sentences:

(7) 今天 是 星期五.

(8) 現在 是 十二点 过 十分

(9) 一个 星期 有 七天

(10) 我的 朋友 四月 三号 来.

3. 回答下边的問題:

3) Answer the following questions:

(11) 你 星期日 学习 不 学习?

(12) 这个 星期 你 哪天 忙, 哪天 不 忙?

五、汉字表 Hànzì biǎo Chinese Characters

1	月	
2	今	
3	天	一 天
4	日	
5	号	口 𠮟 号
6	星	日
		生

7	期	其（一 十 卄 廿 甘 𠀠 其）	
		月	
8	点	占	
		灬	
9	鐘	金	
		童	立
			里
10	过	寸	
		辶	
11	分		
12	刻	亥（丶 亠 亡 𠅃 𠅃 亥）	
		刂	
13	差	丶 丷 䒑 䒑 𦍌 𦍌 ⺶ 差	
14	忙	忄	
		亡（丶 亠 亡）	
15	現	王（一 二 干 王）	
		見	目
			儿
16	时	日	
		寸	

17	候	亻 亻丨 亻丨𠃍 亻丨𠂉 候

第二十六課 Lesson 26

26.1	能願动詞 Optative Verbs	
26.2	有关能願动詞的注意事項 Some Rules Concerning Optative Verbs	

一、生詞 Shēngcí New Words

1.	能	(能动)	néng	to be able, can
2.	会	(能动)	huì	may, to know how to do
3.	要	(动、能动)	yào	to want, to desire
4.	应該	(能动)	yīnggāi	should, ought
5.	用	(动)	yòng	to use
6.	字典	(名)	zìdiǎn	dictionary
7.	認識	(动、名)	rènshi	to know, to recognize
8.	还	(副)	hái	also, too, still
9.	以后	(副)	yǐhòu	afterwards
10.	买	(动)	mǎi	to buy
11.	听	(动)	tīng	to hear, to listen to
12.	好看	(形)	hǎokàn	good-looking
13.	沒关系		méiguānxi	never mind, it does'nt matter
14.	覚得	(动)	juédě	to feel
15.	东西	(名)	dōngxi	thing

二、語法 Yǔfǎ Grammar

26.1. 能願动詞　能願动詞是动詞里的一个附类，它和一般动詞不完全一样，有自己的語法上的特点：不能重叠，不能带詞尾，不能带体詞宾語，常在动詞（或形容詞）前边．这类詞是用来表示可能、能力、願望、要求和意志等等的．

26.1 Optative Verbs (verbs of ability and willingness)

Optative verbs belong to the part of speech of verbs. But they are different from other common verbs, because they have their own grammatical characteristics: they are never used reduplicatively and never followed by any suffix or any substantive object; they are used before verbs or adjectives. The ma n function of optative verbs is to indicate possibility, ability, willingness, demand or intention.

(一)"能"　有时候表示主观能力. 例如:

(1) 能　能 implies subjective ability. e. g.

1. 他 一天 能 看 一本 中文 書.
Tā yìtiān néng kàn yìběn zhōngwén shū.

2. 我 十分鐘 能 写 很 多 汉字.
Wǒ shífēnzhōng néng xiě hěn duō hànzì.

有时候表示客观环境或情理上的允許. 例如:

Sometimes it implies permission under certain conditions. e.g.

3. 我們 不 能 在 圖書館里 說 話.
Wǒmên bù néng zài túshūguǎnlǐ shuō huà.

我 能 跟 你 一起 作 練習 嗎?
Wǒ néng gēn nǐ yìqǐ zuò liànxí må?

(二)"会"　是动詞,但也可以是能願动詞.作为能願动詞,它也表示主观能力. 但是和"能"有所不同:"会"所表示的能力一般是通过学習得到的技巧,所以常和"精通""掌握"这种意思相通. 例如:

(2) 会　会 is a verb, but it is also an optative verb used before a verb or an adjective. When it is used as an optative verb, it also implies subjective ability, but it is different from 能, because 会 means a certain skill acquired through learning, so it is often similar to 精通 (to be well-versed) and 掌握 (to master) in meaning. e. g.

5. 他 会 說 中文.
Tā huì shuō zhōngwén.

6 这个 同志 会 跳 舞.
Zhèigê tóngzhì huì tiào wǔ.

"說中文"和"跳舞"都要学習才会的.

說中文 and 跳舞 in the above examples are skills acquired through learning.

"会"有时候表示客观情势上的可能性. 例如:

会 sometimes implies a possibility under certain conditions. e. g.

7. 他 不 懂 中文, 这本 中文 杂誌 不 会 是 他的.
Tā bù dǒng zhōngwén, zhèiběn zhōngwén zázhì bú huì shì tādê.

8. 他 在 礼堂 看 电影, 不 会 在 圖書館.
Tā zài lǐtáng kàn diànyǐng, bú huì zài túshūguǎn.

(三) "要" "要"和"会"一样, 它可以是动詞. 例如:

(3) 要 Like the word 会, 要 is a verb. e. g.

9. 先生 要 一張 干淨 紙.
Xiānshêng yào yìzhāng gānjìng zhǐ.

作为能願动詞, 有时候表示主观要求. 例如:

When 要 is used as an optative verb, it indicates subjective desire or intention. e. g.

10. 我 要 去 圖書館.
Wǒ yào qù túshūguǎn.

11. 先生 要 看 你的 本子.
Xiānshêng yào kàn nǐdê běnzi.

有时候表示客观的需要. 例如:

It sometimes indicates objective necessity.

12. 学生 要 好好兒地 学習.
Xuéshêng yào hǎohāordê xuéxí.

13. 黑板 要 干淨.
Hēibǎn yào gānjîng.

值得注意的是：在例 13 里，"要" 后边的是形容詞.

Note: 要 in example 13 is used before an adjective.

(四) "应該" "应該" 表示情理上或習慣上的需要，意味着如果不这样，就是不对的、不好的. 例如：

(4) 应該 应該 expresses some demand or necessity dictated by reason or habit. That is to say, it is not right or proper not to do so. e. g.

14. 我們 应該 看 这本 杂誌.
Wǒmên yīnggāi kàn zhèiběn zázhì.

15. 学生 都 应該 努力.
Xuéshêng dōu yīnggāi nǔlì.

注意："应該" 也可以用在形容詞前边.

Note: The optative verb 应該 may be followed by an adjective.

26.2 有关能願动詞的注意事項

26.2 Some Rules Concerning Optative Verbs:

(一) 在选擇式疑問句里，我們并列能願动詞的肯定和否定形式. 例如：

(1) If an optative verb is used in the alternative interrogative sentence, we need only give both the affirmative and the negative forms of the optative verb. e. g.

16. 你 能 不 能 来?
Nǐ néng bù néng lái?

17. 你 要 不 要 跟 我 一起 去?
Nǐ yào bú yào gēn wǒ yìqǐ qù?

当謂語簡短的时候，能願动詞后面的成分也可以出現两次. 例如：

If the predicate is simple and short, the element after the optative verb may be used two times. e. g.

18. 你 能 来 不 能 来?
Nǐ néng lái bù néng lái?

但是应該注意：能願动詞不能只出現一次. 我們不能問"能来不来""应該太多不太多".

Note: In such interrogative sentences, the optative verb has to be repeated. So we cannot say 能来不来 or 应該太多不太多.

(二) 回答問題时，能願动詞能單独作謂語. 例如:

(2) In answering questions, the optative verb may stand alone and be used as the predicate. e. g.

19. 你 要 看 报 嗎?
Nǐ yào kàn bào må?

20. 要.
Yào.

21. 你 会 不 会 用 中文 字典?
Nǐ huì bú huì yòng zhōngwén zìdiǎn?

22. 会.
Huì.

(三) 能願动詞也有連用的可能. 例如:

(3) Two optative verbs may be used in succession. e.g.

23. 学生 应該 会 念 这些 汉字.
Xuéshêng yīnggāi huì niàn zhèixiē hànzì.

24. 他 今天 沒 有 工作, 应該 能 来.
Tā jīntiån méi yǒu gōngzuò, yīnggāi néng lái.

三、課文 Kèwén Text

(a₁) 現在 你們 能 看 中文 报 嗎?
Xiànzài nǐmên néng kàn zhōngwén bào mâ?

(b₁) 不 能, 我們 只 認識 很 少的 汉字, 还 不 能 看 报.
Bù néng, wǒmên zhǐ rènshî hěn shǎodê hànzì, hái bù néng kàn bào.

(a₂) 你們 会 用 字典 不 会?
Nǐmên huì yòng zìdiǎn bú huì?

(b₂) 現在 还 不 会, 以后 先生 要 教 我們. 我們 应該 会 用 字典.
Xiànzài hái bú huì, yǐhòu xiānshêng yào jiāo wǒmên. Wǒmên yīnggāi huì yòng zìdiǎn.

(a₃) 你 有 沒 有 字典?
Nǐ yǒu méi yǒu zìdiǎn?

(b₃) 沒 有 我 一定 要 买 一本. 我 学習 中文, 应該 有 字典.
Méi yǒu, wǒ yídìng yào mǎi yìběn. Wǒ xuéxí zhōngwén, yīnggāi yǒu zìdiǎn.

(a₄) 你們 学習 中文, 只 要 会 說 話、会 看 書 嗎?
Nǐmên xuéxí zhōngwén, zhǐ yào huì shuō huà、huì kàn shū mâ?

(b₄) 不, 我們 应該 能 听、能 說、能 念、能 写.
Bù, wǒmên yīnggāi néng tīng、néng shuō、néng niàn、néng xiě.

(a₅) 你們 也 会 写 汉字 嗎?
Nǐmên yě huì xiě hànzì mâ?

(b₅) 对 了, 我們 会 写 一些. 我們
Duì lê, wǒmên huì xiě yìxiē. Wǒmên

写得　慢，写得　不　好看.
xiědė　màn,　xiědė　bù　hǎokàn.

(a₆) 沒　关系，你們　常常　練習，一定
Méi　guānxỉ,　nǐmėn　chángcháng　liànxí,　yídìng
能　写得　很　好. 你們　觉得
néng　xiědė　hěn　hǎo.　Nǐmėn　juédė
怎么样？　很　忙　嗎？
zěnmȯyàng?　Hěn　máng　mȧ?

(b₆) 我們　觉得　很　忙. 我們　一年
Wǒmėn　juédė　hěn　máng.　Wǒmėn　yìnián
要　学習　很　多　东西，我們　应
yào　xuéxí　hěn　duō　dōngxỉ,　wǒmėn　yīng-
該　很　忙.
gāi　hěn　máng.

四、課外練習　Kèwài liànxí　Home Work

1. 用下边的詞各作一个問句，以后再回答:
1) Write questions with each of the following words, and after that answer them:

(1) 能　(2) 会
(3) 要　(4) 应該

2. 給下边的汉字注上拼音，并比較每組發音的同異:
2) Transcribe the following Chinese characters, and compare the different pronunciation of each group:

(5) 以　意
(6) 詞　字
(7) 看　干
(8) 知　只　枝　誌　紙　志

五、汉字表 Hànzì biǎo Chinese Characters

1	能	厶		
		月		
		匕（乚 匕）		
		匕		
2	要	覀		
		女		
3	应	广 广 广 庐 应		
4	該	言		
		亥		
5	用	丿 冂 月 冃 用		
6	典	丶 冂 冃 由 曲 曲 典		
7	認	言		
		忍	刃（刀 刃）	
			心	
8	識	言		
		戠	音	立
				日
			戈	

9	还	不
		辶
10	以	ㇾ ㇾ 以 以
11	买	乛 ⺈ ⺈ ⺈ 买 买
12	听	口
		斤
13	关	
14	系	丿 ⼛ 幺 幺 系
15	觉	⺍
		見
16	东	一 ⼬ 车 东 东
17	西	

第二十七課 Lesson 27

一、生詞 Shēngcí New Words

1.	上(星期)	(形)	shàng (xīngqī)	last (week)
2.	下(星期)	(形)	xià (xīngqī)	next (week)
3.	了	(尾、助)	lē	(a suffix)
4.	从前	(副)	cóngqián	in the past, formerly
5.	明天	(名)	míngtiān	tomorrow
6.	昨天	(名)	zuótiān	yesterday
7.	回	(动)	huí	to go back, to return
8.	句子	(名)	jùzi	sentence
9.	就	(副)	jiù	then, at once,
10.	呢	(助)	nē	(a particle)
11.	講	(动)	jiǎng	to explain, to give a lecture on, to tell

12.	清楚	(形)	qīngchǔ	clear
13.	复習	(动)	fùxí	to review
14.	詞彙	(名)	cíhuì	vocabulary
15.	語法	(名)	yǔfǎ	grammar
16.	进	(动)	jìn	to enter
17.	城	(名)	chéng	city, town

二、語法 Yǔfǎ Grammar

27.1 完成貌　汉語里一个动作的时間是"过去""現在""未来"，主要地是由时間詞語来表示的．例如：

27.1 The Perfective Aspect　In Chinese, the time of an action, whether it is of the past, present or future, is expressed mainly by a word or word group of time. e. g.

1. 我們 上星期六 看 电影，你們
Wǒmen shàngxīngqīliù kàn diànyǐng, nǐmen
下星期六 看 电影．
xiàxīngqīliù kàn diànyǐng.

动作时間是由时間状語"上星期六""下星期六"来表示的，从动詞"看"的本身，看不出什么时間的形态变化．

The time of action is indicated by the adverbial modifiers of time 上星期六 and 下星期六. The verb 看 has nothing in its morphology to express the time.

但是，汉語里一个动作的情貌是很重要的，动作有开始、进行、持續和完成各种阶段，因此动詞也有各种情貌．今天我們先談完成貌．在汉語里情貌是用詞尾来表現的，而"了"这个詞尾就是表示完成貌的．当我們要强調动作已經完成的时候，动詞的后边就用詞尾"了"．例如：

But in Chinese, the aspect of an action is very important. An action may be in its starting, progressive, continuous or completed state, and a verb may have various kinds of aspects accordingly. In today's lesson, we will discuss only the perfective aspect. In Chinese, aspects are shown by suffixes and the suffix 了 is used to indicate the aspect of a completed action. When we wish to stress the completion of an action, we use the suffix 了 after the verb. e. g.

2. 他 来 了.
Tā lái lẻ.

3. 我們 懂 了.
Wǒmẻn dǒng lẻ.

关于完成貌有两点值得注意:

There are two points to be noticed with regard to the perfective aspect:

(一) 对过去的动作来說，只有特别强調完成情貌的时候，才用詞尾"了". 一般过去时間的动作并不都要用詞尾"了". 例如:

(1) The suffix 了 does not indicate past time. Even if the time of an action is in the past, we do not use the suffix 了, unless we want to emphasize the completion of the action. e. g.

4. 他 一九五四年 在 这兒 工作.
Tā yījiǔwǔsìnián zài zhèr gōngzuò.

5. 从前 他 常常 来.
Cóngqián tā chángcháng lái.

(二) "了" 也强調未来时間动作的完成貌. 例如:

(2) The suffix 了 may also be used to stress the completion of an action in the future. e. g.

6. 明天 你們 来了, 我們 一起 跳 舞.
Míngtiản nǐmẻn láilẻ, wǒmẻn yìqǐ tiào wǔ.

这种的完成貌一般用在表示順序的句子里: 第一个动作完成了，再进行第二个动作.

This kind of perfective aspect is generally used to show the order of actions in a sentence, for the second action only happens after the completion of the first one.

27.2 "了"和宾語　　在有宾語的句子里，用"了"时要注意三点：

27.2 了 and the Object　When we use the suffix 了 in a sentence in which there is an object, the following three points have to be observed:

(一) 詞尾"了"一般地用在动詞之后、宾語之前，特别是宾語带定語的时候．例如：

(1) 了 is generally used after the verb and before the object, especially when the object is modified by an adjective modifier. e. g.

7. 我 昨天 买了 一本 画报.
Wǒ zuótiån mǎilê yìběn huàbào.

8. 星期日 我 看了 那本 杂誌.
Xīngqīrì wǒ kànlê nèiběn zázhì.

△(二) 在簡單的句子里，除了动詞后面用詞尾"了"之外，宾語后边还用表示肯定的語气助詞"了"．例如：

(2) In a simple sentence, the suffix 了 is used after the verb, and the modal particle 了 is used after the object. e. g.

9. 昨天 我 作(了) 練習 了.
Zuótiån wǒ zuò(lê) liànxí lê.

10. 他 回(了) 宿舍 了.
Tā huí(lê) sùshè lê.

这时詞尾"了"可以省去，而助詞"了"便有表示完成的語气．但在宾語带数量詞的时候，要注意"了"的应用：当我們只用詞尾"了"时，表明这类动作已結束；詞尾"了"与語气助詞"了"都用的时候，就表示这类动作还在或还要繼續进行．例如：

In such sentences, the suffix 了 may be omitted, the particle 了 then takes on the meaning of completion. But notice the use of 了, when the object is preceded by a numeral and a measure word. When there is only the suffix 了, we mean that the action is already concluded; when both the suffix 了 and the particle 了 are used at the same time, we mean that the action is still in progression or is being continued. e. g.

11. 我 昨天 作了 八个 句子.
Wǒ zuótiȃn zuòlȇ bágȇ jùzȋ.

12. 我 作了 八个 句子 了, 現在
Wǒ zuòlȇ bágȇ jùzȋ lȇ, xiànzài
要 作 下边兒的.
yào zuò xiàbiȃnrdȇ.

(三) 如果句子宾語簡單, 动詞帶詞尾"了"而宾語后边沒有語气助詞"了", 就覺得語气未完; 这时就要求其他成分来构成一个完整的句子. 例如:

(3) If there is only the suffix 了 after the verb and no particle 了 after a simple object, the sentence is not complete and must be completed by adding other elements. e. g.

13. 我 作了 練習 就 去.
Wǒ zuòlȇ liànxí jiù qù.

14. 他 学了 中文 就 能 看 中文 書.
Tā xuélȇ zhōngwén jiù néng kàn zhōngwén shū.

我們在这里常用表示順序或因果关系的副詞"就".
Here the adverb 就 is always used to express successive actions or the relation of cause and effect.

27.3 完成貌的否定 如果表示一个动作未开始或未进行, 就在动詞的前边加"沒有". 例如:

27.3 The Negative Form of the Perfective Aspect When we wish to express an action that did not take place, we have only to add 沒有 before the verb. e. g.

15. 昨天 他 没（有）来.

Zuótiån tā méi yǒu lái.

16. 星期六 我 没（有）去 圖書館.

Xīngqīliù wǒ méi (yǒu) qù túshūguǎn.

要注意：否定的完成貌"没有"和肯定的詞尾"了"是互相排斥的．我們一定不能說："昨天他没(有)来了"或者"星期六我没(有)去了圖書館".

We have to pay attention to the fact that the affirmative suffix 了 can never be used simultaneously with 没有, which is the negative form of the perfective aspect. Therefore, we must not say: 昨天他没(有)来了 or 星期六我没(有)去了圖書館.

如果动作虽未完成，但是即将完成，就用"还没(有)…呢"，这里"呢"是一个語气助詞．例如：

If an action is not yet completed, and is to be completed very soon, we use the construction 还没(有)…呢 (not yet...), the 呢 here is a modal particle. e. g.

17. 我 今天 还 没（有）看 报 呢!

Wǒ jīntiån hái méi (yǒu) kàn bào nê!

"没有"在动詞前边永远可以省为"没"，但是它独立回答一个問題的时候，就必須是"没有"．例如：

没有 may be always shortened as 没, whenever it is used before a verb, but when 没有 is used independently to answer a question, it should never be shortened. e. g.

18. 先生 来 了 嗎?

Xiānshêng lái lê må?

19. 没 有.

Méi yǒu.

20. 没 来.

Méi lái.

21. 还 没（有）来 呢!

Hái méi (yǒu) lái nê!

27.4 完成貌的选擇式疑問句　用选擇式提問的时候，用"……了(賓語) 沒有"这个方式. 例如:

27.4 The Alternative Interrogative Sentence of the Perfective Aspect If we wish to ask a question using the alternative interrogative sentence, we have only to use this sentence pattern ……了 (object) 沒有. e. g.

22. 报 来 了 沒 有?
Bào lái lê méi yǒu?

23. 你 作了 練習 沒 有?
Nǐ zuòlê liànxí méi yǒu?

这里的"沒有"也不能省为"沒".
Here 沒有 cannot be shortened as 沒 either.

三、課文 Kèwén Text

I

(a₁) 今天的 練習 有 八个 句子, 你 作了 几个 了?
Jīntiândê liànxí yǒu bágê jùzǐ, nǐ zuòlê jǐgê lê?

(b₁) 作了 四个 了.
Zuòlê sìgê lê.

(a₂) 你 会 作 后边兒的 那 四个 嗎?
Nǐ huì zuò hòubiânrdê nèi sìgê mâ?

(b₂) 先生 講得 很 清楚, 我 都 懂 了, 我 会 作.
Xiānshêng jiǎngdê hěn qīngchû, wǒ dōu dǒng lê, wǒ huì zuò.

(a₃) 你 复習了 从前的 詞彙 沒 有?
Nǐ fùxílê cóngqiándê cíhuì méi yǒu?

(b_3) 还 沒 有 复習 呢! 我 明天 复習.
Hái méi yȯu fùxí nė! Wǒ míngtiȧn fùxí.

(a_4) 复習了 詞彙, 你 作 什么?
Fùxílė cíhuì, nǐ zuò shénmȯ?

(b_4) 复習了 詞彙, 我 就 复習 語法.
Fùxílė cíhuì, wǒ jiù fùxí yǔfǎ.

(a_5) 复習了 詞彙 和 語法, 你 还 要 作
Fùxílė cíhuì hé yǔfǎ, nǐ hái yào zuò
什么?
shénmȯ?

(b_5) 复習了 詞彙 和 語法, 我 就 練習
Fùxílė cíhuì hé yǔfǎ, wǒ jiù liànxí
汉字.
hànzì.

II

(a_6) 上星期六 你 作 什么 了?
Shàngxīngqīliù nǐ zuò shénmȯ lė?

(b_6) 我 进 城 了.
Wǒ jìn chéng lė.

(a_7) 你 在 城里 看了 电影 沒 有?
Nǐ zài chénglǐ kànlė diànyǐng méi yȯu?

(b_7) 沒 有, 我 买 东西 了.
Méi yȯu, wǒ mǎi dōngxi lė.

(a_8) 你 买 什么 东西 了?
Nǐ mǎi shénmȯ dōngxi lė?

(b_8) 我 买了 一本 字典 和 很 多 杂誌.
Wǒ mǎilė yìběn zìdiǎn hé hěn duō zázhì.

(a_9) 你 沒 (有) 买 書 嗎?
Nǐ méi (yȯu) mǎi shū mȧ?

(b₉) 沒　有.
Méi　yǒu.

四、課外練習　Kèwài liànxí　Home Work

1. 把下边的句子用汉字写出來，并在完成貌詞尾“了”下面画一横綫:
1) Re-write the following sentences using Chinese characters and underline the suffix 了:
   (1) Zhèigê yuèdê “Rénmín Huàbào” lái lê.
   (2) Wǒ zuòlê liànxí jiù gēn nǐ chàng gēr.
   (3) Tā xīngqīrì méi yǒu jìn chéng, zài xuéxiào fùxí yǔfǎ lê.
2. 用否定式回答下边的問題:
2) Answer the following questions in the negative:
   (4) 你　同屋　回　宿舍　了　沒　有?
   (5) 先生　講　这些　句子　了　嗎?
   (6) 他　用了　这本　字典　沒　有?
3. 完成下边的句子:
3) Complete the following sentences:
   (7) 听了　唱　歌兒……………………………
   (8) 我　进了　圖書館……………………………

五、汉字表　Hànzì biǎo　Chinese Characters

1	明	日
		月
2	昨	日
		乍
3	回	丨　冂　冋　回
4	句	丿　勹　句

5	就	京	
		尤(一ナ九尤)	
6	呢		
7	講	言	
		冓(一 = キ 井 井 冉 冓 冓)	
8	清	氵	
		青	
9	楚	林	木
			木
		疋(乛 丆 下 正 疋)	
10	复	丿 𠂉 亠 复 复	
11	詞	言	
		司(𠃌 𠃍 司)	
12	彙	夕 夕 彑 彖 彙	
13	語	言	
		吾	五
			口
14	法	氵	
		去	

15	进	
16	城	土
		成（厂 万 成 成 成）

第二十八課 Lesson 28

一、生詞 Shēngcí New Words

1.	开始	(动)	kāishǐ	to start, to begin
2.	住	(动)	zhù	to live, to dwell
3.	上(課)	(动)	shàng(kè)	to go to class, to attend class
4.	字	(名)	zì	character
5.	…的时候兒		…dèshíhòur	when…, at the time of
6.	下(課)	(动)	xià(kè)	the class is over, after class
7.	从…起		cóng…qǐ	since…, from the time of
8.	上(月)	(形)	shàng(yuè)	last month, ultimo
9.	从…到…		cóng…dào…	from…to…
10.	已經	(副)	yǐjīng	already
11.	节	(量)	jié	(a measure word)
12.	課	(名)	kè	lesson, class
13.	翻譯	(动、名)	fānyì	to translate, translation
14.	特别	(形)	tèbié	special, particular
15.	帮助	(动)	bāngzhù	to help

16. 教室 (名) jiàoshì classroom

17. 休息 (动) xiūxì rest, to take a rest

二、語法 Yǔfǎ Grammar

28.1 結构助詞"的"(二) 我們已經学过: 当名詞、代詞或形容詞构成定語的时候, 常常需要用結构助詞 "的" 把定語和中心語联系起來 (15.1). 現在我們要考察一下动詞、动詞結构或主謂結构所形成的定語. 首先, 我們看动詞作定語. 例如:

28.1 The Structural Particle 的 (2) We have already learned that when a noun, pronoun or adjective is used to make up an adjective modifier, it is necessary to use the structural particle 的 to join the adjective modifier and the central word together (15.1). Here we shall discuss those adjective modifiers that are made up of verbs, verbal constructions, or subject-predicate constructions (clauses) First of all, let us see how a verb becomes an adjective modifier. e. g.

1. 这本 字典 很 好, 买 的 人 很 多.
Zhèiběn zìdiǎn hěn hǎo, mǎi dê rén hěn duō.

"买" 就是簡單动詞作定語, 再看动詞結构作定語. 例如:

The word 买 in the above example is a simple verb used as adjective modifier. Now let us see how verbal constructions become adjective modifiers. e. g.

2. 上星期 来 的 学生 开始 学習 了.
Shàngxīngqī lái dê xuéshêng kāishǐ xuéxí lê.

3. 他 是 从 城里 来 的 那个 同志.
Tā shì cóng chénglǐ lái dê nèigê tóngzhì.

4. 来得 早 的 人 都 在 前边兒.
Láidê zǎo dê rén dōu zài qiánbiānr.

5. 她 是 教 語法 的 先生.
Tā shì jiāo yǔfǎ dê xiānshêng.

"上星期来" 是动詞带状語作定語, "从城里来" 也是动詞带状語

(介詞結构）作定語．“来得早”是动补結构作定語，“教語法”是动宾結构作定語．虽然每个定語里都有其他成分，但其中动詞是主要的，所以都是动詞結构作定語．

Here, 上星期来 is an adj. modifier composed of a verb and its adverbial modifier, 从城里来 is an adjective modifier composed of a verb and a prepositional construction (phrase) modifying the verb, 来得早 is an adj. modifier composed of a verb and its complement, and 教語法 is an adj. modifier composed of a verb and its object. Although all the above adj. modifiers are composed of different constructions, yet, the one common feature is that in each of them the verb is used as the main element. Therefore, they are all verbal constructions used as adj. modifiers.

最后，主謂結构所形成的定語，又有两类：

Last of all, let us see how subject-predicate constructions become adj. modifiers. Such modifiers may be divided into two kinds:

（一）結构中的謂語是以形容詞为主要成分的．例如：

(1) The construction in which the predicate is composed mainly of an adjective. e. g.

6. 中文 不 好 的 人 不 会 用 这本 字典.
Zhōngwén bù hǎo dė rén bú huì yòng zhèiběn zìdiǎn.

7. 他 是 一个 工作 积極的 同志.
Tā shì yígė gōngzuò jījídė tóngzhì.

“中文不好”“工作积極”都是主謂結构作定語，而其中形容詞“好”和“积極”就是这两个結构里的謂語．

中文不好 and 工作积極 are subject-predicate constructions used as adjective modifiers and the adjectives 好 and 积極 are predicates.

（二）結构中的謂語是以动詞为主要成分的．例如：

(2) The construction in which the predicate is composed mainly of a verb. e. g.

8. 我 喜欢 他 买 的 那本 書.
Wǒ xǐhuȧn tā mǎi dė nèiběn shū.

9. 他們 复習 先生 講 的 語法.
Tāmėn fùxí xiānshėng jiǎng dė yǔfǎ.

“他买”“先生講”都是主謂結构作定語，而其中动詞“买”和“講”就是这两个結构里的謂語. 应当注意的是这种結构不能独立作完整的句子.

他买 and 先生講 are all subject-predicate constructions used as adjective modifiers, and the verbs 买 and 講 are predicates. Notice: such constructions cannot be used independently as complete sentences.

另外还有一种作定語的主謂結构，本身的意思完整（其中的动詞或者有宾語或者沒有宾語），独立存在的时候，就是完整的句子. 例如:

Besides, there is another kind of subject-predicate construction that is complete in meaning by itself, where the verb may or may not carry an object. It is a complete sentence by itself. e. g.

10. 他 住 的 那个 宿舍 在 工厂 外边兒.
Tā zhù dė nèigė sùshè zài gōngchǎng wàibiȧnr.

11. 哪兒 是 他們 上 課 的 地方?
Nǎr shì tāmėn shàng kè dė dìfȧng?

所有上述的定語和中心語之間都需用結构助詞“的”，不能省略.
In all the above sentences, the structural particle 的 has to be inserted between the adjective modifiers and the central words.

当語言环境已經把中心語表示明白的时候，上述所有定語后边的中心語都可以省略. 例如:

When the central words are clearly understood from the context, all the above central words modified by adjective modifiers can be omitted. e. g.

12. 他們 都 在 那兒: 説 話 的 是
Tāmėn dōu zài nàr: shuō huà dė shì
先生, 写 字 的 是 学生.
xiānshėng, xiě zì dė shì xuéshėng.

13. 我 給 他 的 是 一本 書.
Wǒ gěi tå dė shì yìběn shū.

例 12 省略了“人”, 例 13 省略了“东西”.

In example 12, 人 has been omitted and in example 13 东西 has been omitted.

28.2 “…的时候兒” 这是一个常用的結构, 意思相当於英語里的 when 或者 at the time of. 一般用在單詞或較复杂的結构后面, 起状語作用. 例如:

28.2 ……的时候 This is a very common construction eqivalent to the English "when" or "at the time of…". In general, it is placed after a word or a complicated construction used as adverbial modifier. e. g.

14. 工作 的 时候兒, 他 一定 好好兒地
Gōngzuò dė shíhȯur, tā yídìng hǎohāordė
工作.
gōngzuò.

15. 作 練習 的 时候兒, 他 写 汉字
Zuò liànxí dė shíhȯur, tā xiě hànzì
写得 很 清楚.
xiědė hěn qīngchů.

16. 我 回 宿舍 的 时候兒, 他 还
Wǒ huí sùshè dė shíhȯur, tā hái
沒 下 課 呢!
méi xià kè nė!

28.3 “从…起” 这也是一个常常用作时間状語的結构. 例如:

28.3 从……起 It is also a common construction used as adverbial modifier of time. e. g.

17. 他們 从 上月 起 学習 中文.
Tāmen cóng shàngyuè qǐ xuéxí zhōngwén.

18. 我們 从 学習 語法 起, 作了 很 多 練習 了.
Wǒmen cóng xuéxí yǔfǎ qǐ, zuòle hěn duō liànxí le.

19. 从 我 認識 他 起, 我們 常常 一起 学習.
Cóng wǒ rènshi tā qǐ, wǒmen chángcháng yìqǐ xuéxí.

由以上几个例句我們可以知道單詞和比較复杂的結构都可以用在这种結构里.

From the above examples, we see that we may either insert a word or a complicated construction into this construction.

28.4 "从…到…" 这也是一个常常用作时間状語的結构. 例如:

28.4 从……到 This is also a common construction used as adverbial modifier of time. e. g.

20. 我們 从 七点半 到 十点半 学習.
Wǒmen cóng qīdiǎnbàn dào shídiǎnbàn xuéxi.

21. 他 从 一九五二年 到 一九五五年 在 北京 大学 工作.
Tā cóng yījiǔwǔèrnián dào yījiǔwǔwǔnián zài Běijīng Dàxué gōngzuò.

有时候, 也作表示范圍的定語. 例如:

But, it may also be used as adjective modifier indicating limit or scope. e. g.

22. 星期六 我們 复習 从 星期一 到 星期五 的 語法.
Xīngqīliù wǒmen fùxí cóng xīngqīyī dào xīngqīwǔ de yǔfǎ.

三、課文 Kèwén Text

I

上星期 很 忙，我 还 沒 有 看
Shàngxīngqī hěn máng, wǒ hái méi yǒu kàn

你 給 我 的 那本 杂誌 呢！你 給
nǐ gěi wǒ dė nèiběn zázhì nė! Nǐ gěi

我 的 那本 画报 很 有意思. 不 会 中文
wǒ dė nèiběn huàbào hěn yǒuyìsi. Bú huì zhōngwén

的 人 也 能 看 那本 画报.
dė rén yě néng kàn nèiběn huàbào.

II

他們 从 上星期 起，已經 开始 学
Tāmėn cóng shàngxīngqī qǐ, yǐjīng kāishǐ xué-

習 了. 从 八点（过）五分 到 十一点
xí lė. Cóng bādiǎn (guò) wǔfēn dào shíyīdiǎn

四十分，他們 有 四节 課. 上 課 的
sìshífēn, tāmėn yǒu sìjié kè. Shàng kè dė

时候兒，先生 說 中文 說得 很 慢、很
shíhȯur, xiānshėng shuō zhōngwén shuōdė hěn màn、hěn

清楚，他們 都 能 懂 先生 說 的 話.
qīngchǔ, tāmėn dōu néng dǒng xiānshėng shuō dė huà.

复習 的 时候兒，作 翻譯 工作 的 同志
Fùxí dė shíhȯur, zuò fānyì gōngzuò dė tóngzhì

还 特別 帮助 他們.
hái tèbié bāngzhů tāmėn.

III

从 苏联 来 的 学生 都 在 这个
Cóng Sūlián lái dė xuéshėng dōu zài zhèigė

宿舍里 住. 他們 上 課 的 教室 在
sùshèli zhù. Tāmėn shàng kè dė jiàoshì zài

宿舍 旁边兒. 下 課 的 时候兒, 他們
sùshè pángbiānr. Xià kè dė shíhȯur, tāmėn

都 在 教室 外边兒 休息. 休息 的
dōu zài jiàoshi̇ wàibiȧnr xiūxi̇. Xiūxi̇ dė

时候兒, 先生 看 画报, 学生 唱 歌兒.
shíhȯur, xiānshėng kàn huàbào, xuéshėng chàng gēr.

先生 都 喜欢 看 "人民 画报", 学生
Xiānshėng dōu xǐhuȧn kàn "Rénmín Huàbào", xuéshėng

都 喜欢 唱 張 同志 教 他們 的
dōu xǐhuȧn chàng Zhāng tóngzhì jiāo tāmėn dė

中文 歌兒.
zhōngwén gēr.

四、課外練習 Kèwài liànxí Home Work

1. 把下面的句子譯成中文:

1) Translate the following sentences into Chinese:

(1) Those who want to see the film have already gone to the city.

(2) The newspaper he is now reading (literally to see) is yesterday's.

(3) Students who are good in English may read the English magazines.

(4) The place where we are resting is beside the auditorium.

2. 抄写下面的句子, 并塡进"得"或"的"去:

2) Copy the following sentences and fill the blanks with either 得 or 的:

(5) 教 你____那个 先生 教____特別 好.

(6) 学習____多 的 学生 应該 帮助 学習得 少____学生.

(7) 我 同屋 买____东西 都 在 桌子上.

(8) 我 写 从前 学____詞彙, 写____快; 我 写 今天 学____詞彙, 写____慢.

五、汉字表　Hànzì biǎo　Chinese Characters

1	开	二 于 开	
2	始	女	
		台	厶
			口
3	住	亻	
		主（丶 亠 亠 丰 主）	
4	課	言	
		果（曰 旦 果）	
5	到	至	
		刂	
6	已	乛 コ 已	
7	經	糸	
		巠（一 く 巛 巛 巠）	
8	节	艹	
		卩（㇆ 卩）	

9	翻	番	釆（丿 ⺈ 䒑 平 乎 釆）
			田
		羽	
10	譯	言	
		睪	罒
			幸（土 圥 去 坴 幸）
11	特	牜（丿 𠂉 𠂒 牜）	
		寺	土
			寸
12	别	另	口
			力
		刂	
13	帮	邦（一 二 三 丰 邦）	
		巾	
14	助	且（丨 冂 冃 月 且）	
		力	
15	室	宀	
		至	
16	休	亻	
		木	

17	息	自（丿 自）
		心

第二十九課　Lesson 29

29.1	宾語提前 The Inversion of Object
29.2	疑問句 (四) The Interrogative Sentence (4)
29.3	"每" The Pronoun 每

一、生詞 Shēngcí New Words

1.	还是	(連)	háishì	or
2.	每	(代)	měi	each, every
3.	生詞	(名)	shēngcí	new word
4.	小説兒	(名)	xiǎoshuōr [本]	novel
5.	借	(动)	jiè	to lend, to borrow
6.	想	(动、能动)	xiǎng	to think, to want, to intend
7.	还	(动)	huán	to return, to give back
8.	可以	(能动)	kěyǐ	may
9.	謝謝		xièxiè	to thank, thanks
10.	問	(动)	wèn	to ask, to inquire
11.	問題	(名)	wèntí	question, problem
12.	必須	(能动)	bìxū	must, have to
13.	回答	(动、名)	huídá	to answer, to reply
14.	对	(形)	duì	right, correct
15.	告訴	(动)	gàosù	to tell, to inform
16.	方法	(名)	fāngfǎ	way, method

二、語法 Yǔfǎ Grammar

29.1 宾語提前 我們已經知道汉語里一般动詞謂語句的詞序是:

(定語)主語——(状語)动詞——(定語)宾語

29.1 The Inversion of Object We know already that in Chinese the general word order of the sentence with a verbal predicate is:

(Adj. modifier) Subject — (Adverbial modifier) Verb — (Adj. modifier) Object

但在一定的情况下，宾語也可以提到主語之前．現在介紹最常見的两种:

But the object can be put before the subject under certain conditions. Here we shall introduce two kinds of sentences with inverted object:

(一) 在謂語比較复杂(包括較長的宾語)的句子里，宾語提前可以使句子的結构紧凑、意思清楚．例如:

(1) In a sentence in which the predicate is comparatively complicated (or when the object consists of several words), the sentence becomes more compact and clearer in meaning, if the object is transposed to the beginning of the sentence. e. g.

1. 中文 書 我 朋友 看得 很 快.
Zhōngwén shū wǒ péngyǒu kàndê hěn kuài.

2. 先生 説 的 話 我 听得 很 清楚.
Xiānshêng shuō dê huà wǒ tīngdê hěn qīngchǔ.

以上两句都有程度补語．如果不提前宾語，我們就需要重复动詞(如"我朋友看中文書，看得很快"和"我听先生說的話，听得很清楚")；为了語言的簡潔，我們常是把宾語提前的.

In each of the above two sentences, there is a complement of degree. If the objects are not transposed, the verbs have to be reduplicated. (e. g. 我朋友看中文書，看得很快 and 我听

先生的話，听得很清楚). For the sake of compactness, the object is always put at the beginning of a sentence.

这种句子的宾語如果是复数，我們常在謂語前边用副詞“都”．例如:

When the object is a compound object or in the plural form, the adverb 都 has to be used before the predicate. e. g.

3. 練習里的 汉字 他 都 写得 很 好看.
Liànxílidê hànzì tā dōu xiědê hěn hǎokàn.

4. 我 买 的 杂誌 你 都 能 看.
Wǒ mǎi dê zázhì nǐ dōu néng kàn.

(二) 提前宾語可以使宾語突出. 例如:

(2) In order to stress the object in a sentence, we can transpose the object to the beginning of a sentence. e. g.

5. 这个 月的 人民 画报 我 已經 看 了.
Zhèigê yuèdê Rénmín Huàbào wǒ yǐjìng kàn lê.

6. 那个 新 同志的 名字 我 不 知道.
Nèigê xīn tóngzhìdê míngzì wǒ bù zhīdào.

并列結构的句子常要突出宾語，就常把宾語提前. 例如:

The parallel elements in a sentence are always stressed. If they happen to be two objects, we may transpose them to the beginning of the sentence. e. g.

7. 新 杂誌 我 买, 旧 杂誌 我 不 买.
Xīn zázhì wǒ mǎi, jiù zázhì wǒ bù mǎi.

8. 昨天的 語法 他 懂, 今天的 (語法)
Zuótiāndê yǔfǎ tā dǒng, jīntiāndê (yǔfǎ)

他 也 懂.
tā yě dǒng.

并列結构之間的关系可以是对比的（如例 7），也可以是順說的（如例 8）；順說的时候常用副詞"也"．如果不用順說的并列結构，也可以用复合宾語．例如：

The parallel elements are joined together sometimes for contrast (as in example 7) and sometimes according to the sequence of time (as in example 8). In the latter case, the adverb 也 is always used. But a compound object may be used instead of the parallel construction, if it is kind that is based on the sequence of time. e. g.

9. 昨天的 語法 和 今天的 語法 他 都 懂.
Zuótiāndė yǔfǎ hé jīntiāndė yǔfǎ tā dōu dǒng.

这时候在謂語的前边要用副詞"都"．

Note: When the compound object is transposed to the beginning of the sentence, the adverb 都 has to be added before the predicate.

29.2 疑問句（四） 第四种提問的方法是把答案的两种可能并列出来而用"(还是)…还是…"这个結构来联系．这里要注意"还是"的位置，它是放在要問的成分之前的．例如：

29.2 The Interrogative Sentence (4) The fourth kind of the interrogative sentence contains two alternative questions represented by the construction (compound conjunction) (还是)…还是….. The construction 还是…还是 should be placed before the elements concerning which the questions are asked. e. g.

10. (还是) 你 来, 还是 她 来?
(Hái shì) nǐ lái, háishì tā lái?

11. 你 (还是) 来, 还是 不 来?
Nǐ (háishì) lái, háishì bù lái?

例 10 里我們要知道"誰来"，就把"还是"用在主語之前，例 11 里我們要知道"你来不来"，就把"还是"放在謂語之前．

In example 10, we wish to know "who is coming", putting 还是 before the subject of each clause; in example 11, we wish to know whether "you will come or not", with 还是 before the compound predicate.

29.3 "每" "每"的意思是包括整个范圍里的一切个体. 用这个詞的时候, 有两点要注意:

29.3 每 includes all the individual members or elements of a group of persons or things. Two points should be noticed in using the word 每:

(一) 它是指示代詞, 不能和名詞直接联系, 当中要求一个量詞. 例如:

(1) It is a demonstrative pronoun and cannot be directly used with a noun. There should be a measure word. e. g.

12. 每个 学生 都 很 努力 学習.
Méigè xuéshêng dōu hěn nǔlì xuéxí.

13. 每張 桌子 都 很 干淨.
Měizhāng zhuōzi dōu hěn gānjìng.

但是, 有些名詞本身具有量詞性質, 与"每"連用的时候就不用量詞. 例如:

However, some nouns have the function of measure words, so they can be directly used with the word 每. e. g.

14. 我們 每天 八点 过 五分 上 課.
Wǒmen měitiān bādiǎn guò wǔfēn shàng kè.

15. 每課 有 十五个 生詞.
Měikè yǒu shíwǔgè shēngcí.

(二) 当"每"作主語的定語的时候, 謂語經常要用状語"都". 例如:

(2) When the word 每 is used as adjective modifier of the subject, the adverb 都 is always placed before the predicate. e. g.

16. 每个 学生 都 作了 練習 了.
Měigê xuéshêng dōu zuòlê liànxí lê.

17. 每(个) 人 都 应該 会 用 那 本 字典.
Měi(gê) rén dōu yīnggāi huì yòng nèi bén zìdiǎn.

但是，也可以不用“都”. 不用的时候，“每”的意思差不多就和“一”相当了. 例如:、

But 都 may also be omitted. When such is the case 每 takes on almost the same meaning as 一. e. g.

18. 每年 有 十二个 月.
Měinián yǒu shíèrgê yuè.

19. 每个 学生 应該 有 两个 本子.
Měigê xuéshêng yīnggāi yǒu liǎnggê bènzi.

三、課文 Kèwén Text

I

(a_1) 这 两本 小說兒 是 誰的? 是 你的, 还是 張 同志的?
Zhèi liǎngběn xiǎoshuōr shì shéidê? Shì nǐdê, háishi Zhāng tóngzhìdê?

(b_1) 这本 中文的 是 張 同志的, 那本 俄文的 是 我 在 圖書館 借 的.
Zhèiběn zhōngwéndê shì Zhāng tóngzhìdê, nèiběn èwéndê shì wǒ zài túshūguǎn jiè dê.

(a_2) 两本 你 都 看 了 嗎?
Liǎngběn nǐ dōu kàn lê mâ?

(b_2) 对 了, 两本 都 看 了.
Duì lê, liǎngběn dōu kàn lê.

(a_3) 哪本 好？ 还是 中文的 有意思，
Něiběn hǎo? Háishì zhōngwéndė yǒuyìsi,

还是 俄文的 有意思？
háishì èwéndė yǒuyìsi?

(b_3) 都 有意思. 我 都 喜欢.
Dōu yǒuyìsi. Wǒ dōu xǐhuån.

你 想 不 想 看？
Nǐ xiǎng bù xiǎng kàn?

(a_4) 俄文的 想 看，中文的 我 还
Èwéndė xiǎng kàn, zhōngwéndė wǒ hái

不 懂 呢！ 你 哪天 还 这本
bù dǒng nė! Nǐ něitiān huán zhèiběn

俄文的？
èwéndė?

(b_4) 下星期 还. 你 可以 在 这个
Xiàxīngqī huán. Nǐ kěyǐ zài zhèigė

星期里 看.
xīngqīlǐ kàn.

(a_5) 謝謝，我 看了 就 还 你.
Xièxiė, wǒ kànlė jiù huán nǐ.

II

(a_6) 你們 每天 上 几节 課？
Nǐmėn měitiān shàng jǐjié kè?

(b_6) 每天 四节.
Měitiān sìjié.

(a_7) 每天 都 上 四节 課 嗎？
Měitiān dōu shàng sìjié kè må?

(b_7) 对 了，我們 現在 每天 都 上
Duì lė, wǒmėn xiànzài měitiān dōu shàng

四节　课，星期六　也　上　四节　课.
sìjié　kè,　xīngqīliù　yě　shàng　sìjié　kè.

(a_8) 上　課　的　时候兒，先生　問　你们　問題　嗎？
Shàng　kè　dȩ　shíhȯur,　xiānshȩng　wèn　nǐmȩn　wèntí　mȧ?

(b_8) 問，他　每天　都　問.
Wèn,　tā　měitiān　dōu　wèn.

(a_9) 每个　学生　他　都　問　嗎？
Měigȩ　xuéshȩng　tā　dōu　wèn　mȧ?

(b_9) 每个　学生　他　都　問．每人　都　必須　回答.
Měigȩ　xuéshȩng　tā　dōu　wèn.　Měirén　dōu　bìxū　huídá.

(a_{10}) 先生的　問題　你們　都　回答得　对　嗎？
Xiānshȩngdȩ　wèntí　nǐmȩn　dōu　huídádȩ　duì　mȧ?

(b_{10}) 回答得　不　对　的　时候兒，先生　就　告訴　我們．这　是　練習　的　好　方法.
Huídádȩ　bú　duì　dȩ　shíhȯur,　xiānshȩng　jiù　gàosȗ　wǒmȩn.　Zhèi　shì　liànxí　dȩ　hǎo　fāngfǎ.

四、課外練習　Kèwài liànxí　Home Work

1．用“(还是)…还是…”改写下面的疑問句：

I) Re-write the following interrogative sentences with (还是)… 还是：

(1) 你 什么 时候兒（今天，明天） 还 他 这本 字典？

(2) 他 唱 的 是 什么（俄文的，中文的） 歌兒？

2. 用下边两組詞各作一个句子：

2) Make sentences with each of the following groups of words:

(3) 每 小説兒

(4) 每 年

3. 把下边的句子改成宾語提前的句子：

(3) Change the following into sentences with inverted objects:

(5) 我們 可以 借 圖書館的 杂誌，不 能 借 这个 月 来 的 新 杂誌．

(6) 他 回答 先生 問 的 两个 問題，回答得 特别 清楚

(7) 先生 已經 告訴 我們 复習 詞彙 的 方法 了，还 沒有 告訴 我們 复習 語法 的 方法 呢！

五、汉字表 Hànzì biǎo Chinese Characters

1	每	丿 𠂉 𠂉 ⺟ 每 每 每	
2	借	亻	
		昔(一 十 廾 龷 昔)	
3	想	相	木
			目
		心	
4	可		
5	謝	言	
		射	身(丿 亻 介 自 自 身 身)
			寸
6	問		
7	題		
8	必	丶 乚 心 必 必	
9	須	彡	
		頁	
10	答	⺮	
		合	

11	告	ノ ㇐ 牛 生 告
12	訴	言
		斥（斤 斥）

第三十課 Lesson 30

一、語法复習 Yǔfǎ fùxí Review

30.1 过去时和完成貌 时間和情貌是不同的．因为动詞形态不根据时間而根据情貌来变化是汉語的一个特点．这里再从过去时和完成貌的比較来明确一下这个問題．

30.1 The Past Tense and the Perfective Aspect Time and aspect are two different things. One of the characteristic features of the Chinese language is that the morphology of a verb is not determined by time but by aspect. Let us clarify this problem by making a comparison between the past tense and the perfective aspect.

在汉語里，时間一般是由时間状語来表示的，因此过去时間的动作也經常是用表示过去时間的詞語作状語来表示的．例如：

In Chinese, time is generally expressed by an adverbial modifier of time; so a past action is always shown by an adverbial modifier made up of a word or word group expressing some past time. e. g.

1. 我們 <u>从前</u> 常常 唱 中国 歌兒
   Wǒmên cóngqián chángcháng chàng Zhōngguó gēr.
2. <u>一九五六年</u> 他們 在 这个 工厂 工作.
   Yījiǔwǔliùnián tāmên zài zhèigê gōngchǎng gōngzuò.

"唱中国歌兒"和"工作"都是过去的动作，时間是由"从前""一九五六年"表示出来的，动詞本身沒有形态变化．这就是因为汉語里动詞不是根据时間变化的. 因此, 我們决不能因为这些动作是过去的就在动詞后边用"了".

唱中国歌兒 and 工作 are all past actions, the time of the actions being shown by the words 从前 and 1956 年. But the verbs themselves are not inflected. It is because verbs in Chinese do not change in form according to the change of time. Hence, we must never put the suffix 了 after verbs, when the actions are in the past.

汉語动詞的形态是根据动作所处的阶段而变化的, 动作有进行、持續、完成各种阶段, 而"了"就是表示"完成貌"的詞尾. 但是我們要注意: 汉語的情貌詞尾"了"只在强調一个动作处于完成阶段的时候才用. 一个动作虽然是在过去时間完成了, 但是在不要强調完成的时候, 也不用詞尾"了".

In Chinese, the inflection of a verb is determined by the different state of an action. An action may be in its progressive, continuous or complete state, and the word 了 is the suffix indicating the perfective aspect. But we must pay attention to the fact that the suffix 了 is used only when we wish to lay stress on the completion of an action. When we have no wish to emphasize the completion of an action in the past, there is no need to use this suffix.

30.2 完成貌动作的时間 上面談到动作的情貌只是就它所处的阶段而論的. 因此, 无論是过去时間或未来时間的动作都可以有不同的阶段, 有完成貌. 在我們学过的完成貌的句子里, 可以分为两类:

30.2 Time of Action of the Perfective Aspect As mentioned above, the aspect of an action is only determined by the state of the action. Therefore, whether the action is in the past or in the future, it may have different aspects. Sentences of the perfective aspect (we have already learned these) can be classified into two kinds:

(一) 句子里只叙述一个动作, 这个动作是过去时間的. 例如:

(1) When the sentence contains only one action in the past. e. g.

3. 昨天 我 看了 一本 小説兒.
Zuótiån wǒ kànlė yìběn xiǎoshuōr.

（二）句子里叙述两个动作，一般是第一个动作完成以后，再进行第二个动作的．这种句子又可以就时間而分为两类：

(2) When there are two actions in the sentence, in general, the second action takes place only after the completion of the first action. So far as time is concerned, such sentences may be subdivided into two kinds:

(1) 两个动作都發生在过去时間的． 例如：

a) Both actions take place in the past time. e. g.

4. 昨天 他 下了 課，很 快地 就
Zuótiån tā xiàlė kè, hěn kuàidė jiù

去 圖書館 了.
qù túshūguǎn lė.

(2) 两个动作都發生在未来时間的． 例如．

b) Both actions happen in the future. e. g.

5. 明天 我 下了 課，就 回 宿舍.
Míngtiån wǒ xiàlė kè, jiù huí sùshè.

因此，我們可以更明确以下两点：

We may arrive at the conclusion:

（一）在汉語里，动詞形态以情貌为依据，而情貌和时間根本是两回事——完成貌不等于过去时．

(1) In Chinese, the inflection of a verb shows aspect only; time and aspect are entirely two different things— the perfective aspect is not the same as the past tense.

（二）过去时間內有完成动作，未来时間內也有完成动作．当我們强調一个未来动作将在另一个动作完成之后进行的时候，这另一动作就要用完成貌来表示．

(2) There is perfective aspect in the past time as well as in the future. When we wish to emphasize one future action

happening after the completion of another one, the latter should be told by a verb of the perfective aspect.

30.3 "不"和"沒有" "不"和"沒有"都是表示否定的，而"沒有"只能用在动詞謂語句中.
下边就談一下动詞謂語句中的否定:

30.3 不 and 沒有 These two adverbs indicate negation, but 沒有 is only used in the sentence with a verbal predicate. Here we shall deal with the negative forms of the sentence with a verbal predicate:

(一) 用"不"来否定的:

(1) 不 is used under the following conditions:

(1) 經常性或習慣的动作，不論在什么时間，永远用"不"否定. 例如:

(a) All the customary or habitual actions, whatever the time may be, are negated by 不. e. g.

6. 从前 他 不 跳 舞.
Cóngqián tā bú tiào wǔ.

7. 我們 先生 不 說 俄文.
Wǒmen xiānsheng bù shuō èwén.

(2) 未来时間的动作用"不"否定. 例如:

(b) 不 is used to negate all future actions. e. g.

8. 星期日 我們 休息, 不 工作.
Xīngqīrì wǒmen xiūxi, bù gōngzuò.

9. 下星期 他 不 进 城.
Xiàxīngqī tā bú jìn chéng.

只有在特別强調动作沒有完成的时候，才用"沒有". 例如:

Only when we wish to stress an action that is not yet completed, we use 沒有. e. g.

10. 我 必須 在 明天 还 沒 有 上 課 的 时候 練習 这些 汉字.
Wǒ bìxū zài míngtiān hái méi yǒu shàng kè de shíhour liànxí zhèixiē hànzì.

(3) 表示意願的时候用"不"，这也不受时間的限制. 例如:

(c) 不 is used to negate intention or wish regardless of the time. e. g.

11. 休息 的 時候兒 我們 都 唱 歌兒,
Xiūxī dė shíhòur wǒmėn dōu chàng ger,
他 不 唱.
tā bú chàng.

12. 他 不 喜欢 这个 电影, 他 不
Tā bù xǐhuǎn zhèigė diànyǐng, tā bú
看.
kàn.

(4) 在一般的能願动詞和一些表示心理状态的动詞前边，要用"不"否定. 例如:

(d)不 is used before optative verbs or verbs implying mental states. e. g.

13. 开始 学習 的 时候兒, 我 不 会
Kāishǐ xuéxí dė shíhòur, wǒ bú huì
説 中国 話.
shuō Zhōngguó huà.

14. 他 沒 有 告訴 我, 我 不 知道.
Tā méi yǒu gàosů wǒ, wǒ bù zhīdào.

(二) 用"沒有"来否定，表示某一动作未曾开始或进行. 例如:

(2) 沒有 is used to show that a certain action has not happened. e. g.

15. 我 同屋 还 沒 有 回 宿舍 呢!
Wǒ tóngwū hái méi yǒu huí sùshė nė!

16. 我 只 借了 画报, 沒 有 借 小
Wǒ zhǐ jièlė huàbào, méi yǒu jiè xiǎo-
説兒.
shuōr.

二、課文 Kèwén Text

(a₁) 昨天 是 星期日，您 作 什么 了？
Zuótiån shì xīngqīrì, nín zuò shénmô lê?

(b₁) 我 进 城 了．我 看了 一个 朋友．
Wǒ jìn chéng lê. Wǒ kànlê yígê péngyôu.

(a₂) 你的 这个 朋友 是 作 什么 工作 的，您 能 告訴 我 嗎？
Níndê zhèigê péngyôu shì zuò shénmô gōng zuò dê, nín néng gàosû wô mâ?

(b₂) 他 在 学校里 教 書．
Tā zài xuéxiàolî jiāo shū.

(a₃) 他 教 什么？
Tā jiāo shénmô?

(b₃) 他 教 俄文．我 朋友 教 俄文 的 方法 很 好，学生 都 学得 很 快．他們 从 九月 起 开始 学習，已經 会 說、会 写 了．
Tā jiāo èwén. Wǒ péngyôu jiāo èwén dê fāngfǎ hěn hǎo, xuéshêng dōu xuédê hěn kuài. Tāmên cóng jiǔyuè qǐ kāishǐ xuéxí, yǐjīng huì shuō、huì xiě lê.

(a₄) 他們 每天 都 有 課 嗎？
Tāmên měitiān dōu yǒu kè mâ?

(b₄) 都 有．从 星期一 到 星期六 他 每天 講 两节 語法．他 每
Dōu yǒu. Cóng xīngqīyī dào xīngqīliù tā měitiān jiǎng liǎngjié yǔfǎ. Tā méi

天 都 很 忙.
tiān dōu hěn máng.

(a_5) 你 星期日 进 城 了 嗎?
Nǐ xīngqīrì jìn chéng lẻ mả?

(b_5) 沒 有, 我 在 宿舍 看 書 了.
Méi yỏu, wǒ zài sùshè kàn shū lẻ.

我 星期六 从 朋友 那兒 借了
Wǒ xīngqīliù cóng péngyỏu nàr jièlẻ

一本 翻譯 小說兒, 星期日 一天
yìběn fānyỉ xiǎoshuōr, xīngqīrì yìtiān

我 都 看 小說兒 了.
wǒ dōu kàn xiǎoshuōr lẻ.

(a_6) 这本 小說兒 写得 怎么样?
Zhèiběn xiǎoshūor xiědẻ zěnmỏyàng?

(b_6) 这本 小說兒 写得 很 好. 你 要
Zhèiběn xiǎoshuōr xiědẻ hěn hǎo. Nǐ yào

不 要 看?
bú yào kàn?

(a_7) 这个 星期 我 很 忙, 我 不 能 看.
Zhèigẻ xīngqī wǒ hěn máng, wǒ bù néng kàn.

(b_7) 沒 关系, 你 可以 慢慢兒地 看.
Méi guānxỉ, nǐ kěyỉ mànmānrdẻ kàn.

我 不 一定 現在 还 他.
Wǒ bù yídìng xiànzài huán tả.

(a_8) 好, 下星期 我 一定 看.
Hǎo, xiàxīngqī wǒ yídìng kàn.

第三十一課 Lesson 31

一、生詞 Shēngcí New Words

1.	因为…所以…		yīnwèi… suǒyǐ…	because (owing to)… therefore (so)…
2.	要是…就…		yàoshi…jiù…	if, (then)
3.	件	(量)	jiàn	(a measure word)
4.	事(情)	(名)	shì (qing) [件]	matter, business
5.	虽然…但是…		suírán… dànshì…	although…(yet)…
6.	岁	(量)	suì	year (a measure word)
7.	或者	(連)	huòzhě	or
8.	点兒	(量)	diǎnr	bit (a measure word)
9.	書店	(名)	shūdiàn	bookstore
10.	这么	(代)	zènmo	such, so
11.	为什么		wèishénmo	for what, why
12.	專业	(名)	zhuānyè	special field
13.	难	(形)	nán	difficult

14. 怎么	(代)	zěnmô	how
15. 玩兒	(动)	wánr	to play, to amuse oneself
16. 晚上	(名)	wǎnshång	night, evening

二、語法 Yǔfǎ Grammar

31.1 复合句　汉語的复合句有很多种．分句之間的关系也多种多样．現在介紹最基本的三种：

31.1 The Composite Sentence　In Chinese, there are many kinds of composite sentences and the relations between the clauses are also of various kinds. Here in this lesson three common kinds will be introduced as follows:—

(一) 用"因为…所以…"表示因果的．例如：

(1) 因为 … 所以 … expresses cause and effect. e. g.

1. 因为 那本 字典 太 旧，所以 我 沒 有 买．

有时候可以省去"因为"或者"所以"．文义清楚的时候，也可以把二者都省去．例如：

Sometimes, we may omit 因为 or 所以. If the meaning of the context is clear enough, both 因为 and 所以 may be omitted. e. g.

2. 那本 字典 太 旧，我 沒 有 买．

(二) 用"要是…就…"表示条件的．例如：

(2) 要是… 就 … expresses a condition. e. g.

3. 要是 你 不 告訴 我 这件 事(情)，我 就 不 知道．

"要是"可以在第一分句主語的前边或者后边，但是"就"必須用在第二分句的謂語前边."要是"常常省略，而"就"在一般的情况下不能省. 例如：

要是 may be placed either before or after the subject in the first clause, but the word 就 must be placed before the predicate in the second clause. In general, 要是 may be omitted but 就 is always used. e. g.

4. 你 不 告訴 我 这件 事(情)，我 <u>就</u> 不 知道.

但是，当第二分句里有其他状語的时候，"就"也可以省. 例如：

If there is an adverbial modifier in the second clause, 就 may be omitted too. e. g.

5. (要是) 你 不 告訴 我 这件 事(情)，我 <u>一定</u> 不 知道.

(三) 用"虽然…但是…"表示轉折的. 例如：

(3) 虽然 … 但是 … shows an adversative or antithesis. e. g.

6. 他 <u>虽然</u> 不 是 北京 人，<u>但是</u> 北京 話 說得 很 好.

在这种句子里，"虽然"常常省去，但要保留"但是".

In such a sentence 虽然 is often omitted but 但是 is not.

31.2 不带系詞的体詞謂語句　我們知道体詞謂語句的謂語包含系詞和体詞，現在談一种特殊的不用系詞的体詞謂語句. 口語里常有一些簡短的句子是屬于这个类型的，現在只介紹常用的两种：

31.2 The Substantive Sentence without Copula　We have learned that in a sentence with a substantive predicate, the predicate is composed of a copula and a substantive. Here, in this lesson, we shall learn a special form of this kind of sentence in which the copula is not used. In the spoken language, simple and short sentences take this special form. Here, we will introduce the two most common types:

(一) 表示时間或籍貫的. 例如:

(1) When the predicate expresses time or place of birth. e. g.

7. 今天 星期几?

8. 今天 星期一.

9. 你 哪兒(的) 人?

10. 我 北京 人.

(二) 謂語里有数詞的. 例如:

(2) When the predicate contains a numeral or numerals. e. g.

11. 你 二十几岁?

12. 我 二十二岁.

13. 一个 月 多少天?

14. 一个 月 三十天, 或者 三十一天.

上述两类句子肯定句中虽然不带系詞, 但在否定句中一定要用. 例如:

Note: All the examples given above are affirmative sentences, and the copula can be omitted. But in the negative sentences the copula 是 has to be used. e. g.

15. 今天 星期三, 不 是 星期四.

16. 他 十八岁, 不 是 二十岁.

31.3 "一点兒"和"有一点兒" "点兒"是一个表示少量的不定量詞. "一点兒"的意思和"一些"差不多, 但在口語里用得更多. 例如:

31.3 一点兒 and 有一点兒　点兒 (a bit) is a measure word showing an indefinite small quantity. The meaning of 一点兒 is similar to that of 一些. In the spoken language, we prefer to use 点兒. e. g.

17. 我 想 买 一点兒 紙.

这种說法比"我想买一些紙"更合習慣. 这样用的时候, 就是数詞加量詞. 而汉語里量詞前的数詞是"一"的时候, 如果不在句首, "一"就常常省去. 例如:

The above sentence is used more habitually than 我想买一些紙. 一点兒 is composed of a numeral and a measure word. In Chinese, if the numeral before the measure word is 一, except when it is at the beginning of a sentence, it is often omitted. e. g.

18. 我 想 买 点兒 紙.

"有(一)点兒"是一个动宾結构, 口語里常用它作状語来修飾形容詞或动詞. 例如:

有(一)点兒 is a verb-object construction. In the spoken language, it is always used as an adverbial modifier to modify an adjective or a verb. e. g.

19. 他 今天 有 一点兒 不 高兴.

20. 虽然 他 有 一点兒 想 进 城, 但是 很 忙, 不 能 去.

例 19 里"有一点兒"修飾形容詞"高兴", 例 20 里修飾动詞"想".

In example 19, 有一点兒 is used to modify the adjective 高兴, while in example 20 it is used to modify the verb 想.

31.4 "或者"和"还是"　这两个連詞的用法不同:

31.4 或者 and 还是 These two conjunctions are different in use:

(一) "还是"常是用在疑問句里的，而"或者"一般是用在陈述句中的. 例如:

(1) 还是 is used in the interrogative sentence, while 或者 is used in the declarative sentence. e. g.

21. 您 要 借 鋼笔 还是 鉛笔?

22. 鋼笔 或者 鉛笔 都 可以.

这里值得注意的是: 当"或者"联系主語或提前的宾語的时候，謂語前要用"都".

Note: When 或者 is used to join the compound subject or the inverted objects, we must use the adverb 都 before the predicate.

(二) 有时候，"还是"也可能用在一个包含着疑問的陈述句中. 例如:

(2) 还是 sometimes can also be used in a declarative sentence indicating uncertainty. e. g.

23. 他 去 圖書館 了 还是 去 書店 了?

24. 我 也 不 知道 他 去 圖書館 了, 还是 去 書店 了.

像这样的情形，例 24 也可以更簡短地說成: "我也不知道".

In this case, example 24 may be briefly expressed as 我也不知道.

三、課文 Kèwén Text

(a_1) 今天 星期几?

(b_1) 今天 星期五.

(a_2) 你們 今天 上 四节 課 还是 上 三节 課?

(b_2) 我們 今天 上 四节 課.

(a_3) 你們 星期六 也 上 四节 課 嗎?

(b_3) 我們 星期六 也 上 四节 課.

(a_4) 你們 上 这么 多 課, 不 覚得 太 忙 嗎?

(b_4) 虽然 有 一点兒 忙, 但是 沒 关系.

(a_5) 为 什么?

(b_5) 要是 現在 不 上 这么 多 課、不 快快兒地 学, 我們 就 学得 太 少. 要是 中文 学得 太少, 以后 学 專业 的 时候兒, 就 会 覚得 很 难. 所以 我們 現在 都 很 努力.

(a_6) 星期日 你們 怎么 玩兒?

(b_6) 星期日 我們 常常 在 学校 看 电影, 或者 进 城.

(a_7) 这个 星期日, 你 要 作 什么?

(b7) 我 想 进 城. 我 要 买 点兒 东西. 晚上 还 想 复習 語法.

四、課外練習 Kèwài liànxí Home Work

1. 抄写下面的句子，并在括弧里选擇一个适当的詞語塡到空白的位置上:

1) Copy the following sentences and fill the blanks with the correct words given in the parentheses:

(1) 这个 同志 二十岁______二十一岁? 我 也 不 知道 他 二十岁______二十一岁. (“还是”“或者”)

(2) 因为 这个 問題______难, 所以 他 回答得 不 好. (“一点兒”“有一点兒”)

(3) 因为 他 説話 説得______快, 我 只 懂了______. (“一点兒”“有一点兒”)

(4) 我們 今天 晚上______明天 晚上 一起 玩兒? 今天 晚上______明天 晚上 都 可以 (“或者”“还是”)

2. 用下边的詞組各作一个句子:

2) Make sentences with each of the following word combinations:

(5) 因为… 所以…

(6) 虽然… 但是…

(7) 要是… 就…

五、汉字表 Hànzì biǎo Chinese Characters

1	因	冂 冈 因
2	为	丶 丿 为 为
3	所	户（丿 ㇇ 户 户）
		斤
4	件	亻
		牛（丿 𠂉 牛）
5	事	一 𠮛 ⺕ ⺕ ⺕ 事
6	情	忄
		青
7	虽	口
		虫（口 中 虫 虫）
8	然	夕（⺈ 夕）
		犬（大 犬）
		灬
9	但	亻
		旦（日 旦）

10	岁	山（丨 凵 山）
		夕
11	或	一 𠮛 亘 式 或 或
12	者	
13	店	
14	專	叀（一 𠮛 甫 車 叀）
		寸
15	业	丶 丨丨 丷丨 业 业
16	难	又
		隹
17	玩	王
		元（二 元）

第三十二課 Lesson 32

32.1 結果补語
The Resultative Complement
32.2 帶結果补語的动詞的否定
The Negative Form of the Verb Carrying a Resultative Complement
32.3 "着"作結果补語
着 Used as Resultative Complement
32.4 "見"作結果补語
見 Used as Resultative Complement

一、生詞 Shēngcí New Words

1.	完	(动)	wán	to finish
2.	着	(动)	zháo	to catch, to touch, (always used as a complement)
3.	找	(动)	zhǎo	to find, to seek, to look for
4.	見	(动)	jiàn	to see
5.	看見	(动)	kànjiȧn	to see
6.	毛澤东	(名)	Máozédōng	Mao Tse-tung
7.	主席	(名)	zhǔxí	chairman
8.	听見	(动)	tīngjiȧn	to hear
9.	汉俄		hàn-è	Chinese-Russian
10.	那么	(代)	nènmȯ	then, thus
11.	前天	(名)	qiántiȧn	day before yesterday
12.	卖	(动)	mài	to sell
13.	怎么办		zěnmȯbàn	What is to be done?
14.	汽車	(名)	qìchē [輛 liàng]	motor car, automobile
15.	遇見	(动)	yùjiȧn	to meet, to come across

二、語法 Yǔfǎ Grammar

32.1 結果补語　結果补語是在动詞后边补充說明动作的結果的，它本身可以是动詞，也可以是形容詞．例如：

32.1 The Resultative Complement　The resultative complement is used after a verb to denote the result of an action. The resultative complement may be either a verb or an adjective. e. g.

1. 他 已經 作完了 練習 了

2. 我 要 学好 中文．

例 1 里"作"是动詞，它后边的动詞"完"就是結果补語．例 2 里"学"是动詞，后边的形容詞"好"是結果补語．

In example 1 作 is a verb, and it is followed by another verb 完 as the resultative complement. In example 2 学 is a verb, and it is followed by an adjective 好 as the resultative complement.

用結果补語的时候，有两点值得注意：

There are two points to be noticed in using the resultative complement:

(一) 只要詞义配合得上，形容詞或动詞都可以作結果补語，也就是說这种动补結构的組合是相当自由的．

(1) In Chinese, any adjective or verb can be used as a resultative complement so long as the combination or a verb and its complement has some logical meaning. That is to say, this kind of verb-complement construction is often rather loose.

(二) 但在既經組合之后，这个結构便很紧凑：补語直接連在动詞的后边，不用結构助詞．动詞有詞尾或宾語的时候，詞尾或宾語要用在动詞和补語之后而不能拆开动补結构，这是和程度补語不同的地方．由于这个結构特别紧凑，有一些習慣上常用的动补結构(如"打倒""說明"等)，已經發展为复合动詞了．这种現象还在不断地增加．

(2) But once this construction is formd, the verb and its complement become a very close unit. The complement can be

put immediately after the verb without any structural particle. When there is a suffix or an object after the verb, all these elements have to be put after the verb and its complement; one must never split the verb-complement construction. This is different from the complement of degree. It is because such constructions are so closely bound that we have so many verb-complement constructions (such as 打倒 (to overthrow), 說明 (to explain) etc.) already accepted as compound verbs in common use. Such compound verbs are still increasing.

32.2 帶結果补語的动詞的否定　我們知道否定完成的动作用"沒有"(27.3)，有結果补語的动詞也不例外．因为有了結果的动作，一般总是完成了的，現在旣被否定，所以也要用"沒有"．例如：

32.2 The Negative Form of the Verb Carrying Its Resultative Complement　As we know, 沒有 is used to negate a completed action (27.3). This rule is also applicable to the verb with a resultative complement. The reason is that when an action has already born a certain result, it is generally completed. e. g.

3. 我 沒有 看懂 这个 問題，所以 回答得 不 对.

4. 要是 沒有 听清楚 先生的 話，我 就 問.

但是，被否定的这个动作如果是表示条件的或表示意願的，就用"不"(30.3)．例如：

But, if an action denotes condition or will, we have to use 不 in the negative form (30.3). e. g.

5. 不 看懂 問題，就 不 能 回答.

6. 你 不 写清楚，我們 怎么 看？

32.3 "着" 作結果补語　上面談到形容詞或动詞都可以作結果补語. 但是有些动詞經常作結果补語. 这些动詞作結果补語在口語里是常常用到的. 現在介紹几个最常用的, 先談"着".

32.3 "着" Used as Resultative Complement　As mentioned above, almost any adjective or verb can be used as a resultative complement, but some verbs are always used as resultative complements. Here, we shall introduce some of the most commonly used.

"着"是一个动詞, 作謂語用的时候不多, 但常常作結果补語. 作結果补語的时候, 它表示一个动作达到了預期的目的或結果, 所以有"得到""达到"的意思. 例如:

着 is a verb, but it is rarely used as predicate, and often used as resultative complement. As a complement it implies an action that has attained its expected aim or result. So it has the meaning of "attaining" or "reaching". e. g.

7. 我要借圖書館的字典, 但是沒有借着.

8. 那枝旧鋼笔我沒有找着.

"借"和"借着"不同: "借"只是这个动作, 而"借着"才是通过"借"的动作得到了要借的东西, "找着"也和"找"不一样: "找"只是这个动作的进行, 而"找着"才是通过"找"而得到了要找的东西.

借 and 借着 are different from each other in meaning, because 借 is a verb meaning "to lend or to borrow", while 借着 means that something has already been lent or borrowed. 找 and 找着 are also not the same; 找 is a verb meaning "to look for", while 找着 means "one has already got the thing one wants to find".

32.4 "見"作結果补語　"見"是一个动詞, 除了作謂語之外, 也作結果补語. 作結果补語的时候, 經常用在表示感覺的动詞如

"听""看"之类的后边."看"是用眼睛去看，看得見看不見不一定,"看見"才是确实看到了. 例如:

32.4 見 Used as Resultative Complement 見 is a verb. It is not only used as predicate, but also as resultative complement. It is often used as resultative complement to verbs expressing sensuous perception, such as: 听 and 看 etc.

看 is simply "to see", but whether the thing or object is seen or not is uncertain, but 看見 means that the object has really been seen. e. g.

9. 他 每天 都 看 报.

10. 十月 一日 我們 看見了 毛(澤东) 主席.

"听"和"听見"也是如此，二者的区别可以由下边的例句表示出来:

It is the same with 听 and 听見, and their different meanings may be observed from the following examples:

11. 因为 他 沒 有 好好兒地 听, 我 說 的 問題 他 沒 有 听見.

三、課文 Kèwén Text

(a1) 你 昨天 去 書店 了 嗎?

(b1) 去 了. 因为 我 很 想 买 那本 汉俄 字典, 上完 課 我 就 去 了.

(a2) 那么, 你 一定 买着 字典 了.

(b₂) 沒 有，虽然 我 去得 很 早，
但是 沒 有 买着.

(a₃) 为 什么 沒 有 买着？

(b₃) 因为 买 的 人 很 多，所以
沒 买着. 我 同屋 前天 晚上
还 看見 很 多 本，但是 昨天
都 卖完 了.

(a₄) 你 沒 买着 字典，怎么办？

(b₄) 沒 关系，我 已經 借着 了.
回 学校 的 时候兒，我 在
汽車上 遇見了 一个 先生，我
告訴了 他 我 买 字典 的 事.
他 說 要是 我 用 字典，可以
借 他的，因为 他 有 一本，
現在 不 用. 我 很 高兴；虽然
沒 有 买着，但是 借着 了.

四、課外練習 Kèwài liànxí Home Work

1. 用肯定的句子回答下边的問題:

1) Answer the following questions in the affirmative:

(1) 今天 这 一課 你 都 学会 了 嗎？

(2) 这 一課的 語法 你 看懂 了 沒 有?

(3) 黑板上的 句子 你 都 看清楚 了 嗎?

2. 用否定的句子回答下边的問題:

2) Answer the following questions in the negative:

(4) 我 想 借 你的 字典, 你 用完 了 沒 有?

(5) 今天的 練習 你 翻譯好 了 沒 有?

(6) 这些 汉字 你 要是 不 写清楚, 他們 能 看懂 嗎?

3. 用下边的动詞和結果补語作句子:

3) Make sentences with the following verbs and their resultative complements:

(7) 回答 对　　(8) 写 完

五、汉字表 Hànzì biǎo Chinese Characters

1	完	宀
		元
2	着	丶 丷 䒑 丷 ⺷ 坴 ⺶ 着
3	找	
4	見	
5	毛	

6	澤	氵	
		睪	
7	主		
8	席	广+廿	广
			廿(一 十 卄 廿)
		巾	
9	卖	十 土 [illegible] [illegible] [illegible] [illegible] 卖	
10	办		
11	汽	氵	
		气(丿 𠂉 𠂒 气)	
12	車	一 百 亘 車	
13	遇	禺([illegible] [illegible] [illegible] [illegible] [illegible] 禺)	
		辶	

第三十三課 Lesson 33

33.1	"住"作結果补語 住 Used as Resultative Complement
33.2	"开"作結果补語 开 Used as Resultative Complement
33.3	"在"作結果补語 在 Used as Resultative Complement
33.4	"到"作結果补語 到 Used as Resultative Complement

一、生詞 Shēngcí New Words

1.	記	(动)	jì	to remember, to take notes to learn by heart
2.	拿	(动)	ná	to take
3.	掉	(动)	diào	to lose, to miss
4.	开	(动)	kāi	to open (a door) to drive (a car)
5.	門	(名)	mén	door
6.	搬	(动)	bān	to move
7.	坐	(动)	zuò	to sit
8.	站	(动)	zhàn	to stand, to rise to one's feet
9.	到	(动)	dào	to reach, to arrive
10.	劳駕		láojià	excuse me, may I trouble you
11.	輛	(量)	liàng	(a measure word)
12.	错	(形)	cuò	wrong, incorrect, mistaken
13.	热	(形)	rè	hot
14.	剛才	(副)	gāngcái	a short time ago,

15. 窗户 (名) chuānghu window

二、語法 yǔfǎ Grammar

33.1 "住"作結果补語. "住"是个常用动詞，意思是"居住"，可以作謂語. 例如:

33.1 住 Used as Resultative Complement 住 is a very common verb meaning "to live" or "to dwell", and may be used as predicate. e. g.

1. 我 朋友 在 这个 宿舍 住.

但是，作为一个結果补語，它就有了引申的意义. 例如:

But, when it is used as resultative complement, it has an extended meaning. e. g.

2. 我 要 記 二十个 生詞，記住了 十八个，两个 沒有 記住.

3. 那枝 鉛笔 我 沒有 拿住，掉了.

"記住"就是通过"記"使生詞留在記忆里，"沒有拿住"就是虽然拿了，但是沒有能把鉛笔留在手中，所以我們可以說結果补語"住"的意思是通过动作影响目的物、使目的物停留在一定的位置上.

記住 means to have committed the words to memory through the action of 記. 沒有拿住 means that though the action of 拿 has taken place, yet one has failed to hold that pencil in hand. Therefore, the resultative complement 住 possesses the meaning of retaining or keeping the object of an action in a certain place as the result of the action.

33.2 "开"作結果补語　"开"也是个常用动詞，可以作謂語. 例如:

33.2 开 Used as Resultative Complement 开 is also a common verb and may be used as predicate. e. g.

4. 图書館 七点半 开門.

5. 他 会 开 汽車.

"开"也常作結果补語，例如:

It may also be used as resultative complement:

6. 这兒的 椅子 太 多，应該 搬开 两把.

7. 你的 朋友 来了，你 快 开开 門.

"搬开"椅子就是搬椅子而使椅子离开原来的位置，"开开門"就是开門而使关着的門轉入分开的状态. 因此，我們可以說"开"作結果补語表示分散、离开的意思.

搬开椅子 means to move the chair away from its original place. 开开門 is to let the door open, that is to say, to let the door stand wide open. Hence, we may say that 开 used as resultative complement means separation or departure.

33.3. "在"作結果补語　"在"除了作謂語之外，也常在别的动詞后边作結果补語表示存在. 例如:

33.3 在 Used as Resultative Complement 在 is not only used as predicate, but may also be used as resultative complement after some verbs indicating existence. e. g.

8. 我們 坐在 椅子上.

9. 先生 站在 黑板 旁边兒

"坐""站"是动詞，"在"是結果补語. "在"表示人物由于动作而存在于一定的地点. 我們用这个补語的时候，要特別注意；这个补語只能和某些动詞（如"坐""站""住""躺"等）結合，不是所有的动詞都可以这样用. 因此我們不能說"我們学習在北京大学"或者"那个同志工作在哪兒". 这时我們可以把"在"用个介詞，构成介詞結构作状語来說明动作發生的地点，例如可以說"我們在北京大学学習"或"那个同志在哪兒工作".

坐 and 站 are verbs and 在 is the resultative complement. 在 tells us the place where persons or things are as, the result of a certain action. Care should be taken in using this resultative complement. It can only be used after a certain number of verbs, such as 坐, 站, 住 and 躺. Not all verbs can be followed by such a complement. Therefore, we must not say 我們学習在北京大学 or 那个同志工作在哪兒. In such cases, 在 may be used in a prepositional construction used as adverbial modifier, expressing where an action has occurred. Therefore, we have to say 我們在北京大学学習 or 那个同志在哪兒工作.

33.4 "到"作結果补語　"到"是个动詞，常常用作謂語. 例如:

33.4 到 Used as Resultative Complement　到 is a common verb and often used as predicate. e.g.

10. 主席 到 了 嗎?

11. 主席 到 了.

"到"也常用作結果补語.　作結果补語的时候，有"达到"的意思，它的宾語表示动作的終点. 例如:

But 到 is also very frequently used as resultative complement, with the meaning of "attaining" or "reaching". The object following the complement indicates the place where an action has come to an end. e.g.

12. 六点 我 已經 回到 宿舍 了.

13. 先生 講到 这兒 的 时候兒, 問 了 几个 問題.

三、課文 Kèwén Text

I

(a₁) 劳駕, 这輛 汽車 是 去 哪兒 的?

(b₁) 去 北京 大学 的.

(a₂) 什么 时候兒 开?

(b₂) 五点 一刻 开.

(a₃) 什么 时候兒 可以 开到 北京 大学?

(b₃) 六点 过 五分.

II

(a₄) 学完 的 語法 你 都 記住 了 嗎?

(b_4) 都 記住 了. 但是, 我 説 話 的 时候兒, 还 常常 説錯.

(a_5) 学了 的 詞彙 你 能 不 能 都 記住?

(b_5) 不 能, 虽然 我 每天 都 練習, 但是 特别 难的 汉字 还 会 写錯.

III

(a_6) 桌子上的 書 是 你的 嗎?

(b_6) 是 我的. 你 想 在 这張 桌子上 作 練習 嗎?

(a_7) 对了. 我的 練習 还 沒 有 作完, 我 想 在 这兒 作.

(b_7) 好, 我 拿开 我的 書.

IV

(a_8) 你們 不·觉得 热 嗎?

(b_8) 不 觉得. 剛才 有 一点兒 热, 現在 門 和 窗戶 都 开开 了, 不 热.

V

(a$_9$) 上 課 的 时候兒，你 坐在 哪兒？

(b$_9$) 我 坐在 前边兒.

(a$_{10}$) 誰 坐在 你的 旁边兒？

(b$_{10}$) 我 同屋 和 一个 苏联 学生 坐在 我 旁边兒. 我 坐在 他們 中間兒.

四、課外練習 Kèwài liànxí Home Work

1. 注意同音的汉字，把正确的塡进空白里去：

1) Notice the different Chinese characters having the same sound and fill the following blanks with the correct ones:

(1) gāng
- 我____才 看見 他.
- ____笔 掉 了.

(2) zuò
- 我____錯 了 一个 句子.
- 誰____在 汽車上？

2. 抄写下边的句子，并把結果补語"在""住""开""到"塡进适当的空白里去：

2) Copy the following sentences, and fill the blanks with the resultative complements 开，在，住，and 到:

(1) 他 回____宿舍，就 作 練習.

(2) 上 課 的 时候兒，先生 站____黑板 旁边兒.

(3) 那張 紙 我 沒 有 拿____,
掉 了.

(4) 这本 字典 要是 用完 了, 我們
就 拿____.

3. 把下边的句子譯成中文:

3) Translate the following English sentences into Chinese:

(5) It is very hot, so I am standing at the window.

(6) A new motor-car has just stopped in front of the auditorium.

(7) If I had not remembered these Chinese characters, I would have written them wrong.

(8) Since the window is not open, it is a bit hot.

五、汉字表 Hànzì biǎo Chinese Characters

1	記	言
		己 (㇆ コ 己)
2	拿	合
		手 (㇒ 三 手)

3	掉	才	
		卓（丨 卜 占 卓）	
4	門		
5	搬	才	
		般	舟（′ 丿 ⺆ 舟 舟 舟）
			殳（几 殳）
6	坐	从	
		土	
7	站	立	
		占	
8	劳	艹（一 十 廿 艹）	
		力	
9	駕	加	力
			口
		馬	

10	輛	車	
		兩（一 丆 冂 帀 帀 帀 帀 兩）	
11	錯	金	
		昔	
12	热	执	才
			丸（九 丸）
		灬	
13	刚	冈	
		刂	
14	才	一 十 才	
15	窗	穴	宀
			八
		囱（丿 门 向 囱）	
16	户	丶 户	

第三十四課 Lesson 34

一、生詞 Shēngcí New Words

1.	以前	(副)	yǐqián	in the past, ago, before
2.	交	(动)	jiāo	to hand, to give
3.	忘	(动)	wàng	to forget
4.	带	(动)	dài	to bring, to carry
5.	下午	(名)	xiàwǔ	afternoon
6.	报告	(名、动)	bàogào	report, to make a report
7.	走	(动)	zǒu	to go, to walk
8.	台	(名)	tái	platform, rostrum
9.	热烈	(形)	rèliè	warm, enthusiastic
10.	鼓掌	(动)	gǔzhǎng	to applaud, to clap (one's hands)
11.	非常	(副)	fēicháng	uncommonly, extremely
12.	重要	(形)	zhòngyào	important

13.	記	(动)	jì	to take down (in the note-book)
14.	繼續	(动)	jìxù	to continue
15.	种	(量)	zhǒng	(a measure word)

二、語法 Yǔfǎ Grammar

34.1 簡單趨向补語　“来”和“去”这两个动詞除了作謂語以外，还常常作动詞的补語．因为“来”“去”作补語的时候，补充說明动作的趨向，这种补語就叫作趨向补語．如果一个动作是向着說話人（或所談事物）进行的，就在动詞的后边加“来”，如果动作是朝着相反的方向进行的，就在动詞的后边加“去”．例如：

34.1 The Simple Directional Complement　The two verbs 来 and 去 are not only used as predicates, but are also frequently used as complements to other verbs. As complements, 来 and 去 are used to indicate directions of actions, and are called directional complements. If an action proceeds towards the speaker (or the thing or things under discussion), we use the directional complement 来 after the verb. We put the directional complement 去 after a verb, if the action proceeds contrariwise or away from the speaker. e. g.

1. 先生 进 教室 来 了．
2. 先生 进 教室 去 了．

同样一个“先生进教室”的动作，却可以因說話人地位的不同而有不同的补語．当說話人在教室里边，先生进教室的动作是向着說話人进行的时候，这个人就說“进来”，当說話人在教室外边，先生进教室的动作是背着說話人进行的时候，这个人就說“进去”．又如我們在宿舍里，我們就說：

In the above two examples, we can see that the same action in 先生进教室 may have different complements, because the speaker's position in these two sentences is not the same. When the speaker is inside the classroom, and if the action proceeds towards the speaker, he must say 进来. On the contrary, if the action proceeds away from the speaker who is standing outside the classroom, then he must say 进去. As another example, suppose we are in the dormitory, then we must say:

3. 他 回 宿舍 来 了.

如果我們不在宿舍，就要說:

If we are not in the dormitory or away from it, then we must say:

4. 他 回 宿舍 去 了.

34．2 簡單趋向补語与宾語的位置　带趋向补語的动詞可以有宾語，这种宾語又可以分为两种；不同的宾語在句中的位置也不同:

34.2 The Positions of the Simple Directional Complement and the Object　Verbs with directional complements may also have objects. Such objects can be divided into two kinds. Different kinds of objects have different positions in such sentences.

(一) 宾語所表示的事物如果不因动作而移动位置，只能用在动詞之后，补語之前．上面所举例句都属于这一类型．我們絕对不能說“先生进来教室了”或“他回去了宿舍”．

(1) If the thing denoted by the object does not change its position under the influence of an action, then the object is placed before the directional complement and after the verb. All the objects in the above examples are of this kind. We never say 先生进来教室了 or 他回去了宿舍.

(二) 宾語所表示的人或事物，如果因动作而移动位置，一般也放在动詞之后、补語之前．例如:

(2) If the thing denoted by the object changes its position under the influence of an action, it should also be placed after the verb and before the complement. e. g.

5. 我 要 搬 一把 椅子 来.

这和第一种宾語位置沒有区别. 但是，如果动作是完成了的，我們就說:

So in the above example, the position of the object is not different from that of the first kind. But, if the action is completed, we must say:

6. 我 刚才 搬来了 一把 椅子.

这样，动补結构就結合得很紧，把宾語带在后边，很像結果补語的詞序.

Here, the verb and its complement are closely knit, so that the object is placed after them. Such word order is similar to that of the resultative complement and the object.

34.3 "以前" "以前"可以作副詞，用法跟"从前"一样.例如:

34.3 以前 以前 may be used as an adverb, it is just the same in use as 从前. e. g.

7. 他 以前 在 这兒 工作.

"以前" 又可以和單詞、动詞結构、主謂結构組成一个說明时間的結构. 例如:

以前 may also be used after a word, a verbal-construction or a subject-predicate construction (clause), thus forming a construction to indicate time. e. g.

8. 十一点 以前 我 要 上 課.

9. 来 中国 以前, 他 不 会 中文.

10. 上 課 以前, 你 应該 作好 練習.

11. 先生 来 以前, 学生 都 来 了.

这种結构有一个特点，就是："以前"前边的結构肯定和否定都可以用，意思上完全一样．所以上边的三个句子也可以說成：

Note: There is a characteristic feature in such a construction, that is, the construction before 以前, whether affirmative or negative, makes no difference in meaning. Therefore, the above three examples may be re-written as follows:

12. 沒有来中国以前，他不会中文．

13. 沒有上課以前，你应該作好練習．

14. 先生沒有来以前，学生都来了．

34. 4 "以后" "以后"和"以前"一样，除了能作副詞以外也可以和單詞、动詞結构、主謂結构用在一起，組成說明时間的結构．例如：

34.4 以后 Just like 以前, 以后 may be used as an adverb, and may also be placed after a word, a verbal construction, or a subject-predicate construction, thus forming a construction indicating time. e. g.

15. 十五号以后，他們要开始一个新的工作．

16. 工作以后，你应該休息．

17. 这个同志来了以后，很积極地作了很多工作．

18. 听清楚問題以后，他就回答．

"以后"和"以前"不同，它前边的成分，只能是肯定的，不能是否定的.

Note: The elements before 以前 can never be negative in form.

三、課文 Kèwén Text

I

(a1) 張友文 到 哪兒 去 了?

(b1) 回 宿舍 去 了.

(a2) 他 为 什么 現在 回去?

(b2) 我們 今天 要 交 練習，他的 本子 忘在 宿舍里 了.

(a3) 你的 本子 带来 了 嗎?

(b3) 带来 了. 我 沒 有 忘. 我 每天 都 带 本子 来.

(a4) 今天 要 用 字典，你 也 带来 了 嗎?

(b4) 带来 了. 你 看，这本 汉俄 字典 是 我 昨天 从 城里 买来 的.

II

今天 星期六. 我們 下午 在 礼堂 听 报告. 两点半 报告 开始，我 两点过十分就到礼堂去了．那时候兒到的人还不多，我就坐在前边兒．十分鐘以后，听报告的都进礼堂来了．

两点半，作报告的同志从外边兒进来了．他走到主席台上去的时候兒，我們都热烈地鼓掌．他的报告非常重要，很多应該記住的地方，我都記在本子里了．講到四点一刻，我們有五分鐘的休息．休息以后，他繼續講，講到五点二十．我回到宿舍来的时候兒，已經五点三刻了．

这个报告虽然有一点兒長，但是給我的帮助很大．我非常喜欢听这种报告．

四、課外練習 Kèwài liànxí Home Work

1. 把趋向补語"来"或者"去"正确地塡进下边的句子里去：

1) Fill each of the following blanks with a proper directional complement 来 or 去:

(1) 因为 想 借書，我 要 到 圖書館____.

(2) 我 从 朋友 那兒 拿____了 两本画报.

(3) 今天 城里 有 一个 报告，我 必須 进 城____.（説話人在城外）

(4) 我 同屋 从 外边兒 搬____了 一張 桌子.（説話人在里边）

2. 用下边的动詞和宾語各作一个句子，并在每句中用上适当的趋向补語"来"或"去".

2) Make sentences with each group of words (a verb and its object), and use a proper directional complement 来 or 去 in each of your sentences:

(5) 进 書店

(6) 买 东西

(7) 回 学校

(8) 借 鉛笔

3. 抄写下边五組汉字，并在同音汉字中間兒画"＝"，不同音的汉字中間画"≠":

3) Copy the five groups of Chinese characters in the following, and make a " = " mark between characters of the same sound, and " ≠ " between those that are different:

(9) 带 太

(10) 午 五

(11) 張 掌

(12) 記 繼

(13) 重 鐘

五、汉字表 Hànzì biǎo Chinese Characters

1	交		
2	忘	亡	
		心	
3	带	一 十 卄 卌 丗 带	
4	午	丿 𠂉 午	
5	走		
6	台		
7	烈	列	歹（一 歹）
			刂
		灬	
8	鼓	壴（士 吉 吉 吉 壴）	
		支	

9	掌	尚			
		手			
10	非	丿 ㇒ ⺕ ⺕ ⺕刂 非 非 非			
11	重				
12	繼	糹			
		𢇍（ㄑ ⺈ 幺 𢆶 丝 𢇁 𢇍）			
13	續	糹			
		賣	士		
			買	罒	
				貝	目
					八
14	种	禾			
		中			

第三十五課　Lesson 35

一、生詞　Shēngcí　New Words

1.	話剧	(名)	huàjù	drama, stage-play
2.	首都	(名)	shǒudū	capital
3.	剧場	(名)	jùchǎng	theatre
4.	班	(名)	bān	class
5.	同学	(名)	tóngxué	school-mate
6.	出發	(动)	chūfā	to start, to set out
7.	开演	(动)	kāiyǎn	to perform, to give a performance
8.	吃	(动)	chī	to eat
9.	晚飯	(名)	wǎnfàn	evening meal, supper
10.	大家	(代)	dàjiā	all
11.	演員	(名)	yǎnyuán	actor, actress

12. 演	(动) yǎn	to perform, to play the role of...
13. 差不多	(副) chàbůduō	more or less, almost
14. 了解	(动) liǎojiě	to understand
15. 情况	(名) qíngkuàng	state, situation, case

二、語法 Yǔfǎ Grammar

35.1 用"(是)…的"的动詞謂語句 当我們要强調一个动作的完成的时候，就在表示动作的动詞后边用詞尾"了"(27.1). 当我們已經肯定这个动作是已經完成了的，只是要特別强調这个动作發生的时間、地点或动作的方式等等的时候，我們就用"(是)…的"这个結构. 例如:

35.1 The Verbal Sentence with (是)…的 When we wish to stress a completed action, we add the suffix 了 after the verb (27.1). But when it is understood that the action has been completed, and we wish especially to emphasize the time, place or manner of its completion etc., then we use the construction (是)……的. e. g.

1. 他 (是) 昨天 来 的.

在这里，我們对"他来"这个动作的完成十分肯定，强調的是时間状語"昨天". 又如:

Here, it is quite clear that the action in 他来 is completed, and the emphasis is laid on the adverbial modifier 昨天. Another example is:

2. 我 (是) 在 圖書館里 复習 的.

这里我們对"复習"的完成沒有疑問，只是要强調介詞結构所构成的处所状語"在圖書館里". 再如:

There is no doubt about the completion of the action 复習. What is stressed here is the prepositional construction 在圖書館里, used as an adverbial modifier of place. Another example is:

3. 她(是)跟我一起去的.

这里强調的是"跟我一起"这个表示动作方式的状語. 所以我們說这种动詞謂語句里，一定包含着一个說明动作时間、地点、方式或其他状語. 同时要注意在动詞后边不要再用表示完成的詞尾"了".

What is emphasized here is the prepositional construction 跟我一起, an adverbial modifier expressing the manner of the action. Therefore, it is clear that in such kind of sentence with a verbal predicate there must be an adverbial modifier indicating the time, place or manner of the action expressed by the verb. Notice the suffix 了 is no longer required after the verb, though the action is completed.

35.2 "(是)…的"句的否定 当我們肯定一个动作已經完成而要强調指出这个动作不是在某一时間、地点或不是通过某各方式等完成的时候，就用否定的"是…的"即"不是…的". 例如:

35.2 The Negative Form of the Verbal Sentence with (是)……的 When we are certain that an action is completed, but wish to emphasize that the action was not completed at a certain time or place or in a certain manner etc., we use the negative form of 是……的, that is to say, the construction 不是…的. e. g.

4. 她不是昨天来的，是前天晚上来的.

5. 我不是在圖書館里复習的.是在宿舍里复習的.

6. 她不是跟我一起去的，她是跟謝同志一起去的.

要注意的是: 肯定句中"是"可以省略，而否定句中一定用"不是…的"，"是"不能省略.

What is to be noticed is that in the affirmative sentence the word 是 can be omitted; while in the negative sentence the word 是 in 不是……的 can never be omitted.

35.3 "(是)…的"句中的宾語　如果这种句子有宾語，宾語常常放在"的"字之后．例如：

35.3 The Object in the Verbal Sentence with (是)…的 When there is an object in such kind of sentence we often place it at the end of the sentence. e. g.

7. 我（是）前天 进 的 城.

8. 他 不 是 在 这兒 买 的 字典.

但是，也可以把宾語放在动詞之后、"的"字之前，尤其是人称代詞作宾語的时候．例如：

But we may also place the object after the verb and before the word 的, especially when the object is a personal pronoun. e. g.

9. 我（是）前天 进 城 的.

10. 我（是）昨天 看見 他 的.

35.4 疑問句(五)　第五种提問的方法就是把表示疑問的"是不是"用在陈述句里．"是不是"可能有下面三种位置：

35.4 The Interrogative Sentence (5) The fifth kind of interrogative sentence is formed by placing the interrogative construction 是不是 in a declarative sentence. As to its position, there are three possibilities:—

(一)"是不是"放在全句的开始．例如：

(1) 是不是 placed at the beginning of a sentence. e. g.

11. 是 不 是 你們 都 住在 学校里？

12. 是 不 是 这本 小說兒 很 有意思？

(二)"是不是"放在全句的末尾．例如：

(2) 是不是 placed at the end of a sentence. e. g.

13. 你們 都 住在 学校里，是不是？

14. 这本 小説兒 很 有意思，是不是？

(三)"是不是"放在謂語中所要問的成分之前. 例如:

(3) 是不是 placed before the question concerned (in the predicate). e. g.

15. 你們 是不是 都 住在 学校 里？

16. 这本 小説兒 是不是 很 有意思？

三、課文 Kèwén Text

(a_1) 上星期六 你（是）怎么 玩兒 的？

(b_1) 我 晚上 看了 一个 話剧.

(a_2) 你（是）在 哪兒 看 的 話剧？

(b_2) 在 城里边兒——首都 剧場.

(a_3) 你（是）跟 誰 一起 去 的？

(b_3) 跟 我們 班上的 先生 和 同学 一起 去 的.

(a_4) 你們（是）什么 时候兒 出發 的？

(b_4) 七点 一刻 开演，我們（是）吃了 晚飯 以后 六点半 出發 的.

(a5) 这个 話剧 怎么样?

(b5) 很 好, 大家 都 很 喜欢 看 这个 話剧.

(a6) 你 現在 看 中国 話剧 是 不 是 都 能 懂?

(b6) 还 不 能 都 懂. 但是 因为 演員 演得 好, 說 話 說得 清楚, 我 差不多 都 懂 了.

(a7) 是 不 是 你 常常 看 話剧?

(b7) 对了. 我 非常 喜欢 看. 因为 看 話剧 可以 多 了解 中国的 情况.

(a8) 这个 話剧 長 不 長? 你們 (是) 几 点 回 学校 来 的?

(b8) 話剧 不 太 長, 我們 (是) 差不多 十一点半 回到 宿舍 的.

四、課外練習 Kèwài liànxí Home Work

1. 把下边的句子改为强調状語的"(是)…的"句:

(1) Change the following into sentences using (是) … 的, emphasizing the adverbial modifiers:

(1) 我的 朋友 从上月起 翻譯 这本 書.

(2) 他 跟 那个 同学 一起 去 了.

(3) 昨天 那个 演員 在 北京 剧場 演
話剧.

2. 用否定句回答下边的問題:

(2) Answer the following questions in the negative:

(4) 你 是 不 是 一九五六年 到 这个
班上 来 的?

(5) 你 是 不 是 在 同学 那兒 借 的
小説兒?

3. 用"是不是"改写下边的問題:

(3) Re-write the following sentences using 是不是:

(6) 这个 問題 非常 重要 嗎?

(7) 先生 已經 了解了 他的 学習
情况 了 嗎?

五、汉字表 Hànzì biǎo Chinese Characters

1	剧	居	尸
			古(一 十 古)
		刂	
2	首		
3	場	土	
		昜(日 旦 昘 昜 昜 昜)	

4	班	王	
		刂（丿 刂）	
		王（一 二 千 王）	
5	出	乚 凵 屮 出 出	
6	發	癶（フ ヲ ヺ ヺ 癶）	
		弓	
		殳	
7	演	氵	
		寅（宀 宀 宙 寅）	
8	吃	口	
		乞（丿 𠂉 乞）	
9	飯		
10	家	宀	
		豕（一 ア 丆 豕 豕 豕 豕）	
11	員	口	
		貝	
12	解	角（丿 ク 𠂊 角 角 角）	
		刀牛（刀 刃 刄 刄 刀牛）	
13	况	冫	
		兄	口
			儿

第三十六課 Lesson 36

一、語法复習 Yǔfǎ fùxí Review

36.1 提問的五种方法　我們学过五种疑問句(13.3、15.3、19.1、29.2、35.4)，这五种疑問句几乎概括了汉語里主要的提問方法. 現在根据用途，把几种疑問句复習一下:

36.1 The Five Kinds of Interrogative Sentences　We have learned five kinds of interrogative sentences (13.3, 15.3, 19.1, 29.2, 35.4) covering almost all the chief methods of asking questions in Chinese. In this lesson, let us review their different uses.

(一) 用"嗎"的疑問句和选擇式的疑問句　这两种疑問句用得最多. 当我們很客观地詢問一件事情的时候，当我們对可能的回答不作預先的估計的时候，我們就用"嗎"或者选擇式. 例如:

(1) The Interrogative Sentence with the Particle 嗎 and the Alternative Interrogative Sentence　These two kinds of interrogative sentences are very common in use. When we are very objective in inquiring about a matter or thing, and when we have not taken into consideration whether the expected answer be in the affirmative or in the negative, we prefer to use these two kinds of interrogative sentences. e. g.

1. 那些 汉字 他 都 念得 对 嗎?
2. 那些 汉字 他 都 念得 对 不 对?
3. 汽車 开来 了 嗎?

4. 汽車 开来了没有?

(二) 用疑問詞的疑問句 当我們要特别地知道"誰""什么""哪兒""什么时候兒""怎么样""怎么""多少"等等未知因素的时候，我們就用疑問詞提問. 例如:

(2) The Interrogative Sentence with An Interrogative Word When we wish especially to know who, what, where, when, now, how much etc., we must use interrogative words in asking these questions. e. g.

5. 你 今年 二十几岁?

6. 先生 講到 什么 地方 了?

用了疑問詞的疑問句，就不能再用"嗎". 回答这种問題的时候，必須針对着疑問詞，答案的位置和問題里疑問詞的位置要相当. 例如:

We cannot use the particle 嗎 in an interrogative sentence in which there is an interrogative word. In answering such a question, one must aim at what is asked by the interrogative word, and the position of the answer in the sentence should be the same as that of the interrogative word. e. g.

7. 我 今年 二十五岁.

8. 先生 講到 这个 地方 了.

(三) 用"(还是)…还是…"的疑問句 当提問人估計到答案有兩种 (或更多) 可能的时候，用这个方法提問. 例如:

(3) The Interrogative Sentence with (还是)…还是 When the person asking the question thinks that the answer may be given in two or more ways, he may use this kind of interrogative sentence. e. g.

9. 你們 复習得 怎么样? 有 問題 还是 沒 問題?

10. 你 現在 还是 到 圖書館 去 还是 回 宿舍 去?

(四)用"是不是"的疑問句 当提問人要进一步地明确某件事的"是"与"不是"的时候，用这个方式. 例如:

(4) The Interrogative Sentence with 是不是 When the person asking the question wishes to make sure whether a certain fact or matter is real or not, whether it is right or wrong, he may use this kind of interrogative sentence. e. g.

11. 那个 話剧 很 短，是 不 是?

12. 是 不 是 那个 話剧 很 短?

13. 那个 話剧 是 不 是 很 短?

36.2 "(是)…的" 的动詞謂語句和体詞謂語句(二) 当我們要强調一个动作是何时、何地或如何完成的时候，就用"(是)…的"結构作动詞謂語句. 例如:

36.2 The Verbal Sentence with (是)…的 and the Sentence with a Substantive Predicate (2) When we wish to emphasize when, where, or how an action was completed, we use the verbal construction of (是) … 的. e. g.

14. 我 (是) 九月 一号 来 的.

15. 他 (是) 在 北京 大学 学 的 中文.

16. 他 (是) 在 北京 大学 学 中文 的.

这种句子和体詞謂語句(二)在結构上有相似的地方，因为体詞謂語句(二)也用"是…的"結构. 例如:

The sentence structure of such kind of sentence is similar to that of the sentence with a substantive predicate (2), because the construction 是 … 的 is also found in the latter. e. g.

17. 这本 杂誌 是 九月 一号 来 的.

18. 他是在北京大学学中文的.

但是这两种句子还是不同的:

But there is a difference between these two kinds of sentences:

（一）从結构上来看　体詞謂語句的系詞"是"絕对不能省略，而动詞謂語句的"是"常常省略．在体詞謂語句里，作定語的动宾結构（如"学中文"）用在助詞"的"之前；而动詞謂語句如果有宾語的时候，虽然宾語可以在"的"之前，它也常在"的"之后．

(1) So far as the sentence structure is concerned, the copula 是 is absolutely necessary in the sentence with a substantive predicate, but it is often omitted in the sentence with a verbal predicate. In the former, the adjective modifier composed of a verb-object construction (such as 学中文) should be used before the particle 的; while in the latter, if there is an object, it is often put after 的, though it may also be put before it.

（二）从意义上来看　动詞謂語句是叙述动作的，用"(是)…的"結构的动詞謂語句是叙述动作的时間、地点、方式等等的．体詞謂語句則是判断主語的．例如"他(是)在北京大学学的中文"主要地叙述"学中文"的地点，而"他是在北京大学学中文的"就判断"他"是怎样的一个人．

(2) So far as the sentence meaning is concerned, the sentence with a verbal predicate is used in describing an action, but the verbal sentence with the construction (是) … 的 is used to tell about the time, place or manner of an action. The sentence with a substantive predicate is used to form a judgement on the subject, for example, the sentence 他 (是) 在北京大学学的中文 chiefly tells where he learned Chinese, but the sentence 他是在北京大学学中文的 is used to describe what kind of a person he is.

36.3　結果补語小結　从学習結果补語开始(32.1)，我們先后遇見了不少結果补語．現在把它們总結如下:

36.3 A Summary on the Resultative Complement Since we first learned about the resultative complement (32.1), we have now come across many more such complements. Here all the resultative complements are summarized as follows:

結果补語 Resultative comple-ments	引 申 义 The extended meanings	已經学过的結构 Constructions we have already learned
着	to gain to reach	买着 to have bought 借着 to have lent or borrowed 找着 to have found
見	to receive something through one's sense perception	看見 to have seen 听見 to have heard 遇見 to meet
住	to keep the object of an action	拿住 to hold 記住 to bear in mind
开	to leave, to depart, to separate	搬开 to move away 拿开 to take away 开开 to open
在	to be at a certain place as the result of an action	坐在 to sit on 站在 to stand on 住在 to live in 記在 to keep in mind 忘在 to forget
到	the goal of an action	回到 to go back 講到 to explain to (汽車)开到 to drive to 走到 to walk to
会		学会 to have learned to do
完		作完 to have done 卖完 to sell out 用完 to use up 写完 to have written
懂		看懂 to understand by reading 听懂 to understand by listening
对		回答对 to answer correctly (right) 念对 to read correctly (right)

錯		說錯 to speak wrongly 写錯 to write wrongly
好	to attain or achieve the ideal result or effect	作好 to make well 学好 to study well 翻譯好 to translate well
清楚		听清楚 to hear clearly 看清楚 to see clearly 写清楚 to write clearly

以上的結果补語，有的是动詞，有的是形容詞．但是，只要意思配合得上，都可以和动詞一起构成这种动补結构．

Of all the resultative complements mentioned above, some are verbs and some are adjectives. But any verb or adjective may be used after another verb to form a verb-complement construction, if only there is some logical meaning in such a combination.

关于这种动补結构，要注意以下三点：

Special attention should be paid to the following three points:

（一）动詞与补語結合得很紧，有的已經变成一个詞了．因此动詞的宾語或詞尾，只能在补語之后，不能在动詞和补語之間．例如：

(1) Verbs and their complements are so closely knit together that some of them have even become compound verbs. So all the verb suffixes and objects have to be placed after complements, and not between verbs and their complements. e. g.

19. 他 翻譯完了 两本 小說兒．

20. 你 应該 写清楚 你的 名字．

（二）許多結果补語，正像上表所列出的，有了引申意义．例如：

(2) Many resultative complements, as shown in the above list, possess extended meanings. e. g.

21. 上 課 的 时候兒，大家 要 坐好．

"坐好"的"好"意思是很規矩、不乱动；而

The word 好 in 坐好 here means "sitting in one's place without stirring", while in the following example:

22. 他 作好 練習 了.

这里的补語"好"就有"完了"的意思.

the complement 好 means "finished".

(三) 結果补語在汉語里的应用是很广泛的. 有时候虽然我們可以只用动詞不用补語, 但在習慣上就要用动补結构. 例如我們如果說"我懂了今天的語法", 虽然在語法上沒有錯誤, 但是要用动补結构就覺得更好一些. 所以我們更常說:

(3) In Chinese, the resultative complement is very extensively used. Although a verb is sometimes enough to express an idea without complement, it is better idiomatically to use a verb-complement construction. For example, if we say 我懂了今天的語法 it is of course grammatically correct, but it will be much better if we add a complement. Therefore, we prefer to say:

23. 今天的 語法 我 听懂 了.

24. 今天的 語法 我 看懂 了.

二、課文 Kèwén Text

I

(a_1) 你 看, 走到 台上 去 的 那个 同志 是 誰? 是 作 报告 的 嗎?

(b_1) 不 是, 作 报告 的 同志 还 沒 有 来 呢. 这 是 今天的 主席 方明 同志.

(a₂) 方明 同志？我 常常 听見 这个 名字.

(b₂) 对，他 从 一九五二年 起 在 这兒 工作，所以 很 多 人 都 知道 他. 你 看，作 报告 的 同志 来 了.

II

(a₃) 剛才的 問題 你 都 回答 了 嗎？

(b₃) 都 回答 了. 只 有 八个 問題，是 不 是？

(a₄) 是，但是 我 只 回答对了 七个，后边兒的 那个 我 不 太 会，虽然 写了 一点兒，但是 一定 写錯 了. 你 是 怎么 回答 的？

(b₄) 我 是 这么 回答 的，你 看.

III

(a₅) 你 到 哪兒 去 了？

(b₅) 我 到 先生 那兒 去 了.

(a₆) 先生 住在 什么 地方？

(b_6) 他 住在 学校 旁边兒的 宿舍里.

(a_7) 从前 他 住在 城里, 是 什么
时候兒 搬来 的?

(b_7) 他 是 上月 搬到 城外 来 的.
你 不 知道 嗎?

(a_8) 不 知道. 要是 知道, 我 早
去 他 那兒 了.

第三十七課 Lesson 37

37.1	序数 Ordinal Numerals
37.2	概数 Approximate Numbers
37.3	錢的計算 The Counting of Money

一、生詞 Shēngcí New Words

1.	第	(头)	dì	(a prefix)
2.	年級	(名)	niánjí	(year) class
3.	哥(哥)	(名)	gē(gẻ)	elder brother
4.	元	(量)	yuán	dollar (a measure word)
5.	角	(量)	jiǎo	ten cents (a measure word)
6.	分	(量)	fēn	cent (a measure word)
7.	塊	(量)	kuài	(a measure word)
8.	毛	(量)	máo	(a measure word)
9.	錢	(名)	qián	money
10.	上午	(名)	shàngwǔ	morning, the forenoon
11.	合作社	(名)	hézuòshè	co-operative store
12.	样兒	(名)	yàngr	shape, sort, style
13.	又	(副)	yòu	again
14.	一共	(副)	yígòng	totally, all together
15.	找	(动)	zhǎo	to return (change), to look for

16. 糖　　(名) táng[塊;斤 jīn]　sugar, candy
17. 水菓　　(名) shuǐguǒ[斤]　fruit
18. 出　　(动) chū　to go (come) out

二、語法 Yǔfǎ Grammar

37.1 序数 "第" 是表示数目顺序的詞头. 当我們要表示序数的时候, 就把这个詞头用在数詞的前边, 那个数目就变成了序数. 例如:

37.1 Ordinal Numerals In Chinese, the woıd 第 is the prefix used to indicate the order of numbers. Ordinal numerals are formd by placing the prefix 第 before the cardinal numerals. e. g.

1. 我 坐在 第二輛 汽車上.
2. 每年的 第一个 月 叫 一月.

这里 "第一" "第二" 都是序数. 用序数的时候我們要注意以下两点:

In the above sentences, 第一 and 第二 are ordinal numerals. The following two points must be observed in using ordinal numerals:

(一) 一般的序数与基数一样: 与名詞連用的时候, 要用量詞, 如例 1 里的 "輛" 和例 2 里的 "个".

(1) Just like cardinal numerals, ordinal numerals in general require measure words when they are joined with nouns, such as the measure words 輛 in example 1 and 个 in example 2.

(二) "第二" 不能說成 "第两".

(2) 第二 cannot be 第两.

除了一般的序数以外, 序数也有一些例外的情况. 有时候数詞前面虽然沒有詞头, 也可能是表示序数. 以下介紹常見的几种:

Besides the general ordinal numerals, there are some exceptions. That is to say, sometimes no prefix is used before certain numerals, yet they are ordinal numerals. Some of the exceptional ordinal numerals in common use are as follows:

(一) 表示年、月、日、时的时候，数詞都沒有詞头"第"，但也表示順序. 例如:

a) None of the numerals indicating the year, the month, the day and the hour take a prefix, nevertheless, they imply the order of time. e. g.

3. 二月 二日

就是一年里的第二个月的第二天. 由此我們更可以知道，在序数里，不管有沒有詞头"第"，都只能用"二"，不能用"两".
The above example means the second day of the second month in a year. Hence it is clear that 二 must be used instead of 两 in expressing an ordinal number, whether there is the prefex 第 or not.

(二) 事物的等級也不用詞头"第". 例如:

b) We do not use the prefix in expressing different classes of things. e. g.

4. 一年級 学生

就是第一年級的学生.
It means first year students.

(三) 亲屬称呼也常常不用詞头"第". 例如:

c) In general, the prefix is not used in calling members of the family and relatives. e. g.

5. 三哥(哥)

就是第三个哥哥.
It means the third elder brother.

以上这些情况，虽然說明序数也可能不带詞头"第"，但并不意味着沒有詞头的序数就不能区别于一般的基数: 基数在名詞之前的时候，必然带量詞，而不用詞头的序数，在名詞前边是不用量詞的. 这是和用"第"表示序数不同的地方，应該注意. 例如上边的"二月""三哥"就是不用詞头"第"的序数，都不用量詞. 如果說"two months""three brothers"就要說成"两个月""三个哥哥".

Although from the above exceptions we know that there are some ordinal numerals actually used without the prefix, this does not mean that ordinal numerals without the prefix may be confused with the general cardinal numerals. We must notice that cardinal numerals carry measure words when they are used before nouns, but ordinal numerals without the prefix do not require any measure word when they are used before nouns, e. g., the numerals in 二月 and 三哥 are ordinal numerals without the prefix 第, so we do not use any measure word. If we say "two months" and three elder brothers", they should be translated as 两个月 and 三个哥哥.

37.2 概数 汉語里有不少方法表示概数，下边介紹几种最常用的方法:

37.2 Approximate Numbers In Chinese, there are many ways of indicating approximate numbers. Here, we shall introduce only the most common ones:

(一) 把两个邻近的数目直接联系在一起. 例如:

(1) The use of two neighbouring numerals. e. g.

6. 他 写錯了 三四个 汉字.

7. 我 朋友 这个 月 十七八号 到 北京 来.

8. 这个 教室 有 二三十把 椅子.

"三四个" 就是 "三个或者四个", "十七八号" 就是 "十七号或者十八号", "二三十把" 就是 "二十几把或者三十把左右".

三四个 means "three or four", 十七八号 means "the seventeenth or eighteenth" and 二三十把 means "more than twenty or around thirty".

(二) 用 "几" 来代表不确定的数字，譯成英語就是 several. 例如:

(2) The use of the word 几 (several) to indicate an indefinite number. e. g.

9. 教室里 那 几个 窗户 都 开开了.

10. 我們 每天 学 十几个 生詞.

11. 这 几十个 学生 都 要 学習 这个 專业.

(三) 在一个数目的后边用"多"表示超过那个数目."多"和量詞位置的关系有以下两种情况:

(3) The use of the word 多 after a numeral indicates more than the number shown by that numeral. The positions of the measure word and the word 多 are shown in the following:

(1) 概数是整数的时候,"多"用在量詞或不带量詞的名詞前边. 例如:

a) If the approximate number is a part of a large number, 多 is used before the measure word or before a noun not requiring a measure word. e. g.

12. 我們 学了 二十多課 語法 了.

13. 三十多年 以前, 毛 主席 在 北京 大学 工作.

(2) 概数是整数以后的零数的时候,"多"就用在量詞或不带量詞的名詞后边. 例如:

b) If the approximate number is a fraction of the whole, 多 is used after the measure word or a noun not requiring a measure word. e. g.

14. 他 昨天 复习了 两课多 語法.

15. 他 (是) 三年多 以前 到 中国 来 的.

37.3 錢的計算　汉語里錢的計算單位是"元""角""分",口語里更常用"塊""毛""分".在最后一位的后边,常常用"錢".例如:

37.3 The Counting of Money　In Chinese, the units of currency are 元, 角 and 分, while in the spoken language they are called 塊, 毛 and 分 respectively. After the last unit we often use the word 錢. e. g.

16. 3.00元——三元——三塊(錢)

17. 0.50元——五角——五毛(錢)

18. 0.08元——八分——八分(錢)

19. 1.45元——一元 四角 五分——一塊 四毛 五(分錢)

20. 25.20元——二十五元 二角——二十五塊 二(毛錢)

上面提到的关于"多" 字的用法,也完全适用于錢的計算.例如:

The rules of the use of 多, stated above, are also suitable for money expressions. e. g.

21. 他 有 三十多塊 錢.

22. 他 有 五塊多 錢.

三、課文 Kèwén Text

上午 十一点 四十(分), 我們 上完了 第四节 課. 回 宿舍 的 时候兒, 在 圖書館 前边兒, 我 遇見了 一个 二年級的 学生. 他 要 到 合作社 去. 我的 練習 本子 用完 了, 必須 买 几本 新的. 所以 我 就 带了 两三塊錢 跟 他 一起 去 了.

合作社 在 学生 宿舍的 旁边兒. 我 进去 就 問: "同志, 有 練習 本子 沒有?" 卖 东西 的 同志 回答: "有, 您 要 什么 样兒的? 都 在 这兒."

我 看見了 一种 我 喜欢 的, 就 問 他: "那种 本子 多少錢?" 他 說: "两毛 二 一本". 我 告訴 他: "我 要 六本", 就 給了 他 两塊錢. 他 給 我 本子 以后, 又說: "一共 一塊 三毛 二, 找 您 六毛 八".

这时候兒，我的 朋友 已經 买好了 糖 和 水菓．我 拿了 找来 的 錢 和 本子 就 跟 他 一起 出来 了．

四、課外練習 Kèwài liànxí Home Work

1. 抄写并回答下边的問題：

1) Copy and answer the following questions:

(1) 今天 几月 几号？

(2) 你 是 几年級 学生？

(3) 一年級 一共 有 多少 学生？

2. 把下边的概数用汉字表示出来：

2) Write out the following approximate numbers in Chinese:

(5) thirty or forty

(6) twenty five or six

(7) more than fifty (use 几)

(8) more than eighty (use 多)

3. 用汉字表示下列錢数（用口語和書面語两种方式）：

3) Write out the following sums of money in Chinese (both the oral and written forms):

(8) 0.27元　(9) 8.95元　(10) 36.00元

(11) 2.17元　(12) 0.04元　(13) 13.50元

五、汉字表 Hànzì biǎo Chinese Characters

1	第	⺮	
		弟（ㄱ コ 弓 弔 弟）	
2	級	糹	
		及（丿 ア 乃 及）	
3	哥		
4	元		
5	角		
6	塊	土	
		鬼（丿 由 鬼 鬼）	
7	錢	金	
		戔	戈
			戈
8	合		
9	社		
10	又		
11	共	一 十 卄 龷 共	
12	糖	米（丶 丷 䒑 半 米 米）	
		唐（广 户 户 庐 庚 唐）	
13	水	亅 刁 水 水	
14	菓	艹	
		果	

第三十八課 Lesson 38

38.1 兼語式
The Telescopic Form
38.2 动詞重叠
The Reduplication of Verbs
38.3 "又…又…"
The Construction 又…又…
38.4 "也…也…"
The Construction 也…也…

一、生詞 Shēngcí New Words

1.	請	(动)	qǐng	please
2.	讓	(动)	ràng	to let
3.	討論	(动、名)	tǎolùn	to discuss, discussion
4.	又…又…		yòu…yòu…	(compound connective)
5.	也…也…		yě…yě…	(compound connective)
6.	开(会)	(动)	kāi (huì)	to hold (a meeting)
7.	会	(名)	huì	meeting
8.	叫	(动)	jiào	to call, to shout
9.	通知	(动、名)	tōngzhī	to inform, information
10.	談	(动)	tán	to talk, to tell
11.	介紹	(动、名)	jièshào	to introduce, introduction
12.	自己	(代)	zìjǐ	oneself, self
13.	經驗	(名)	jīngyàn	experience

14.	方面	(名)	fāngmiàn	respect, side
15.	意見	(名)	yìjiàn	opinion
16.	提	(动)	tí	to raise, to express
17.	欢迎	(动、名)	huānyíng	to welcome, welcome
18.	准备	(动、名)	zhǔnbèi	to prepare, preparation

二、 語法 Yǔfǎ Grammar

38.1 兼語式　动詞謂語句里有一种比較复杂的形式——兼語式. 这种句子的謂語里除了动詞和宾語以外，宾語后边还有其他成分. 这个成分是說明宾語的动作或状态的，它和宾語之間有主謂关系. 因为这种句子里的宾語又兼有作它后边成分的主語的作用，所以叫作兼語；又因为兼語后边的成分与兼語有主謂关系，这个成分就叫作兼語的謂語，而这种句子就叫作兼語式. 例如：

38.1 The Telescopic Form　There is a kind of sentence with a verbal predicate that is rather complicated in construction ——the telescopic form. In the predicate of such a sentence, there is some other element following the object, besides the verb and its object. Such an element describes the action or state of the object, so that the relation between the object and such an element becomes one of subject and predicate. Since the object has at the same time the function of being the subject of the other element following it, it is called the double-function word. Moreover, since there exists between the object and the other element the relation of subject and predicate, such an element is also the predicate of the double-function word. This is why we call it a sentence in the telescopic form. e. g.

1. 我 請 你 来.
2. 这件 事情 讓 我 很 高兴.

"我""这件事情"是主語，"請""讓"是动詞，"你""我"是兼語，"来"和"很高兴"就是兼語的謂語．在这里"你""来"和"我""很高兴"都有主謂关系．因此，我們可以說兼語式都有下边的型式：

主語——动詞——兼語——兼語的謂語

└————謂語————

我 and 这件事 are subjects, 請 and 讓 are verbs, 你 and 我 are double-function words, and 来 and 很高兴 are the predicates of the double-function words. We can see that there exists between 你 and 来, 我 and 很高兴 the relation of subject and predicate. Therefore, all the sentences of the telescopic form have the following sentence pattern:

Subject — Verb — the Double-function Word —
the Predicate of the Double-function Word

这种句子里的动詞常是"請""讓""叫"等一类的詞，而兼語的謂語和一般句子一样，它可以是体詞、形容詞、动詞或我們尙未学到的主謂結构．

The verbs used in such sentences are always 請, 讓, 叫 etc. The predicate of the double-function word, as in other sentences, may be a substantive, an adjective, a verb or a subject-predicate construction which we shall learn later.

38.2 动詞重叠　我們知道形容詞可以重叠 (20.2)，动詞也可以重叠．动詞重叠表示动作經历的时間短促．例如：

38.2 The Reduplication of Verbs　We have learned that adjectives can be used reduplicatively (20.2). Here we shall learn the reduplication of verbs. In Chinese, the reduplication of verb implies a short and quick action. e g.

3. 我 想 看看 小說兒.

4. 他 請 他 朋友 在 宿舍里 坐坐.

因为說話的人在心理上有短促的感覚，有时候也表示輕松和随便. 例如:

In such cases, the speaker has the feeling that the action is short and quick; so the reduplication of a verb may in some cases also express some informal or random action. e. g.

5. 这个 星期日 上午, 我 复習复習 生詞、看看 报, 就 已經 十二点 了.

有时候又可以表示尝試、試行、試作. 例如:

Sometimes it may also express an attempt or trial.

6. 我 覚得 这本 小説兒 很 有意思, 你 看看.

7. 你們 应該 討論討論 这个 問題.

关于动詞重叠，有三点要注意:

Special attention should be paid to the following three points:

(一) 重叠單音动詞的时候, 当中可以加"一", 意思不变. 例如:

(1) When the monosyllabic verb is used reduplicatively, we may insert the word 一. e. g.

8. 他 想 看一看 小説兒.

9. 他 請 他 朋友 在 宿舍里 坐一坐.

(二) 复音动詞重叠的时候, 以詞为單位. 例如:

(2) The dissyllabic verb repeats its bound-form. e. g.

10. 你 应该 休息休息.

11. 这个 方法 很 好, 我 要 学习学习.

这一点是与形容詞有区别的. 同时要注意复音动詞重叠的时候, 不能插入"一"字.

The reduplication of the dissyllabic verb should be clearly distinguished from that of the dissyllabic adjective. At the same time, notice that the word 一 is never inserted when a dissyllabic verb is reduplicated.

(三) 遇見动宾結构, 只能重叠动詞部分, 不能重叠宾語. 例如:

(3) As to a verb-object construction, we only reduplicate the verb and not the object. e. g.

12. 現在 你們 可以 唱唱 歌兒.

当然这时候也可以在單音的动詞之間插上"一". 例如:

Of course, we can insert the word 一 when monosyllabic verbs are reduplicated. e. g.

13. 現在 你們 可以 唱一唱 歌兒.

38.3 "又…又…" 汉語里常用这个結构联系并列成分来特别强調两种情况或两种特性的同时存在. 例如:

38.3 又……又…… In Chinese, we often use this construction (compound connective) to connect two parallel elements and to stress that the two states or characteristics exist at the same time. e. g.

14. 他 又 是 我的 先生, 又 是 我的 朋友.

15. 这張 桌子 又 新、又 大.

16. 这个 同志 又 会 中文、又 会 俄文.

17. 他 說 中文 說得 又 快、又 清楚.

用这个結构的时候要注意:

There are two points to be observed in using this construction:

(一) "又" 必須放在謂語或程度补語的前边.

(1) 又 has to be placed before the predicate or before the complement of degree.

(二) 如果有两个以上的并列成分, 就把 "又" 在每个成分的前边用一次. 例如:

(2) When there are more than two parallel elements, we have to use 又 before each of the elements. e. g.

18. 他 写 汉字 写得 又 快、又 清楚、又 好看.

38.4 "也…也" 这个結构也是联系并列成分的. 在一般的情况下, 它經常联系以动詞构成的并列結构. 例如:

38.4 也…也… This construction is also used to connect two parallel elements. In general, it is always used to connect two parallel elements composed of verbs. e. g.

19. 他 会 中文——也 能 説，也 能 写.

20. 昨天 星期日，我 也 玩兒 了，也 学習 了.

三、課文 Kèwén Text

(a_1) 今天 开 会，你 知道 了 嗎？先生 叫 我 通知 你.

(b_1) 謝謝. 我 已經 看見 那个 通知 了. 下午 三点 开，是 不 是？

(a_2) 是 三点. 你 能 不 能 来？

(b_2) 能 来. 但是 为 什么 开 这个 会，我 还 不 太 清楚.

(a_3) 先生 要 和 大家 一起 討論討論 学習 問題. 他 想 讓 大家 学 得 又 多、又 快、又 好，所以 他 要 和 大家 談一談. 他 还 要 請 張友文 同学 介紹介紹 自己的 經驗.

(b₃) 張友文的 学习 方法 一定 很好: 他 学习得 特别 好, 但是 他 不 觉得 忙, 他 每天 也 学习 了, 也 休息 了.

(a₄) 所以 这 是 一个 很 重要的 会, 大家 应該 好好兒地 听听 他的 經驗. 学习 方面的 意見, 你們 也 可以 提一提.

(b₄) 还 要 提 意見 嗎? 我 沒 有 意見, 怎么办?

(a₅) 先生 非常 欢迎 大家的 意見, 他 叫 你們 准备 意見, 你 可以 好好兒地 想一想.

(b₅) 对, 我 准备准备.

四、課外練習 Kèwài liànxí Home Work

1. 用下边的动詞各作一个句子，在句子里重叠动詞:

1) Make sentences with each of the following verbs and repeat the verbs in your sentences:

(1) 討論

(2) 問

2. 完成下边兼語式的句子:

2) Complete the following telescopic sentences:

(3) 我們 請 新 同学________.

(4) 先生 叫 我________________.

(5) 他 說 的 話 讓 我____.

3. 用"也…也…"或"又…又…"把下边句子譯成中文:

3) Translate the following sentences into Chinese, using 也 … 也 … or 又 … 又 … :

(6) The Capital Theatre is big and good.

(7) The elder brother has bought sweets and fruits from the co-operative store.

五、汉字表 Hànzì biǎo Chinese Characters

1	請		
2	讓	言	
		襄（丶 亠 [illegible] [illegible] [illegible] [illegible] [illegible] [illegible] [illegible] [illegible] [illegible]	
		襄）	
3	討	言	
		寸	
4	論	言	
		侖（人 亼 [illegible] [illegible] 合 [illegible] 侖）	
5	通	甬（乛 マ 甬）	
		辶	
6	談	言	
		炎	火
			火
7	介	人 [illegible] 介	
8	紹	糸	
		召	刀
			口
9	自		

10	己	
11	驗	馬
		僉（人 亼 佥 僉）
12	面	一 丆 丙 丙 而 而 而 面
13	提	扌
		是
14	迎	丿 ⺊ 卬 迎
15	准	冫
		隹
16	备	夂
		田

第三十九課 Lesson 39

39.1	主謂謂語句 The Sentence with a Clause Predicate	
39.2	主謂結构作主語 The Subject-Predicate (clause) Construction Used as Subject	
39.3	主謂結构作宾語 The Subject-Predicate (clause) Construction Used as Object	
39.4	"有的" The Expression 有的	

一、生詞 Shēngcí New Words

1.	身体	(名)	shēntǐ	body
2.	头	(名)	tóu	head
3.	疼	(动)	téng	to ache, to feel pain
4.	希望	(动、名)	xīwàng	to hope
5.	有的		yǒudê	some
6.	全面	(形)	quánmiàn	over-all, whole
7.	發展	(动,名)	fāzhǎn	to develop, development
8.	極了		jílê	very, extremely
9.	病	(名、动)	bìng	disease, illness, to fall ill
10.	医院	(名)	yīyuàn	hospital
11.	大夫	(名)	dàifû	doctor, physician
12.	藥	(名)	yào	medicine
13.	也許	(副)	yěxǔ	perhaps, probably

14. 好　(动)　hǎo　to recover

15. 成　(动)　chéng　to become

二、語法 Yǔfǎ Grammar

39.1 主謂謂語句　除了体詞謂語句、形容詞謂語句和动詞謂語句以外，还有一种主謂謂語句．这种句子的謂語是由主謂結构构成的．例如：

39.1 The Sentence with a Clause Predicate　In Chinese, besides the sentence with a substantive predicate, the sentence with an adjectival predicate and the sentence with a verbal predicate, there is another kind of sentence that is composed of a clause predicate, that is to say, there is a subject-predicate construction (clause) in the predicate. e. g.

1. 他 身体 好.

2. 我 头 疼.

主語是“他”和“我”，而主謂結构“身体好”和“头疼”是“他”和“我”的謂語．因为这两个謂語里边有主謂結构，这种句子就是主謂謂語句．

The subjects of these two sentences are 他 and 我, and the subject-predicate construction 身体好 and 头疼 are the predicates of 他 and 我. Since the predicates contain subject-predicate constructions, such sentences are called sentences with clause predicates.

主謂謂語句有一个特点：句子的主語和主謂謂語里的主語所指人或事物都有一定的关系，后者常常是前者所屬的部分．例如例 1 的“身体”是屬于“他”的，例 2 的“头”是屬于“我”的．从意义上来看，主謂謂語句具有描写的性質．

The characteristic feature of the sentence with a clause predicate is that there is a relation between the person or thing denoted by the subject of the subject-predicate construction and the person or thing denoted by the subject of the whole sentence, that is to say, what is denoted by the subject of the predicate is always part of the person or thing denoted by the subject of the whole sentence. For instance, in example 1 身体 belongs to 他 and in example 2 头 belongs to 我. So far as the sentence function is concerned, the clause-predicate sentence is descriptive in nature.

39.2 主謂結构作主語　主謂結构也能作句子的主語. 例如:

39.2 The Subject Predicate Construction Used as Subject The subject-predicate construction may be used as subject in a sentence. e. g.

3. 身体 好 很 重要.

4. 他 不 努力 学習 是 不 对 的.

如果独立出来，这两个例句里的"身体好""他不努力学習"都是完整的句子. 但是在这里，就是全句的主語.

身体好 and 他不努力学習 in the above two examples are independent sentences when they stand alone. Here, they are used as subjects only.

39.3 主謂結构作宾語　主謂結构也常常作句子的宾語. 例如:

39.3 The Subject-Predicate Cons ruction Used as Object The subject-predicate construction is also very often used as object in a sentence. e. g.

5. 我 希望 你 能 来.

6. 大家 都 知道 他 要 到 苏联 去.

在这两个句子里，主謂結构"你能来"和"他要到苏联去"就只是宾語.

The subject-predicate construction, 你能来 and 他要到苏联去 are used as objects in these two sentences.

主謂結构作宾語的句子，与兼語式相似而实不同:

Note: The sentence in which the object is a subject-predicate construction seems similar to the sentence of the telescopic form, but actually they are different.

(一) 兼語式的动詞有使动意义，如"使""讓""叫"等等,而主謂結构一般作"看見""听見""知道"等沒有使动意义的动詞的宾語.

(1) Verbs used in the telescopic sentence are always causative verbs, such as 使, 讓, 叫 etc.; the subject-predicate construction is generally used as the object of such verbs as 看見, 听見 知道 etc., which are not causative in meaning.

(二) 兼語式动詞以兼語为对象，它和兼語的謂語有相应的关系. 主謂結构作宾語的句子，动詞以整个主謂結构作对象，它和这个結构里的謂語沒有必然的相应关系.

(2) The object of the verb in the telescopic sentence is the double-function word. There is some connection in meaning between the verb and the predicate of the double-function word. But in a sentence in which the object is a subject-predicate construction, the object of the verb is the whole construction, and there is no connection whatever between the verb and the predicate of the construction.

(三) 兼語式的兼語和前边的动詞結合得很紧，其間不但不能插入附加成分，語气上也不能停頓. 主謂結构作宾語的时候，它的主語和动詞的关系比較松散，語气上一般有停頓，尤其是在主謂結构比較長的时候.

(3) The double-function word of the telescopic sentence is so closely knit together with the main verb before it that there should be no other element between them, and no pause when spoken. But, when a subject predicate construction is used as the object in a sentence, the subject in the construction and

the main verb of the sentence are not so closely knit. There is generally a pause between them especially when the subject-predicate construction is comparatively long.

39.4 "有的"　我們常常用"有的"修飾名詞，表示无定．例如：

39.4 有的　We often use the word 有的 to modify nouns, expressing indefinite designation. e. g.

7. <u>有的</u> 班 学生 多，<u>有的</u> 班 学生 少．

8. <u>有的</u> 同学 已經 出發 了．

当語言环境已經把中心語表示得很清楚的时候，中心語常被省略．例如：

When the central word is clearly indicated by context, it can be omitted. e. g.

9. 他 有 不 少 經驗，<u>有的</u> 非常 好．

10. 他 提了 很 多 意見，<u>有的</u> 对，<u>有的</u> 不 一定 对．

"有的"和少数中心語已經形成了穩固的詞組，"的"就可以省去，"有的人""有的时候兒"經常說成"有人""有时候兒"，不必用"的"．例如：

The word 有的 and some central words have become bound-forms, and the word 的 may be omitted. Instead of saying 有的人 and 有的时候兒 we often say 有人 and 有时候 without the word 的.

11. 有人 带 字典 来 了，有人 沒 带.

12. 有时候兒 中国 同学 帮助 我. 有时候兒 我 自己 学習.

三、課文 Kèwén Text

I

1. 他 身体 好，工作 好，学習 好，是 一个 全面 發展 的 学生.

2. 这个 先生 經驗 多，方法 好.

3. 先生 了解 学生的 学習 情况 是 非常 重要 的.

4. 他 来 很 好，他 不 来 也 沒 关系.

5. 我 听見 你們 討論得 热烈 極了.

6. 先生 知道 有人 要 听 报告，所以 今天 不 开会.

7. 昨天的 話剧，有的 演員 演得 好，有的 演得 不 很 好.

8. 有的 同学 以后 还要 繼續 学習 中文.

II

(a1) 張友文 为 什么 沒 有 来?

(b1) 他 病 了.

(a2) 什么 病?

(b2) 他 头 疼. 他 說 他 今天 不 上 課, 要 在 宿舍 休息休息.

(a3) 为 什么 他 不 到 医院 去? 他 要是 現在 找 大夫 看看, 吃 一点兒 藥, 也許 明天 就 能 好.

(b3) 我 告訴 他 了. 他 說 头 疼 沒 关系, 不 一定 要 找 大夫.

(a4) 他 这么 想, 有 点兒 不 对. 有 时候兒 头 疼 也 能 發展成 大 病. 我 希望 你 下 課 以后 跟 他 說一說, 一定 叫 他 到 医 院 去.

四、課外練習 Kèwài liànxí Home Work

1. 抄写下边的句子，把句子里的主謂結构标出主語或宾語来:

2) Copy the following sentences, and under-line the subjects or objects in the subject-predicate (clause) constructions:

(1) 他 知道 他 要 作好 工作 就 必須 了解 全面 情况.

(2) 大家 一起 討論 給 我 很 大的 帮助.

(3) 他 很 希望 他 能 在 这兒 繼續 学習.

2. 把下面的句子翻譯成中文:

2) Translate the following sentences into Chinese:

(4) I hope I can find that doctor.

(5) He knows that the doctor in that hospital has more experience.

(6) On Saturday evening some (people) attended a meeting (literally hold a meet), and some (people) danced.

(7) Some school-mates are well-prepared but some are not well-prepared.

3. 抄写下边的汉字、詞語和句子，填入适当的拼音，并注意汉字的一字多音現象:

(3) Copy the following Chinese characters, word groups and sentences, fill the blanks with proper phonetic spellings, but notice that one Chinese character may be pronounced differently in different context:

(8) 大 {北京 ____学 / 医院里的 ____夫}

(9) 都 {首____ 剧場 / 我 ____ 懂 了.}

(10) 了 {他 ____解 情況. / 朋友 来 ____.}

(11) 还 {我 也 借 書, 也 ____書. / 报 ____ 沒 有 来 呢!}

五、汉字表 Hànzì biǎo Chinese Characters

1	身	
2	体	亻
		本
3	头	丶 ⺀ 丷 头 头
4	疼	
5	希	丿 乂 㐅 肴 希
6	望	丶 亠 亡 㐌 㐌 望
7	全	入 (丿 入)
		王

8	展	尸 尸 尸 屈 屈 屈 展 展	
9	病	疒	
		丙（一 丆 丙 丙）	
10	医	一 矢 医	
11	院	阝	
		完	
12	夫	二 扌 夫	
13	藥	艹	
		樂	白
			幺（𠃋 幺 幺）
			幺
			木
14	許	言	
		午	
15	成		

第四十課 Lesson 40

40.1 强調过去經驗的詞尾"过"
The Suffix 过 Emphasizing Past Experience
40.2 动詞的量詞"次"
The Verbal Measure Word 次
40.3 "下兒"
The Verbal Measure Word 下兒
40.4 宾語和动量詞的位置
The Positions of the Object and the Verbal Measure Word

一、生詞 Shengcí New Words

1.	过	(尾)	guò	(a suffix)
2.	治	(动)	zhì	to cure, to heal
3.	次	(量)	cì	(a measure word)
4.	下兒	(量)	xiàr	(a measure word)
5.	鐘	(名)	zhōng	clock, bell
6.	敲	(动)	qiāo	to knock
7.	对不起		duìbûqǐ	Excuse me, I'm sorry, I beg your pardon.
8.	表	(名)	biǎo	watch
9.	停	(动)	tíng	to stop
10.	带	(动)	dài	to wear, to put on
11.	有名	(形)	yǒumíng	famous, noted
12.	参加	(动)	cānjiā	to take part, to join
13.	晚会	(名)	wǎnhuì	evening party
14.	座位	(名)	zuòwèi	seat

15. 舒服 (形) shūfu comfortable

16. 意思 (名) yìsi meaning

17. 查 (动) chá to look up

二、語法 Yǔfǎ Grammar

40.1 强調过去經驗的詞尾"过" 在动詞謂語句中，如果是要强調在过去时間內曾經發生过某种动作（一次或多次），就在动詞的后边用詞尾"过"。例如：

40.1 The Suffix 过 Emphasizing Past Experience In a sentence with a verbal predicate, when we wish to stress an action in the past (that had happened once or several times), we add the suffix 过 after the verb. e. g.

1. 他 从前 来过。
2. 我 去过 那个 書店。

就是强調过去曾經有"来"和"去"的經驗。如果有結果补語或趋向补語，"过"用在补語之后。例如：

In the above two examples, we emphasize 来 and 去 as past experiences. If there is a resultative complement or a complement of direction, the suffix 过 should be placed after them. e. g.

3. 那个 大夫 治好过 这种 病。
4. 我的 朋友 到 苏联 去过。

我們知道强調完成的时候用"了"，又强調經驗、又强調完成的时候，就可以并用"过"和"了"，而把"过"放在"了"的前边。例如：

As we know the suffix 了 is used to indicate the perfective aspect, so 过 and 了 can be used together when stress is laid on the completion of an action as a past experience. Generally speaking, the suffix 过 precedes the suffix 了. e. g.

5. 他 前天 来过 了.

6. 那本 小説兒 我 已經 看过 了.

否定句中，我們用"沒有"直接加在帶"过"的动詞的前边. 这与完成貌不同："过"在否定式中必須保留，而"了"不能. 例如：

In the negative sentence, we put the negative adverb 沒有 immediately before the verb carrying the suffix 过. It differs from the perfective aspect in that the suffix 过 has to be retained in the negative sentence, but the suffix 了 must be dropped. e. g.

7. 他 沒 有 来过.

8. 我 沒 有 看过 那本 小説兒.

这种句子，用选擇式提問的时候，採取下边的方式：

In turning such sentences into alternative interrogative sentences, we do the following:

9. 他 来过 沒 有？

10. 你 看过 这本 小説兒 沒 有？

有宾語的时候，宾語常常提前. 例如：

When there is an object, it is often placed at the beginning of the sentence. e. g.

11. 这本 小説兒 你 看过 沒 有？

12. 那个 演員 你 看見过 沒 有？

40.2 动詞的量詞"次" 汉語除了名物有量詞 (14.1) 以外，动作也有量詞. 但是它們的用法并不一样：名量詞和数詞結合起来用在名詞的前边作定語，而动量詞和数詞用在动詞的后边作补語. "次"是一个常用的动量詞，应用范圍很广. 例如：

40.2 The Verbal Measure Word 次 In Chinese, besides nominal measure words (14.1), there are also verbal measure words. But they are not the same in use: the nominal measure words and numerals are used together as adjective modifiers before nouns, while the verbal measure words and numerals are used together as complements after verbs. 次 is one of the common verbal measure words. e. g.

13. 上星期 他 来了 两次.

14. 我 看过 一次 中国 話剧.

40.3 "下兒" 也是一个常用的动詞的量詞. 有时候它表示具体的动量——动作的單位. 例如：

40.3 下兒 It is also a verbal measure word, but sometimes it has a concrete meaning——the frequency of the action. e. g.

15. 鐘 敲了 三下兒.

但更多的时候，它和"一"連用，表示动作經历时間的短促. 例如：

But it is more often used together with 一 showing that an action has lasted only for a very short time. e. g.

16. 我 要 想 一下兒 这个 問題.

17. 我 必須 准备 一下兒 那个 报告.

当"下兒"表示具体的动量（动作的單位）的时候，前边可以用任何数詞. 但在表示动作經历时間短促的时候，"下兒"只能和数詞"一"連用. 我們知道，动詞重叠常有动作經历时間短促的意思(38.2)，而"一下兒"用在动詞后边就跟动詞重叠所表示的意思一样. 例如例 16 和例 17，就完全可以用重叠动詞的方式来表示:

When 下兒 is used to indicate the frequency of an action, we may use any numeral before it; but when it is used to indicate that an action has lasted for only a short time, we can only use 一 before it. We know that when a verb is used reduplicatively, it always indicates that the action has lasted for only a little while (38.2). 一下兒 used after a verb plays the same role as the reduplication of the verb. Therefore, examples 16 and 17 can be expressed equally well by reduplicating the verbs:

18. 我 要 想(一)想 这个 問題.

19. 我 必須 准备准备 那个 报告.

40.4 宾語和动量詞的位置　如果句子里有宾語，用动量詞的时候，要注意它的位置.

40.4 The Positions of the Object and the Verbal Measure Word　When there is an object in a sentence, we have to pay attention to the position of the verbal measure word.

(一) 如果宾語是名詞构成的，量詞一般要用在宾語之前. 例如:

(1) If the object is a noun, the measure word, in general, must be placed before the object. e. g.

20. 他 哥哥 去了 一次 北京 医院.

21. 我 在 这个 合作社 买过 五六次 东西.

22. 先生 想 了解 一下兒 他的 学習 情况.

（二）如果宾語是代詞，动量詞必須用在宾語之后. 例如:

(2) When the object is a pronoun, the measure word should be placed after the object. e. g.

23. 他 住在 医院 的 时候兒，我 看过 他 三次.

24. 我 到 这兒 来过 两次.

25. 先生 叫 我 帮助 他 一下兒.

三、課文 Kèwén Text

I

(a₁) 对不起，我的 表 停 了. 我 想 問 一下兒：現在 几点 几分？

(b₁) 我 今天 沒 有 带 表. 但是，剛才 我 听見 鐘 敲了 两下兒. 我 想 現在 差不多 是 两点 过 四五分鐘.

II

(a₂) 星期六 晚上 你 去 首都 剧場 了 嗎？

(b₂) 沒 有.

(a_3) 为什么 沒有 去？你 不 知道 那个 話剧 非常 有名 嗎？

(b_3) 知道．但是，我 已經 看过 两次 了，所以 沒 有去．

(a_4) 首都 剧場 你 也 去过 嗎？

(b_4) 对了，也 去过．我 在 那兒 参加过 一次 晚会 那个 剧場 又 新 又 大，座位 很 舒服．

III

(a_5) 劳駕！这个 字 念 什么？是 什么 意思？你 告訴 我 一下兒．

(b_5) 对不起，我 沒 学过 这个 字，我 也 不 知道．

(a_6) 你 有 字典 嗎？

(b_6) 我 有，你 查 一下兒．

(a_7) 你 看 这个 字 在 这兒，講得 很 清楚．

(b_7) 对了，我們 以后 要是 遇見 不

認識 的 字，就 应該 查 字典.

四、課外練習 Kèwài liànxí Home Work

1. 給下边的句子作出問題来：

1) Write interrogative sentences for the following declarative sentences:

(1) 那个 大夫 治过 这种 病.

(2) 到 北京 大学 以后，他 参加过 晚会.

2. 用"一下兒"改写下边的句子：

2) Re-write the following sentences using 一下兒:

(3) 这个 意見 很 重要，大家 应該 討論討論.

(4) 你 听听，这个 表 停 了 沒 有？

3. 把"两次"用在下边的句子里：

3) Put the words 两次 into the following sentences:

(5) 他 在 合作社 买过 水菓.

(6) 我 在 晚会上 遇見过 他.

4. 把"过"或"了"塡到下边的空白里去：

4) Fill the following blanks with 过 or 了:

昨天 我 参加____一个 会. 在 会上 听____一个 报告. 这个 作 报告 的 同志 是 一个 很 有名的 人. 从前 我 听____他的 报告. 这 两次 他 都 講得 很 好.

五、汉字表 Hànzì biǎo Chinese Characters

1	治	氵
		台
2	次	
3	敲	高
		攴（丨 ⺊ 攴）
4	表	一 二 丰 丰 声 表 表 表
5	停	亻
		亭（丶 亠 古 高 亭 亭）
6	参	厶
		大
		彡
7	加	
8	座	广
		坐
9	位	亻
		立
10	舒	舍
		予（乛 マ 予 予）

11	服	月
		艮
12	查	木
		旦

第四十一課 Lesson 41

41.1	介詞"为" The Preposition 为
41.2	介詞"替" The Preposition 替
41.3	介詞"給" The Preposition 給
41.4	"先...再..." The Construction 先...再...

一、生詞 Shēngcí New Words

1.	为	(介)	wèi	for
2.	共产主义	(名)	gòngchǎnzhǔyì	Communism
3.	奋斗	(动)	fèndòu	to struggle, to strive for
4.	进步	(名、形、动)	jìnbù	progress, progressive to progress
5.	服务	(动)	fúwù	to serve
6.	建設	(动、名)	jiànshè	to construct, to build
7.	社会主义	(名)	shèhuìzhǔyì	Socialism
8.	替	(动、介)	tì	to replace, to substitute, instead of, for...
9.	給	(介)	gěi	for
10.	先...再...		xiān...zài...	first... then...
11.	組織	(动、名)	zǔzhī	to organize organization
12.	联欢	(动)	liánhuān	to hold a party, to hold a reunion
13.	封	(量)	fēng	(a measure word)

14. 信	(名) xìn [封]	letter
15. 寄	(动) jì	to post, to mail
16. 早上	(名) zǎoshång	morning
17. 接到	(动) jiēdào	to receive
18. 国家	(名) guójiā	country

二、語法 Yǔfǎ Grammar

41.1 介詞"为" "为"是一个常用介詞，我們学过的"为什么"就是一个介詞結构．"为"的宾語常是指人或事物的名詞．这种介詞結构，有时候說明动作的目的，有时候說明一种情况存在的原因，有时候說明服务的对象．例如：

41.1 The Preposition 为 为 is one of the commonly used prepositions. We have learned that 为什么 is a prepositional construction. Its object is always a noun denoting persons or things. Such a prepositional construction may describe the purpose of an action, the reason of the existence of a certain state, or the object of service. e. g.

1. 中国 人民 为 共产主义 奋斗．
2. 大家 都 为 你的 进步 高兴．
3. 我們 要 为 人民 服务．

例 1 的"共产主义"是"奋斗"的目标，例 2 的"你的进步"是"高兴"的原因，例 3 的"人民"是服务的对象．带有这种結构的句子往往用于比較正式的場合．而且这种結构一定要用在状語的位置，不能放在句尾．我們一定不能說"中国人民奋斗为共产主义"．"为"的宾語有时是一个动宾結构．例如：

In example 1 共产主义 is the object or purpose of 奋斗; in example 2 你的进步 is the reason for 高兴; and in example

3 人民 is the object of 服务. Sentences with such constructions are frequently used in a rather formal situation. Moreover, such constructions have to be put where adverbal modifiers usually stand, and are never allowed at the end of a sentence. We must not say: 中国人民奋斗为共产主义. The object of the preposition 为 may be a verb-object construction. e. g.

4. 中国 人民 为 建設 社会主义 努力 工作.

41.2 介詞"替" "替"可以是一个动詞，有"代替"的意思. 例如:

41.2 The Preposition 替 替 may be used as a verb and suggests the meaning of "to be in the place of". e. g.

5. 張 先生 今天 有 事 不 能 上 課，謝 先生 替 他.

但是，"替"也常常可以是一个介詞. 例如:

But 替 is often used as a preposition. e. g.

6. 謝 先生 替 張 先生 上 課.

7. 哥哥 替 我 买了 一本 小説兒.

8. 我 替 他 找着了 他的 表.

在上边的句子里"替張先生""替我""替他"都是介詞結构作状語.

In the above examples, 替張先生, 替我 and 替他 are all prepositional constructions used as adverbial modifiers.

41.3 介詞"給" 我們知道"給"是一个动詞，它也是一个常用的介詞，經常带着宾語作状語. 例如:

41.3 The Preposition 給 We have already learned that 給 is used as a verb. But it is also often used as a preposition and serves as an adverbial modifier together with its object. e. g.

9. 我给朋友开門.

10. 先生給我們講語法.

在这里"給朋友""給我們"都是状語，所以这样的介詞結构必須放在动詞之前. 我們旣不能說"我开朋友門"和"先生講我們語法"，也不能說"我开門給朋友"和"先生講語法給我們".

Here, 給朋友 and 給我們 are adverbial modifiers, therefore such prepositional constructions have to be placed before verbs. We can not say: 我开朋友門 or 先生講我們語法. Neither can we say: 我开門給朋友, or 先生講語法給我們.

"給"和"为"都可以譯作 for，但是在表示服务对象之外，"为"还可以表示动作的目的或原因，而"給"只能表示服务对象. 表示目的或原因的句子都不能用"給".

給 and 为 can be both translated into "for" in English, and may both introduce an object of service; but 为 can also indicate the aim or reason of an action, while 給 can only indicate the object of service. Therefore 給 can never be used to express the aim or reason of action in any sentence.

"給"有时候可以代替"替". 例如:

給 sometimes may be used instead of 替. e. g.

11. 他从城里給我买来了一本書.

在一定的語言环境下，这个"給我"就可以是"替我"的意思.

Under certain circumstances 給我 may have the meaning of 替我.

41.4 "先…再…" 当我們要强調地指出两个动作进行的順序的时候，我們用"先…再…"这个結构. 第一个动詞放在"先"的后边，"先"有"首先"的意思. 第二个动詞放在"再"的后边，"再"有"然后"的意思. 例如:

41.4 先… 再… The construction 先… 再… is used to lay stress on the order of two actions; the first verb should be placed after the word 先 (first) and the second verb should be placed after the word 再 (then). e. g.

12. 我們 应該 先 复習 語法 再 作 練習.

13. 我們 現在 先 学 中文, 以后 再 学 專业.

三、課文 Kèwén Text

I

1. 他 为 参加 討論 会 准备了 不 少 意見.

2. 我們 为 欢迎 新 来 的 同学 組織了 一个 联欢 会.

3. 我 替 他 买了 一些 水菓 来.

4. 張 先生 有 病 的 时候兒, 这个 先生 替 他 上过 一次 課.

5. 要是 您 認識 他, 我 想 請 您 給 我們 介紹介紹.

6. 这个 很 有 經驗 的 大夫 給 他 治好了 病.

7. 到朋友那兒的时候兒，你应該先敲門，再进去.

II

我哥哥給我写了一封信. 这封信是两个星期以前寄来的. 今天早上寄到了. 我同屋知道我希望接到信，所以就替我拿来了. 我哥哥在信里写了很多我們国家建設的情况，也談到了自己的工作. 他叫我先学好中文，再学習專业. 学好專业就可以好好兒地为人民服务. 我看了信，非常高兴，我同屋也为我高兴.

四、課外練習 Kèwài liànxí Home Work

1. 把适当的介詞塡到下边的句子里去:

1) Fill the blanks with proper prepositions:

(1) 我想請您____我講講这个生詞的意思.

(2) 他的 报告 很 好, 我們 听完了 都___他 鼓掌.

(3) 我 今天 不 能 到 你們 宿舍 去, 希望 你 能___我 通知 一下兒 你的 同屋.

(4) 他___写 这封 信, 今天 沒 有 休息.

2. 把下面的句子譯成中文:

2) Translate the following sentences into Chinese:—

(5) The teacher has already explained for me the meaning ot this word.

(6) My elder brother has borrowed a Chinese-English dictionary for me from the university library.

(7) The teacher has talked several times with me in order to see my point of view.

3. 抄写下边的詞語,給划綫的汉字註出拼音,并比較这些汉字的写法:

3) Copy the following words and word groups, transcribe the underlined Chinese characters, and compare their different ways of writing:

(8) 身体 / 本子

(9) 我們 / 找 大夫

(10) 从前 / 以前

(11) 大 汽車 / 太 慢

(12) 自己 / 已經

(13) 一張 紙 / 長 桌子

五、汉字表 Hànzì biǎo Chinese Characters

1	产	丶 亠 亣 产	
2	义	丿 乂 义	
3	奋	大	
		田	
4	斗	丶 ⺀ 三 斗	
5	步	丨 ⺊ 𠁣 止 𣥂 𣥄 步	
6	务	夂	
		力	
7	建	聿（ㄱ ⺕ 彐 ⺺ 𦘒 聿）	
		廴（㇋ 廴）	
8	設	言	
		殳	
9	替	㚘	夫
			夫
		日	

10	再	一 冂 冉 再	
11	組	糹	
		且	
12	織	糹	
		戠	
13	封	圭	土
			土
		寸	
14	信	亻	
		言	
15	寄	宀	
		奇	
16	接	扌	
		妾	立
			女

第四十二課 Lesson 42

42.1 四种句子
Four Kinds of Sentences
42.2 名量和动量
Nominal Measure Words and Verbal Measure Words
42.3 "了"和"过"
了 and 过

一. 語法复習 Yǔfǎ fùxí Review

42.1 四种句子 按照謂語的結构，句子可以分为四种:

42.1 Four Kinds of Sentences In Chinese, sentences may be divided into four kinds according to their construction.

(一) 体詞謂語句 这种句子是說明或判断"是什么""等于什么""具有什么屬性""屬于什么类别"的. 謂語里边都包含着体詞或体詞結构. 最常見的一种是用系詞"是"的 (13.1). 例如:

(1) The Sentence with a Substantive Predicate This kind of sentence is used to describe or judge of the subject "what it is", "to what it is equivalent", "of what quality" and "of what kind". In the predicate there must be a substantive or a substantive construction. The copula 是 is most frequently used in the sentence (13.1). e. g.

1. 他 是 一年級 那班的 先生.
2. 今天的 晚会 是 欢迎 会.

也有用"叫"的体詞謂語句 (19.2). 例如:

叫 may be used instead of 是 (19.2). e. g.

3. 那个 剧場 叫 首都 剧場.

4. 那个 話剧 叫 什么 名字?

又有很大一部分体詞謂語句在系詞"是"的后边是一个用"…的"組成的体詞結构 (17.1). 例如:

Yet, there are a number of sentences of this kind, where a substantive construction in the form of …的 is used after the copula 是 instead of a simple substantive (17.1). e. g.

5. 这个 意見 是 張 同志 的.

6. 桌子上的 表 是 他的.

7. 那封 信 是 一个 朋友 寄来 的.

8. 他 談 的 經驗 是 很 重要的.

除了上述的体詞謂語句以外,还有一些不用系詞的 (31.2). 例如:

Besides the above-mentioned sentences, there are still some other sentences in which the copula is not used (31.2). e. g.

9. 这个 同志 五十多岁.

10. 明天 十月 三十.

11. 那个 鐘 十五塊 錢.

但是, 在否定句中这种句子也一定要用系詞.

But all the above sentences in the negative form must use the copula.

(二) 形容詞謂語句 (14.3)　这种句子以形容詞为謂語, 是描写主語的. 例如:

(2) The Sentence with an Adjectival Predicate (14.3)　In this kind of sentence the predicate is an adjective, describing the subject. e. g.

12. 他 新 买 的 表 非常 好看.

13. 从 上月 起，他 学习 方面的 进步 很 大.

14. 这次 他 写 的 信 特别 長.

(三) 动詞謂語句 (16.1) 这种句子以动詞为謂語，是叙述动作的. 例如:

(3) The Sentence with a Verbal Predicate (16.1) In this kind of sentence the predicate is a verb and is used to describe an action. e. g.

15. 誰 在 外边兒 敲 門?

16. 新 中国 建設得 很 快.

17. 她 (是) 在 合作社 买 的 水菓.

18. 我 請 他 替 我 拿 一点兒 藥 来.

19. 我 希望 我 能 很 快地 学好 中文.

(四) 主謂謂語句 (39.1) 这种句子的謂語是由主謂結构构成的. 例如:

(4) The Sentence with a Clause Predicate (39.1) The predicate of this kind of sentence is made up of a subject-predicate construction. e. g.

20. 首都 剧場 座位 舒服.

21. 这个 医院 大夫 多.

42.2 名量和动量 我們知道汉語里有一个特殊的詞类——

量詞. 在指代詞或数詞与名詞連用的时候，必須以名量詞为中介(14.1). 例如:

42.2 Nominal Measure Words and Verbal Measure Words

We know that there is a special part of speech in Chinese——the measure word. When a demonstrative pronoun or numeral is used before a noun, there must be a measure word to connect them (14.1). e. g.

22. 我 刚才 接到 一个 开 会 的 通知.

23. 这辆 汽車 是 誰 叫 来 的?

名量詞以外，我們也学到了动量詞 (40.2)，它是和动詞連用的. 只是我們要注意: 名量詞用在名詞的前边，而动量詞用在动詞的后边. 例如:

We have also learned the verbal measure words (40.2), and know that they are used together with verbs. But there is one point to be noticed, the nominal measure words are used before nouns and the verbal measure words are used after verbs. e. g.

24. 他 去过 两次 北京 剧場.

25. 我 忘了 表 在 哪兒, 要 找 一下兒.

另外，还有一点可以比較的: 名量詞前的数詞，如果是“一”的时候，只要数詞不在句首，“一”永远可以省去. 例如:

Besides, there is one more difference: when the numeral before the nominal measure word is 一, it is always omitted except at the beginning of a sentence. e. g.

26. 我 想 給 您 提 个 意見.

27. 他 为 听 报告 买了 个 本子.

但在动量詞前，数詞是“一”的时候，一般不能省去“一”．例如:

But, before the verbal measure word 一 is generally not omitted. e. g.

28. 北京 圖書館 我 只 去过 一次.

42.3 “了”和“过” “了”和“过”两个都是动詞詞尾．“了”是表示动作完成的，而完成了的动作常常是过去的．“过”是表示經驗的，而經驗一定是过去的．因为它們都和过去的动作有联系，所以容易混淆．实际上二者是有区别的:

42.3 了 and 过 了 and 过, as we know, are two verbal suffixes. 了 is used to indicate the completion of an action; a completed action always happens in the past. 过 is used to indicate experience, experience also refers to past action. Since both bear relation to past actions, they are easily confused, though they are actually different from each other.

(一) 当我們要强調已經完成了什么动作的时候，就在动詞的后边加詞尾“了”．例如:

(1) When we wish to stress a completed action, we use the suffix 了 after the verb. e. g.

29. 在 联欢 会上, 主席 請 他 唱了 一个 歌兒.

30. 他 为 我們 准备了 不 少的 水菓 和 糖.

(二) 当我們强調曾有某种經驗的时候，我們就在那个动詞后边加“过”．例如:

(2) When we wish to place special stress on a certain experience in the past, we use the suffix 过 after the verb. e. g.

31. 先生 到 我們 宿舍 来过 很 多 次.

32. 我 从前 沒 有 参加过 这么 大 的 晚会, 这 是 第一次.

在以上两組句子里, 用"了"的不能换"过", 用"过"的不能换"了", 因为所强調的不同. 有时候又强調完成、又强調經驗的时候, 也可以"了""过"并用. 例如:

It is only because the point of emphasis is different, that in the above two groups of examples we cannot use the suffixes 了 and 过 interchangeably. However, when we wish to emphasize the completion of the action as well as the action as past experience, then 了 and 过 may be used together. e. g.

33. 那本 小説兒 虽然 看过了, 我 还 想 看.

34. 听过了 这个 报告 的 人 都 説 这个 报告 好.

偶然有些句子可以用"了", 也可以用"过", 但是我們必須体会不同的詞尾有不同的强調之点. 例如:

Occasionally in some sentences either 了 or 过 may be used, but we must understand that different suffixes imply different point of emphasis. e. g.

35. 他 到 那个 書店 去 了, (所以 不 在 宿舍里).

36. 他 到 那个 書店 去过, (所以 他 認識 書店 在 什么 地方).

二、課文 Kèwén Text

I

(a₁) 方东 同志, 先生 叫 我 通知 你 今天 下午 听 报告.

(b₁) 什么 报告?

(b₂) "国家 建設 方面的 几个 問题". 你 去 不 去?

(b₂) 一定 去. 这个 报告 应該 听听. 你 知道 誰 給 我們 講 嗎?

(a₃) 高子清 同志. 我 听过 一次 他 的 报告. 他 講得 好 極了.

(b₃) 在 哪兒 講? 是不是 在 礼堂?

(a₄) 不 在 这兒. 在 人民 大学. 这个 报告 是 为 三四个 大学 組織 的.

(b₄) 我 还 沒有 去过 人民 大学 呢!

(a₅) 沒 关系, 我 去过, 我 認識. 我 可以 跟 你 一起 去.

(b₅) 好 極了. 报告 几点 开始?

(a₆) 两点半. 現在 我 先 回去, 一点半 再 来.

II

我 到 中国 来的 时候兒, 有 八九个 朋友 都 跟 我 說: "到了 中国, 你 要 常常 給 我們 写 信. 我們 希望 知道 你的 情况, 也 希望 知道 中国的 情况. 中国 是 我們的 好 朋友, 我們 应該 多多地 了解 中国的 人民 和 中国的 建設."

到了 中国 以后, 因为 我 学习 很忙, 只 給 他們 写过 两三次 信. 但是 已經 接到过 他們 十几封 了. 这个 星期日 上午 我 准备 写 信. 我 要 告訴 他們 中国 人民 怎么样 为 社会 主义 建設 奋斗. 我 也 要 告訴 他們 自己 在 学习 中文 方面 有了 一些 进步.